RESCUING HORACE WALPOLE

RESCUING
HORACE WALPOLE

Wilmarth S. Lewis

Published for the Yale University Library

by Yale University Press   New Haven and London

1978

Designed by John O. C. McCrillis and set in Baskerville
type. Printed in the United States of America by The
Meriden Gravure Company, Meriden, Connecticut.

Published in Great Britain, Europe, Africa, and Asia
(except Japan) by Yale University Press, Ltd., London.
Distributed in Australia and New Zealand by Book & Film
Services, Artarmon, N.S.W., Australia; and in Japan by
Harper & Row, Publishers, Tokyo Office.

Library of Congress Cataloging in Publication Data

Lewis, Wilmarth Sheldon, 1895–
    Rescuing Horace Walpole.

    1. Walpole, Horace, 4th Earl of Orford, 1717–1797.
2. Great Britain—Nobility—Biography. I. Title.
DA483.W2L43   828'.6'09 [B]   78–7590
ISBN 0–300–02278–6

Contents

List of Illustrations

RESCUING HORACE WALPOLE

The Fantasy

Two years ago the Almighty called me into His office and said, "I am going to destroy every object in your house except one, and you have twenty minutes to choose it."

I replied, "Lord, I don't need twenty seconds. I'll take Bentley's Drawings and Designs for Strawberry Hill."

The Almighty nodded solemnly. "For that answer you may save twenty-five more objects." After a pause He added, "You seem a little dazed, but I know you're not very good at arithmetic." In a louder voice He explained, "Twenty-*five* and *one* make twenty-*six,* and what I'm telling you is you may save twenty-*six* objects." He paused to see if I understood. Then He continued, "I don't care what they are—books, manuscripts, pictures, furniture—anything you like."

I managed to say, "Sir, I hope I may have more time to choose them."

"How much time do you want?"

"At least a year."

"A year!" His voice was very terrible.

"I think, Sir, I can make the choices fairly quickly, but I would like to write them up as I go along."

And that's the end of the fantasy and the beginning of this book.

The Problem:
Which Twenty-six Objects?

To understand my problem you must know something about Horace Walpole and my library. An account of both appears in *Collector's Progress,* which was published by Alfred Knopf in 1951. I wrote it to answer the question How did you get started on Horace Walpole? *Collector's Progress* shows that I was a born collector, beginning with house flies at the age of six and moving on to stamps at ten. It also tells how while travelling in England in the summer of 1922 I went into every bookshop I came to and pored over its shelves, buying inexpensive eighteenth- and nineteenth-century editions of the English classics, and learning more about books than I had learned at school and college. The following summer I bought at York for thirty-five shillings the book that is the foundation of my library, John Heneage Jesse's *George Selwyn and His Contemporaries,* 4 volumes, 1843. I had never heard of it, but the avuncular bookseller assured me, "it should be in every gentleman's library, Sir."

Inside the front cover of this copy's first volume is a pocket containing thirty-two pages of manuscript comment on the letters by Lady Louisa Stuart, a lady as unknown to me then as were Jesse and Selwyn themselves, but who I subsequently learned was a daughter of George III's first Prime Minister, Lord Bute. The sort of thing she wrote was, "The Coventry children—Lady Maria *was* 'marked for life,' and, I think, the ugliest *young* woman I ever beheld. Lady Anne had not the same strong appearance of disease but was scarcely pretty, nor would have been held at all so, if—if—one must speak out—if a modest woman; a part she disdained playing from her first beginning. Both sisters married, and both were divorced." Lady Louisa led me into the great world of the eighteenth century where I found Horace Walpole at its center. By then I had become so engrossed in the period I couldn't wait until the summer of 1924 for my next trip to England and hurried over in February.

On the 28th of that month when walking up Chancery Lane I came to

3

a gloomy Victorian building in which there was to be a book auction the following day. I stared at it dubiously. Should I go in? I went in and found myself in the sale room of Hodgson's, the modest competitor of Sotheby's and Christie's. The forthcoming sale was of the Milnes Gaskell library in which were a few books printed at Walpole's private press at Strawberry Hill and six of his letters to John Pinkerton, the Scottish historian. Dim as my knowledge of Walpole was, I realized he belonged in my growing library and bought the letters the next day. What, I have often wondered, would my life have been if instead of going into Hodgson's that February morning I had walked on? The collector may reach his specialty by divine direction, as I did, but the great opportunity must present itself in a congenial field. Had I found a roc's egg in Chancery Lane I should not have become an ornithologist, owing to a nasty encounter with a bantam rooster that turned me against birds, but Walpole's six letters fell, so to say, on fertile ground because I had been prepared for the eighteenth century by Boswell's *Life of Johnson,* Chauncey Brewster Tinker at Yale, and Lady Louisa Stuart.

One of the six Walpole letters I bought at Hodgson's begins:

Strawberry Hill. July 31, 1789 [when Walpole was in his seventy-second year]. Having had my house full of relations till this evening, I could not answer the favour of your letter sooner; and now I am ashamed of not being able to tell you that I have finished reading your *Essay on the Ancient History of Scotland.* I am so totally unversed in the story of original nations, and I own always find myself so little interested in savage manners, unassisted by individual characters, that though *you* lead me with a firmer hand than any historian through the dark tracts, the clouds close round me the moment I have passed them, and I retain no memory of the ground I have trod. I greatly admire your penetration, and read with wonder your clear discovery of the kingdom of Stratclyde—but though I bow to you as I would to the founder of an empire, I confess I do not care a straw about your subjects, with whom I am no more acquainted than with the ancient inhabitants of Otaheite. Your origin of the Picts is most able; but then I cannot remember them with any precise discrimination from any other hyperborean nation: and all the barbarous names at the end of the first volume and the gibberish in the Appendix was to me as unintelligible as if I repeated abracadabra, and made no impression on me but to raise respect of your patience, and admire a sagacity that could extract meaning and *suite* from what seemed to me the most indigestible of all materials. You rise in my estimation in proportion to the disagreeable mass of your ingredients . . .

and so on for another page and a half. Walpole had come alive.

I bought Mrs Paget Toynbee's edition of his letters and read its seven-

Strawberry hill
July 31st at night
1789.

Dear Sr

having had my house full of relations till this Evening,
I coud not answer the favour of yr letter sooner; & now I am ashamed
of not being able to tell you that I have finished reading your Essay on the
ancient history of Scotland. I am so totally unversed in the Story of original
Nations, & I own always find myself so little interested in savage manners,
unassisted by Individual Characters, that tho you lead me with a firmer
hand than any Historian thro the dark tracks, the clouds close round me the
moment I have passed them, & I retain no memory of the ground I have trod.
I greatly admire yr penetration, & redde with wonder yr clear discovery of the
Kingdom of Strateclyde — but tho I bow to yours as I woud to the founder of an Em=
=pire, I confess I do not care a straw about yr subjects, with whom I am no
more acquainted than with the ancient Inhabitants of Otaheite. your Origine
of the Piks is most able; but then I cannot remember them with any precise dis=
crimination from any other Hyperborean Nation: And all the barbarous
Names at the end of the first Volume & the Gibberish in the Appendix was to
me as unintelligible as if I repeated Abracadabra, & made no impression on me
but to raise respect of yr patience, & admire a Sagacity that coud extract mea=
=ning & suite from what seemed to me the most indigestable of all materials. you
rise in my estimation in proportion to the disagreable mass of yr Ingredients.

Horace Walpole to Pinkerton, 31 July 1789.

teen volumes straight through, discovering long before the end that
Macaulay's famous essay on Walpole is a caricature. Macaulay wrote it as
a review of Walpole's correspondence with Horace Mann. His manuscript, which I own, was dashed off by a young man flinging untruths
about like confetti. Examples of his brilliance, all untrue, are that Walpole "cared about a miniature of Grammont more than about the American
Revolution," that "his features were covered by mask within mask," and
that he was "a gentleman-usher at heart." Mary Berry who knew Walpole
as well as anyone wrote that Macaulay's "hasty and general opinion" was
"entirely and offensively unlike the original." As to Macaulay's remark
that Walpole "sneered at everybody," she pointed out that "sneering was
not his way of showing dislike." She conceded that "he had very strong
prejudices, sometimes adopted on very insufficient grounds, and he therefore often made great mistakes in the appreciation of character; but
when influenced by such impressions," she went on, "he always expressed
his opinions directly, and often too violently. The affections of his heart
were bestowed on few," she also conceded, "but they were singularly
warm, pure, and constant, characterized not by the ardor of passion, but
by the constant preoccupation of real affection." Miss Berry's answer was
forgotten and Macaulay's essay still damages Walpole's reputation.

As I read volume after volume of Walpole's letters he became a companion who led me about the great world with wit and wisdom. I shared
his love of friends, books, pictures, the theatre, and collecting. I delighted
in what he called the "touches of nature" that he discovered in people and
in his reading; I sympathized with his dread of the gout, which first
attacked him in middle age and reappeared every other year with increas-
ing severity. I was impressed by his determination from the age of eighteen
to record the history of his time for people like himself in the future.
"Giant Posterity" was a lifelong concern. "I have even begun a treatise or
panegyric on the great discoveries made by posterity in all arts and sci-
ences," he wrote, "wherein I shall particularly descant on the delightful-
ness of having whole groves of hummingbirds, tame tigers taught to fetch
and carry, pocket spying-glasses to see all that is doing in China, with a
thousand other toys, which we now look upon as impracticable, and
which pert posterity would laugh in one's face for staring at, while they
are offering rewards for perfecting discoveries, of the principles of which
we have not the least conception!" It was flattering to have him say that
the next Augustan Age would dawn on our side of the Atlantic. Finally,
his devotion to his family and friends was moving, and so was his sym-

pathy with underdogs—blacks, debtors, and Americans. Macaulay made Walpole an underdog whom I grew increasingly eager to defend.

I was encouraged by Byron who said Walpole was 'the father of the first romance [*The Castle of Otranto*] and of the last tragedy [*The Mysterious Mother*] in our language" and was "surely worthy of a higher place than any living writer, be he who he may." Walter Scott granted him "the applause due to chastity and precision of style"; Carlyle called him "an irrefragable authority," and Saintsbury said after dismissing Macaulay's "cocksure dexterity" that Walpole was the key to the society of his day and that his letters would make an excellent third to the Bible and Shakespeare for one stranded on a desert island. I agreed with Henry Adams that one of the charms of reading him is "that he is so extremely like ourselves." When Chauncey Tinker confirmed my belief that Walpole was undervalued I began to think of collecting him seriously. Fortunately, I didn't know how vast a subject he is, for had I known I would have believed it was beyond me. Until I read the letters I had heard only of them and *The Castle of Otranto,* not of *A Catalogue of Royal and Noble Authors, Anecdotes of Painting in England, The Mysterious Mother, Historic Doubts on the Life and Reign of Richard III,* his verses, essays, and memoirs. Nor had I heard of his private press—the first in England— that began with Gray's *Odes* in 1757 and ended with Hannah More's *Bishop Bonner's Ghost* thirty-two years later. My knowledge of Strawberry Hill and its place in the Gothic Revival was hazy. I knew nothing of its library, pictures, and "curiosities" that made it famous throughout Europe.

In *Collector's Progress* I tell how in December 1924 I was drawn by divine guidance into Scribner's Bookstore in New York, just as I had been drawn into Hodgson's, and how I found there a small collection of the Strawberry Hill Press's "detached pieces," how I bought it against the strong advice of a sage elder brother, and how I went ahead as if my life depended on my forming the finest collection of Walpole in existence, which, in fact, it did. The time was propitious because, apart from Dr Johnson and his circle, the eighteenth century was not collected and the books that Walpole wrote, printed, and owned, his letters and manuscripts, were lying about unwanted at a hundredth of what they may fetch today. I went to England nearly every year until the War, made friends with the antiquarian booksellers and read their catalogues from the letter *W.* As their small world became aware of the young American who was collecting Horace Walpole with fanatical zeal more and more of the books

written, printed, and owned by him appeared. Things got easier still when
the Depression brought the Golden Age of collecting in this century. Fortunately, I realized from the first that I should collect the books Walpole
owned because he read and annotated them. We now have a third of his
library, some eighty percent of the original collection that has been
located.

After the War, I embarked on what I later called "Lewis's Folly."
Donald Wing, the head of the Yale Library Purchasing Department, reported to me all the English books from 1751 to 1800 not at Yale that
were offered in booksellers' catalogues. I got several hundred in the next
few years before I unfortunately stopped; "unfortunately" because these
books have proved to be extraordinarily helpful. The subjects range
from how to build chimneys that don't smoke and the Norwich Directory
for 1783 to *How to Live for Many weeks, months, or years, Without
Eating any Thing Whatever*. Many of these "background books" appear
to be the only copies in this country and are the ones most frequently requested from us by readers in the Beinecke Library at Yale. We also have
thousands of unpublished eighteenth-century letters and our collection
of satirical prints, originals and photostats, from 1740 to 1800 is larger
than the British Museum's for the same period. Whereas their collection
has no detailed cross-reference cards, ours has over 60,000.

The local attitude towards my growing library was shown by the Farmington postmistress who observed shrilly while shoveling out the first 302
volumes of the *Gentlemen's Magazine*, "Here you go on, Mr Lewis, buying *books* and all the world crying for *bread!*" Despite this reproof the
library has grown like the chambered nautilus, building more stately
mansions as the swift seasons roll. In 1928 William Adams Delano designed the first of our additional libraries and when Dr Rosenbach, the
greatest of booksellers, stood in its doorway, mouth agape, he said, "This
is the most beautiful library in the world." Five other libraries and two
stack rooms have been added since with a capacity of upwards of 40,000
books. We have protected them with a fire-alarm system so sensitive that
until it was calmed down it brought the local volunteer firemen in their
steel helmets, rubber boots, and axes whenever anyone smoked under one
of the gadgets that set the whole thing off. Our chief "security" against
marauders are two standard French poodles. Although we have opened
the house to hundreds of visitors through the years only one object has
been stolen, a delightful sketch by Jackie Onassis at the age of sixteen, of
her Aunt Annie Burr Lewis.

From 1924 to 1932 I bought only Walpole's unpublished letters, copies of which I sent Paget Toynbee for the supplements that he made to his wife's edition, but in 1932 I had an inspiration that affected the rest of my life. On getting to London that year I hurried round as usual to Maggs Bros. to see what they had put aside for me. For once there was nothing, "No, nothing at all this time, I'm afraid," said Mr Ernest Maggs. Although he was quite ready to have me go I lingered, and then came my inspiration: "It's just occurred to me I ought to have an example of Walpole's hand for every year of his writing life." "Oh, *well!*" said Mr Maggs briskly and ordered up forty letters the firm had been unable to sell since they had bought them eleven years earlier. Mr Maggs and I were equally pleased when I bought all forty for less, as he confided to me, than the firm paid for them. In the next six weeks I got sixty-five more Walpole letters from other booksellers in London and New York, all of whom were thankful to be rid of them at about three pounds apiece. In 1974 Maggs sold one Walpole letter to another bookseller for £350.

When I collated my newly purchased letters with the Toynbees' text of them, feeling rather impertinent to be doing so, I found that they and Walpole's earlier editors had not only been careless in transcription, but had cut out passages they considered "improper," wounding to the descendants of those unflatteringly mentioned, or just plain dull. An untampered text was a third reason why a new edition of the letters was needed. The first reason was to include the letters to Walpole, of which few had been printed apart from Mme du Deffand's. The letters to Walpole not only answer questions that can't be answered in any other way. Without them it is like listening to only one side of a telephone conversation. The second of the three reasons for a new edition was expressed by a reviewer of the letters to Lady Ossory in 1848: "What the reader most indispensably needs," he wrote, "and what registers and magazines cannot supply, is the explanation of small events, slight allusions, obscure anecdotes, traits of individual character, the gossip of the circle, and all the little items and accidents of domestic, social, and political life, which constitute in a most peculiar degree the staple of Walpole's correspondence—the most frequent occasions and chief objects of either his wit or his sagacity, and without some knowledge of which his best letters would be little more than a collection of riddles." The new edition could be done only in a library like Yale's that is especially strong in eighteenth-century newspapers, magazines and collections of contemporary novels, biographies, plays, poems, and pamphlets. The unique material at Farmington would enrich and enlarge the work. My wife and I were ready to finance such an edition if Yale sponsored it. Yale did so and work began 1 July 1933, with one assistant, Dayle Wallace, who had just taken his Ph.D. under Tinker in the Yale Graduate School. I believed naively that the project would be finished by 1950 and not run to more than thirty volumes similar to the small octavos of the Toynbee edition, whereas it will reach forty-eight volumes twice the size of the Toynbee volumes, and will not be finished before 1979. The originals of about half of its seven thousand letters are at Farmington with photostats of the remainder in other hands. Over sixteen hundred letters will be printed for the first time. Lost correspondences may yet turn up—in 1955 two hundred new letters to Walpole appeared out of the blue in Ceylon—but discovery of another large unpublished correspondence is unlikely. Only the keenest Walpolians will read our forty-eight volumes and their million footnotes straight through, yet the Yale Walpole will have to be consulted by all scholars of the period, no matter what their subject is. I once said this in a public talk, stating that you will find in Walpole's letters everything except—I searched for a comic exception—"except bee-keeping," and the next unpublished letter I got was entirely on that subject. As our subscribers live round the world I hope that even a universal cataclysm will spare a set somewhere, perhaps the one at Lima or Oslo, Rondebosch or Osaka, and so enable the study of Walpole and his time to begin anew.

Most of the library was acquired in England, but Walpoliana have been found in Lima, Guernsey, Belfast, The Hague, Geneva, Marburg, Luxor, Cape Town, Colombo, Melbourne, Dunedin, Honolulu, Vancouver, Los Angeles, Chicago, Ann Arbor, and Athens, Georgia. Gifts and bequests have been made by friends and strangers. Thirty-five public institutions in this country, England, Ireland, and Canada, have given or exchanged unique Walpoliana (directly to me or through Yale), for permanent deposit in the Lewis Walpole Library.* They have done so because they

* They are, in the chronological order of their gift or exchange: Yale; Mercantile Library, New York; University of Michigan; Folger Shakespeare Library; University of Chicago; Oriental Institute, Luxor, Egypt; University of Illinois; New York Public Library; Harvard; Library of Congress; Newberry Library, Chicago; Lakeside Press, Chicago; Vancouver Public Library; Century Association, New York; Virginia Historical Society; American Antiquarian Society; College of St Mark and St John, London; University of Liverpool; Essex Institute, Salem, Mass.; Library Company of Philadelphia; Pierpont Morgan Library; Columbia; Wesleyan; Queens University, Belfast; Eleutherian Mills-Hagley Foundation, Del.; University of Virginia; Art Institute of Chicago; National Gallery, Washington; Washington Cathedral; Bryn Mawr; American Philosophical Society; University of Southern California; Cleveland Public Library; Northwestern University; Reform Club, London. These names have been painted by the Bensons of Newport, R.I. on five panels in the East Library, with space left for additions.

have known that my house and everything in it will one day be Yale-in-Farmington.

On my death there will be a Curator and a twelve-man Board of Managers, half of whom will be ex-officio members of the University and half "Successor Members" by analogy with the Successor Fellows of the Corporation who founded Yale in 1701 by giving their books. I have named the first six Lewis Walpole Successor Fellows in my will. They are in full accord with my views of the Library's future use and I trust and pray that they and their successors will not be thwarted by any misguided functionary of the University who would like to use the Library's income for purposes he believes are more important. It is a great comfort to think of these friends protecting the Library throughout the ages against Philistines who have little sympathy with the Library's reason for being. As one who has sat on many similar boards, including the Yale Corporation, I know how effective such a lobby of devoted and solvent persons can be.

It has taken more than a year to decide on the twenty-six objects the Almighty is permitting me to save and to write them up. He let me mention the runners-up for each choice, but punished me with sessions in the Hartford Hospital for doing it.

The order in which the Choices of *Rescuing Horace Walpole* will appear follows Walpole's life more or less chronologically and is not the order of my preference for them.

Choice 1

The Manuscript of "Short Notes of the
Life of Horatio Walpole"

The full title Walpole gave this 7000-word manuscript is, "Short Notes of the Life of Horatio Walpole youngest son of Sir Robert Walpole Earl of Orford and of Catherine Shorter, his first wife." He probably began writing it about 1746 and continued, off and on, until 1779. It begins: "I was born in Arlington Street near St James's London Sept. 24, 1717, O.S. My godfathers were Charles Fitzroy Duke of Grafton, and my Uncle Horatio Walpole; my godmother, my Aunt, Dorothy Lady Viscountess Townshend. I was inoculated for the smallpox in 1724," an event reported in the *London Journal* of 10 October 1724, because it meant that the Prime Minister was endorsing the new practice.

Miss Berry took "Short Notes" after Walpole's death in her third of his manuscripts and sold it years later to her publisher, Richard Bentley (1794–1871). Most of it was printed rather apologetically for the first time in Bentley's edition of Walpole's letters to Horace Mann, 1844. The unknown editor deleted passages that give Walpole's income, when he began and ended each year of his memoirs, a row with his Uncle Horace over money, how he got Lord Waldegrave to marry his niece Maria Walpole, and how he took care of his nephew Lord Orford during his fits of insanity. The full text was printed first in the Yale Walpole with 361 footnotes, some of them quite long. "Short Notes" is the most important Walpole manuscript I know of.

The story of how I got it begins with the start of the Yale Walpole in July 1933, when my wife and I went to Paris to learn from Seymour de Ricci how to find all the letters to and from Walpole in existence. De Ricci was the King of Provenance with 30,000 sale catalogues in his flat and a fabulous memory for owners, dealers, and auctions. My first question was, Where are William Cole's letters to Walpole? because we had started with Walpole's letters to him. De Ricci answered promptly that

Short Notes
of the life of
Horatio Walpole
youngest Son of
Sr Robert Walpole Earl of Orford
and of
Catherine Shorter, his first Wife.

I was born in Arlington street near
St James's London Sept. 24. 1717. O.S. my
Godfathers were Charles Fitzroy Duke of
Grafton, & my Uncle Horatio Walpole;
my Godmother, my Aunt Dorothy Lady
Viscountess Townshend.

In 1725 I went to Bexley in kent with
my Cousins the four younger Sons of
Lord Townshend & with a Tutor, Edward
Weston, one of the Sons of Stephen Bishop
of Exeter, & continued there some months.
The next summer, I had the same education
at Twickenham, Middlesex; & the
intervening winters I went every day
to study under mr Weston at Ld Townshend's.
April 26. 1727. I went to Eton school,
where mr Henry Bland, (since Prebendary
of Durham) Eldest son of Dr Henry Bland,
master of the School, & since Provost of Eton
& Dean of Durham, was my Tutor.

+ I left Eton school Sept. 23. 1734. and
march 11th 1735 went to King's college
Cambridge. My public Tutor was mr John
Smith; my private mr Anstey, afterwards
mr John Whaley was my Tutor. I went to
Lectures in civil law to Dr Dickins of
Trinity hall. to mathematical lectures to
blind Professor Saunderson, for a short time:
afterwards mr Trevigar read lectures to me
in mathematics & philosophy. I heard Dr
Battie's anatomical lectures. I had learned
French at Eton; I learned Italian at Cambridge
of Signor Piazza. at home I learned to dance
& fence; & to draw of Bernard Lens, master
to the Duke & Princesses.

I was inoculated for the
small pox in 1724.

+ Since this man
v. next page.

The first page of Walpole's "Short Notes." From the original manuscript.

they had been bought at the Strawberry Hill Sale in 1842 by the publisher Henry Colburn and that I should get in touch with the grandson of his partner Richard Bentley of the same name who lived at The Mere, Upton, Slough, Bucks.

Fortunately, I followed his advice; fortunately, too, I kept Mr Bentley's letters to me, and fortunately, for the third time, I was able to recover five of my letters to him when they were sold at Sotheby's in 1975. They have refreshed and corrected my memory of one of the most helpful and delightful people I have ever met in Walpoleshire and show the importance of having both sides of a correspondence.

My first letter to Mr Bentley, written 20 August 1933, on Brown's Hotel letter-paper, begins:

Dear Sir:

I am a Research Associate of Yale University engaged upon a new (and I hope definitive) edition of the correspondence of Horace Walpole which will eventually be published by the Clarendon Press. I am, of course, trying to get as many originals of the letters or photostats of them as possible, both to and from Walpole.

"At the Strawberry Hill sale in 1842 a number of letters to Walpole were bought by Henry Colburn. They were lots 135, 136, and 138, of the Sixth Day's sale. Lot 135 I am particularly anxious to trace because it contained upwards of 160 letters to Horace Walpole from Wm. Cole. Mr W. Roberts of Clapham Hill (lately of *The Times*) yesterday suggested to me that these might now be in your possession or that you might know where they are. If you can give me any help in this matter I shall be very grateful. . . .

I shall be here until Sept. 19 or 20 and will gladly motor out any time that it is convenient for you to see me.

Yours sincerely,
W. S. Lewis.

Mr Bentley replied August 28 that he did not have Cole's letters, which proved to be in the Victoria and Albert Museum, but he invited me down to lunch any day the following week; furthermore, he called twice at Brown's without warning. I wrote to say how very disappointed I was to have missed his calls. "It was all the more disappointing in that I could perfectly well have been here had I known you were coming. Now comes your kind letter and I feel that I have put you to a great deal of trouble." I ended, "You are very kind to ask me down for lunch between the 1st and 6th, but, as luck would have it, my wife and I start off on a course of visits this week-end to owners of letters. Everyone has been so

very kind and helpful to me in this business that I think it must succeed."
And there the matter might have rested and I have missed one of the two
richest collections of Walpole's letters and manuscripts then in existence
had I not nearly a year later read a footnote in a book I rarely opened
and learned that the originals of Horace Mann's letters to Walpole (887
in number), were in the possession of Mr Richard Bentley of Upton,
Slough. I hadn't mentioned them and he hadn't volunteered that he owned
them, waiting quite properly, as my wife pointed out to me, to see what
sort of person this young man from Yale was. My letter that reopened our
correspondence is unfortunately missing, but Mr Bentley's reply to it on
30 July 1934, is before me. In my missing letter I apparently assumed he
did not want to part with the originals, but hoped he would let me reproduce them at my expense.

"Dear Mr Lewis,

"Though we were unsuccessful in meeting face to face it is very
pleasant to be again in touch with you. We have a common interest
WALPOLE (in red)
and you are doing a great work—and one would gladly—however slightly
—help you in it." It would be very expensive, he pointed out, "as much
as £300 or £400 to reproduce photographically? Perhaps you might wish
to consider afresh if it is desired to embark upon so expensive a form of
collation?" My letter in which I repeated that I really must edit Walpole's
letters from the originals or have photostats of them if possible is also
missing and so is the postcard of a palm tree that I sent Mr Bentley from
California in the summer of 1934, knowing that any Englishman of Mr
Bentley's generation was stirred by the sight of a palm tree. He replied
in an eight-page letter that he had been pleased to hear from me "on the
shores of the Pacific—and to know that you were having a needed rest
(for I gather you are a very strenuous worker) and the pleasant companionship of a brother ordinarily somewhat out of reach. Coming back
eastwards you must by this time be immersed in the great occupation of
annotating Walpole. The number of years covered—and the variety of
topics and incidents—makes one admire your courage and assiduity in
confronting a work of such magnitude. The reward however is great—
almost every page bristles with interest—and tracking the veiled allusions,
or minor events of the day, now forgotten, tests the skill like a chess
problem. Then Mann's letters to Walpole: These 'lie somewhat heavily
on my chest'!" He was torn between wanting to help me and wanting to
keep the originals; he was concerned about the expense of photostats. He

was writing, he said, in the historic house of the Herschels and reminded me that the lenses of Sir William's telescope were ground by hand and not by machinery and signed himself with very kind regards from his wife and himself. I turned the final page and read, "Would the University feel disposed to spend £100 on Mann?" The letters reached Farmington in time to be a Christmas present from my wife, as I wrote him. Their disposition, Mr Bentley replied, "caused much pleasure . . . AND may I say so without intrusion—the very charming manner in which the documents come into your hands."

During the following months before we met at Upton in July 1935 our correspondence rose to the regularity and fullness of Mann's and Walpole's. Their letters were concerned with the rise and fall of ministries and the marching and countermarching of armies across Europe; Mr Bentley and I were concerned with the minutiae of editing. As you have noticed, his epistolary style was enlivened by block letters and red ink. He darted off the main highway of our subject into bypaths that led to the Duke of Wellington and Henry VII's Queen. Pamphlets by him began arriving, including *A brief Note upon the Battle of Sainte and Mauron, 1351 and 1352* and *Upwards of Sixty Years' Rainfall at Upton, Slough, Buckinghamshire, including hail, sleet, snow, hoar frost or mist.* Our acquaintance was well advanced when my wife and I reached London and found a letter waiting for us at Brown's to confirm our visit to Upton. "The 12:15 from Paddington on Tuesday next [in red ink]. Excellent. You should discover on the platform at Slough an octogenarian with white whiskers (and a projecting white moustache) looking out as passengers descend from the train—on the lookout for *you*."

Our visit to Slough had a double purpose. I wanted to thank Mr Bentley in person for letting me have Mann's letters and I hoped to find Walpole's correspondence with William Mason, the biographer of Gray and a poet held in higher esteem by Walpole and the eighteenth century than by us. The Bentley firm had published the Walpole-Mason correspondence in 1851, since when the original letters had disappeared. Could one or both sides of their correspondence be at Upton? The answer, Michael Sadleir told me, would be in a book there that recorded brief accounts of the Bentley publications and their manuscripts. Mr Bentley was loath to show it, Michael said, but he would if pressed, one might almost say if cornered, remove it from its hiding-place, answer the specific question asked, and put it away again, not letting it out of his hands. That is, our visit was an Aspern Papers mission and the success of it depended on discovering what that book said about the manuscripts in the Walpole-Mason correspondence.

We had no trouble identifying Mr Bentley on the platform at Slough with his projecting white moustache. He was a short stout figure in a black and white checked suit and a square bowler hat on the lookout, as he promised to be, for us. Greetings swiftly over, we were hurried to a massive touring-car and rolled away to The Mere, a large pseudo-Elizabethan house set in ample grounds. In its hall was a grandfather clock with a notice, "True Time—False Time is one hour in advance." Mr Bentley led us to the library that had a long table on which was a life-size iron black boy dressed as a jockey. It was so lifelike that in the rather dim light we were startled. Mr Bentley was enchanted. "What do you think he once did?" he asked. We couldn't imagine. "Blew up!" said Mr Bentley, "when a parlormaid moved him too near the fire." He had been so skillfully mended that, as we could see for ourselves, there was hardly a trace of the mishap. We were not told of any repairs to the parlormaid.

At the end of the table were sherry and biscuits. We sat ceremoniously, and our host launched into the story of Queen Victoria's wedding. At the climax when the organ stalled he dropped into dialogue and acted out the consternation of Sir Somebody Something who was responsible for the failure. During this narration a lady appeared and hurried round to sit beside Mr Bentley, listening to him dutifully with lowered eyes. He paid no attention to her and it was some time before we learned that the newcomer was Mrs Bentley.

Our host was in no hurry to reach Walpole, and that being clear, importunity was to be avoided. Nothing could have been less like the Venetian palace where the Aspern Papers were hidden than The Mere, but on that day there was the same hope of discovery on the part of the visitor and the same reticence on the part of the owner to gratify it.

An opening occurred when we went into the neighboring drawing-room, for on its walls were several copies by G. P. Harding of miniatures formerly at Strawberry Hill. Not to have noticed or commented on them would have been a mistake. The comment having been made without ill effect, I went on to observe that owners of books and manuscripts may not know they own them. "There might be," I said, "letters from or to Walpole right here in this house." Mr Bentley's steady stare suggested I had been precipitate and I did not bring up the Walpole-Mason correspondence until a second opening occurred at lunch. This time, greatly

daring, I came right out with, "The Walpole-Mason letters were published by Bentley's. Could the originals be here?"

"I have a book," said Mr Bentley, brushing aside my boldness as if it
were a crumb, "that will answer that question."

We were interrupted by a message from the gardener, which Mr
Bentley read aloud: "Upton, Slough, Bucks, July 16, 1935, 2:05. True
Time. 79 ½° F."

"You see," Mr Bentley exulted, "it's almost *80!*"

In a few minutes an excited maid brought a second report from the
gardener that the thermometer had just crossed 80. Pleased astonishment
went round the table. 80! A *very* warm day!

Lunch was of eight courses and lasted until 3:30 False Time. With the
disappearance of the strawberries I ventured to ask our host: "And now
the book?"

Mr Bentley looked at me stonily. "You must see the house first."

We followed him and Mrs Bentley through several bedrooms and came
to rest in an upstairs sitting-room where our host opened a cabinet from
which he took a purse that he handed my wife. "Money, it is said, is the
root of all evil; yet we can't do without money, and a purse is as convenient a way to carry it as any other. Now, madam, look inside that
purse." My wife opened it and out flew a spring, which Mr Bentley retrieved promptly from the floor. Other speeches and surprises followed
before we moved on. Mr Bentley anticipated my question. "But you
haven't seen Windsor!" He pointed to stairs up which we climbed into a
cupola with a view of Windsor through the trees, Mr Bentley prudently
waiting below. As we came down he pointed to the wall and began
rapidly. "You would say, Mr Lewis, that this is the end of the house?"

"I would."

"Let us see." He pressed a button, a door slid back revealing another
wing of the house fitted up as a ship; port and starboard lights, oars, state-
rooms, life preservers. A telephone to the kitchen—or galley when called
from this quarter—received orders that began with "Ahoy!"

"Now," said Mr Bentley with a crafty glance, "the book!" He led us
back to the dining-room, where the sizable ledger was hidden in a cupboard. Mr Bentley got it out and sat with it on the arm of a large stuffed
chair.

"What year did you say the Mason letters were published?"

"1851."

He struggled with the book, which was hard to handle sitting in that
position. "Here, you take it," he said.

The book was in my hands! I turned to "The Correspondence of Horace Walpole, Earl of Orford, and the Rev. William Mason. Now first published from the original MSS. Edited, with notes, by the Rev. J. Mitford. In Two Volumes. London: Richard Bentley, Publishers in Ordinary to Her Majesty, 1851." I came to the end of the page and read: "The originals of Mason's letters to Walpole are now [1900] in the possession of Mr Richard Bentley of Upton, Slough, Bucks." As I read this last aloud, Mr Bentley fell over into the chair, his short legs sticking above the arm. He was breathing heavily. "What a very pertinacious young man!" I heard him whisper.

"Have you given the letters away?" I asked.

"No."

"Have you sold them?"

"No."

"Then they must still be here!"

There was a pause. "Time for tea," said Mr Bentley firmly, struggling up out of the chair and taking the book away from me.

Letters sped back and forth from Upton to Brown's following our visit to The Mere. Mr Bentley wrote, "Six possible fields of research are open. (Four libraries in the house itself, one a hundred yards away easterly and one a hundred yards distant north westerly. Total six.) Nos 1-2. 4.5.6. do *not* contain the missing letters. No. 3 *possibly* might or should.

"So infected by your ardour I sent for a worthy carpenter to attack certain piles of parcels in Library III. The shelf-books in 'no time' revealed NIL but certain oak 'coffins' or 'double-coffins' wider and deep seemed a suitable hiding place. I sat at their side and gave a critical glance at *each* [underscored in red ink] parcel as it was extracted. It was an interesting review—mainly William IV or (very) early Victorian period—later than Mason. The excellent man in endeavouring to 'preserve *exactly* the same order' in replacement occasionally tripped—and a dossier, say of Thomas Campbell would get interposed between letters of (say) Ingoldsby or of Theodore Hook *—to the puzzlement of someone perhaps in years to come—or (had he been present) would have agonized the exact eye of Michael Sadleir! But—no find! [in red ink.]"

One of my rescued letters is an answer to a postcard with an ambiguous reference in red to Mason's letters to Walpole and a letter of July 23 in which Mr Bentley reported, "The chase goes on—at intervals—between inrushes of visitors—because I feel that you are RIGHT, i.e., if the books

" * Elastic bands, when petrified or fossilized with age, are very untrustworthy. Bursting, their contents would mingle like 'Cocktails,' one author with another!"

have *not* left Upton (which I am sure is the case)—they must be here still [in red]—only 'tis a large field to explore." I answered, "My dear Mr Bentley, On getting back from Norfolk last night I found your two communications. I read the postal first and concluded from it that the letters had been found. Sad disillusionment when I opened the letter! However, Library No. 3 does not yet seem exhausted—I only hope you will not be when this is over! How very good of you to get in the worthy carpenter —miner for the moment, digging for pure gold!

"When we were nearing Liverpool Street last night," I went on, "I asked my wife, 'Do you think I shall find a letter from Mr Bentley on getting home [i.e., Brown's]?' She (who is somewhat clairvoyant) answered, 'Yes, but he won't have found them yet. But he will find them and I think he'll probably bring them up to town himself.' So you see I am still full of hope and confidence. As they were there a mere 33 years ago and as you don't remember giving them away they must be, as you say, still there. What an appetite this delay has given! No letters will be more appreciated when they do turn up."

On the 28th Mr Bentley reported that, libraries one to six having drawn blank, "I did at last what I should have done at first!" he turned to the Sage of Uckfield "with most helpful results. Mason was seen here (in MS I mean) barely a dozen years ago—so now it is certain that he must be still here, even though not at 'No. 3.' . . . Now the searchlight has to be turned at every free interval upon subsidiary or supplemental collections—and *now* with a certainty of ultimate success."

And then on the 31st arrived a "Greetings Telegram" for Professor Lewis in a gold envelope with the message printed by hand, "Eureka, Mason. Bentley." This was followed by a letter:

My dear Professor

> You were right
> I was right
> Wayne Williams [the Sage of Uckfield] was right.

All are satisfied [in red ink]

MASON *IS* [in red ink] AT UPTON.

Good modest man—in no crimson jacket like the Florentine Ambassador—lay low in a plain drab leather jacket, and hid himself in the recesses of a Book case cupboard 'upstairs' as Williams said—and I thought . . . but *not* in Library 3 or Library 4.

In a triumphant moment I ventured to hurl a telegram at you—and even stipulated with the Post office that it should be delivered to you in a gilt envelope.

Now what happens? You will wish to have photostat copy made at once? *OR* you may wish to carry back the originals to augment your Walpole collection at Farmington. . . . Perhaps at half the Mann figure, say 50 guineas. This only if you *WANT* it.

A second letter was written on the same day in answer to my golden greetings telegram of grateful acceptance.

Dear Professor Lewis,

I had hardly despatched a letter to you this afternoon when an excited maid—her eyes fixed upon a salver—came into the room and handed me a 'golden object' with due importance.

The Duke of Marlborough pencilled the news of his great victory on the back of his washerwoman's bill (being away from his desk) and hurried the splendid news off to Queen Anne in England.

You—Sir—have eclipsed the Duke and sent a superb message of triumph on the finding of 'Mason' after 150 years or more!

and he said he would bring the letters up to Brown's on Friday. He came with the letters, all 110 of them, in their "plain, drab, leather jacket."

Just before we sailed there arrived a bon voyage message:

> August 15 1935
> Natal day of Napoleon I

My dear Lewis,

Yale really *MUST* [in red ink] arrange to have the great statue at the entrance to New York illuminated [in red ink] as the Europa enters that harbour.

What a *chain* of

> Victory!

and he spelled out in red the names of Walpole's correspondents whose letters I had found in England during the summer, COLE, MONTAGU, MANN, MASON, OSSORY.

After we got home letters and postcards poured in with excellent advice about editing and shrewd guesses and surmises about Walpolian problems. Mr Bentley was a constant reader of *Notes and Queries,* in which dozens of our queries raised by the Cole correspondence were appearing, and he reported whatever he thought might be helpful. Then, quite suddenly in February 1936, he died.

When we got to London in 1937 Robin Flower, Deputy Keeper of Manuscripts at the British Museum and one of the greatest early friends of the Yale Walpole, told me of the Walpole manuscripts that he found at Upton when he went down to appraise the library for tax purposes. The letters were not in libraries one to six, but in a remote passageway, a collection of Walpole's manuscripts that corresponds in importance to the Boswelliana found in the croquet box at Malahide Castle. There were about a hundred unpublished letters, including those to John Chute, Walpole's first history, *The War with Spain*, 1739, his Journal for 1769, the last memoirs from 1783 to 1791, Sir Robert Walpole's last words, and many notes for the earlier memoirs written on scraps of paper. There were also Walpole's *Hieroglyphic Tales* with two unprinted ones, "An abstract of the Kings and Queens of England," the draft for Walpole's "Account of my Conduct relative to My Places," "The History of Madame du Barry, Mistress of Louis Quinze," and out-topping all in importance, the "Short Notes" of his life. Did Mr Bentley know they were there and was he waiting for me to pursue the quest at Upton further? That is not, I think, impossible. In any event, Mrs Bentley's trustees let me have all the manuscripts, thanks to her friendly offices and those of John Hodgson, he who had knocked down to me in his sale room my first Walpole letters to Pinkerton; but the Upton saga was not finished. Peter Cunningham's correspondence with the first Bentley about his edition of Walpole's letters turned up and so did Miss Berry's letters to Bentley about her books and much besides, all of which Mrs Bentley gave me.

Walpole's letters to Mason are still missing; promising leads in Yorkshire and Wales came to nothing. I hope they may yet appear, but if I had to choose between them and the "Short Notes" I would choose the "Short Notes" without hesitation.

Choice 2

Sir Robert and Lady Walpole by Eccardt and Wootton in a Grinling Gibbons Frame

This frame hung in the Blue Bedchamber, as we learn from Walpole's *Description of Strawberry Hill:* "In a frame of black and gold carved by Gibbons, Sir Robert Walpole and Catherine Shorter; small whole lengths; by Eccardt, after Zincke: the hounds and view of Houghton by Wootton, Sir Robert is sitting; by him, on a table, is the purse of the chancellor of the exchequer, leaning against busts of George 1st and 2d to denote his being first minister to those kings: by Lady Walpole are flowers, shells, a pallet and pencils, to mark her love of the arts." William Cole, Horace Walpole's contemporary at Eton and Cambridge and his chief antiquarian correspondent, noted in his "Account of Some Pictures at Strawberry Hill" now in the British Library, "under the table stands a flower pot, and by Lady Walpole a grotto of shells. I remember when I was a school-boy at Eton, calling on Mr Walpole at Chelsea, where Sir Robert, his father, then lived, I found him learning to draw, with Mr Lens the painter with him; and he then showed me a most beautiful grotto of shell work in the garden, on the banks of the Thames, designed by his mother: probably this alludes to that grotto. The frame of this picture cost £30, being most exquisitely carved, painted black, and gilt, having all sorts of flowers, fruits, birds, and at top figures of boys."

In his *Anecdotes of Painting in England* Walpole calls Gibbons (1648–1720) "An original genius" who was "a citizen of nature. . . . There is no instance of a man before Gibbons who gave to wood the loose and airy lightness of flowers, and chained together the various productions of the elements with a free disorder natural to each species." How did the frame get to Strawberry Hill? I have been saying for years that it was originally around a mirror at Houghton, Sir Robert's house in Norfolk, and that Walpole admired it so much his father gave it to him, a plausible explanation, but I can't prove it. In *Aedes Walpolianae*, 1747, Walpole's *catalogue*

Sir Robert and Lady Walpole by Eccardt and Wootton in a black and gold frame carved by Grinling Gibbons.

raisonné of his father's great collection of pictures at Houghton, he speaks of Gibbons's carvings there, but doesn't mention the frame. Walpole's copy at Farmington of *A Description of Strawberry Hill* "with such prices as I can recollect" says nothing about the £30 or where the frame came from, but we know that it was bought at the Strawberry Hill sale in 1842 by Lord Lansdowne and that it was No. 77 in Lansdowne House, Berkeley Square, until 1930 when it was sold at Christie's and given me by my wife.

Walpole's parents lived apart much of the time. There is at Farmington a letter from Sir Robert to his wife dated 10 July, 1702, when he was twenty-six and their eldest son, Robert, was only a year. The letter begins, "My Dearest Dear" and continues with mock devotion and surprise that she could have written him such unpleasant letters. "I am blind, cannot, would not, see anything in my dearest self but what is most agreeable," etc., etc. The hearty, red-necked Robert Walpole could be cutting and cruel. He and his wife came together occasionally. Edward was born in 1706, Horace in 1717. One hundred and twenty years after Horace's birth Lady Louisa Stuart printed the gossip of her day that he was not the son of Sir Robert, but of Carr Lord Hervey. How, the skeptics asked, could the red-faced, lusty Sir Robert have such a pale epicene son? Horace, it was noted, was more like the Herveys than the Walpoles. He wrote in his first Common Place Book (Choice 4), "Lady Mary Wortley Montagu said there were three sexes: Men, women, and Herveys." His mother's affair with Carr Lord Hervey was no secret, but if the Walpoles had doubts about Horace's paternity when he was born they rose above them: he was named for Sir Robert's younger brother who stood godfather for him; Lady Townshend, his father's sister, was his godmother and paid for the christening. It is not unlikely, as Romney Sedgwick pointed out, that the gossip about Horace's paternity came from John Lord Hervey's statement that Sir Robert believed his grandson and heir, George third Earl of Orford, was illegitimate.

Horace was brought up by his mother who lavished on him what he later called "extreme partiality." We get some idea of this from the bills now at Farmington for his toys that came to £39.11.9 and for two suits that cost £71, a total that is the equivalent of heaven knows how much today. Those bills were thoughtfully reported to me by J. H. Plumb; they were among the Walpole papers at Houghton that the late Lord Cholmondeley deposited in the Cambridge University Library for the use of scholars. The Cholmondeleys very kindly let me have them with other bills paid to Master Horace's writing master, schoolmaster, and footman, together with eight of his Exchequer account books kept in the 1750s. His first letter to his mamma, written when he was eight, is also at Farmington. It hopes that she, his papa, and all his "cruataurs" are "wall," a concern that reflects a lifelong devotion to his parents and pets. He shared his mother's love of flowers and painting. At Farmington are three well drawn water-color copies of Watteau that he signed with his initials and dated 1736, 1737, 1738. We can picture Lady Walpole admiring the first and perhaps the second before she died in 1737 in Horace's twentieth year. So overwhelmed was he by her death that his friends feared for his sanity. The Dean and Chapter of Westminster Abbey permitted him to raise a cenotaph in the Henry VII Chapel to her memory. The drawing of it with a note by Walpole, "Design for Lady Walpole's tomb in Westminster Abbey by Rysbrack," was given me by Fritz Liebert.

On his wife's death Sir Robert promptly married Maria Skerrett, the mother of his daughter Mary, and Horace "got out of a house I could not bear." The new Lady Walpole died a few months later in childbirth. Seven of her books found their way into Horace's library; one of the three at Farmington is a copy of *Paradise Lost*. It was a wedding present from Lady Mary Wortley Montagu with the passage on the felicities of marriage transcribed on a fly-leaf by her. Walpole kept this book under lock and key in the Glass Closet of his library with the books he didn't want everyone to see.

While he was on the Grand Tour Sir Robert had him made a Member of Parliament for a family borough and so Horace was able to fight for his father in the final battle of Sir Robert's twenty-one year rule as Prime Minister. After Sir Robert fell in 1742 and became Earl of Orford, Horace was his constant companion until Sir Robert died three years later. Dr Ranby, Sir Robert's physician, in *A Narrative of the Last Illness of the Right Honourable the Earl of Orford*, 1745, acknowledged his indebtedness to "the journal of one of Lord Orford's sons," who was undoubtedly Horace. The journal has disappeared and Horace did not annotate his three copies of Ranby's printed *Narrative* at Farmington, but we do have Sir Robert's last words that Horace recorded on a scrap found at Upton. The "Lixivium" mentioned in the note was a violent concoction for the stone that was given Sir Robert by his earlier physician, Jurin. The note begins, "Dear Horace, this Lixivium has blown me up, it has tore me to pieces," and ends, "Tis impossible not to be a little disturbed at going out of the world, but you see I am not afraid." Sir Robert left Horace £5000, his house in Arlington Street, and an extra place in the Customs that brought his income to £8000 in 1784, a sum equal to perhaps $400,000 today without taxes. As long as he lived he wrote of his father's superiority to all other men and berated his enemies with unabated dislike.

Horace's much older brothers, Robert and Edward, detested their mother's favorite little boy. No letters between him and Robert have been found, but there is at Farmington a gift from Robert that Horace kept locked in his library's Glass Closet, "Callot's pocket-book, with a great number of exquisite original drawings by himself: a present to Mr Walpole from his brother Robert Earl of Orford: very valuable," an acknowledgment Walpole repeated on a fly-leaf of the book itself. When it was sold in 1842 for one of the highest prices in the library, the underbidder was William Beckford whose letters at Farmington to his bookseller show how badly he wanted the book. Sotheby's re-sold it in 1938. Philip Hofer and I were in London at the time and agreed not to bid against each other; but which of us should have it? The question was settled at a stag dinner given by Boies Penrose when somebody suggested sensibly that we cut for it. I see now the strong light on the card table and the white shirts of the diners standing round it as I leaned over and cut the ten of clubs and Phil cut the six of diamonds, and I remember the congratulations of the company. They proved premature because at the sale Dr Rosenbach soared above the limit that Phil and I had naively assumed was ample and bought the book for Lessing Rosenwald whom I didn't know at the time. After we had become close friends during the War Lessing was distressed to hear of the fiasco. "You ought to have it," he said, "but I've given it to our National Gallery." The Gallery was understandably loath to part with it until two fortunate things happened: Miss Agnes Mongan of the Fogg Museum at Harvard, the authority on Callot, said that the drawings were not by him and Lessing was elected to the National Gallery Board. At his first meeting he moved that the book be given to Yale for permanent deposit at Farmington, and that is how it rejoined sixty of its former neighbors in the Glass Closet.

Walpole had much more to do with Robert's son, George 3rd Earl of Orford, who is remembered chiefly for selling his grandfather's collection of pictures to Catherine of Russia. In his day he was celebrated as the last falconer in Britain, for driving four red deer in a phaeton, and for staging a race for £500 between five turkeys and five geese from Norwich to London. His style is shown in the "voyage" of nine boats that he conducted through the Fens with himself as Admiral of the Fleet and his mistress Patty Turk as its Vice-Admiral. "When the bridges on the smaller rivers and dykes were too low," Wyndham Ketton-Cremer wrote in *A Norfolk Gallery,* "the crew dismantled them, to the dismay of the local inhabitants: and it can only be hoped that they were properly reerected before the fleet moved on." The unabridged manuscript of Walpole's "Short Notes" tells us that Orford first went mad in 1773. His mother, a great heiress who lived in sin at Florence, asked Walpole to take charge of him and his affairs, and was seconded by the "Old Horace" branch of the family at Wolterton, Edward refusing to be bothered with his ailing nephew. Horace surprised himself and everyone else by his business skill, selling horses and dogs and dealing with "the rascally attorneys" and "rookery of harpies" who had been battening on his profligate nephew. Orford recovered his senses, and then with small thanks to his Uncle Horace got back the dismissed harpies. He was intermittently insane until he died in 1791. Horace then became, so he said, "the poorest earl in England." How little the new honor meant to him may be gauged by his not taking his seat in the House of Lords and by his verses,

Epitaphium Vivi Auctoris 1792.

An estate and an earldom at seventy-four!
Had I sought them or wish'd them, 'twould add one fear more,
That of making a countess when almost four-score.
But Fortune, who scatters her gifts out of season,
Though unkind to my limbs, has still left me my reason;
And whether she lowers or lifts me, I'll try
In the plain simple style I have liv'd in, to die;
For ambition too humble, for meanness too high.

There are so many memorials at Farmington of Horace's second brother, Edward, and his family that I have put him in Choice 3.

Walpole's half-sister Mary, the daughter of Sir Robert and Maria Skerrett before they were married, is a shadowy figure; we don't even know the year of her birth, but she wasn't much younger than Horace. When her father became Earl of Orford she was legitimated by George II and was created an earl's daughter, an unprecedented act that submitted her to public abuse. Horace wrote that the wives and daughters of his father's enemies "declare against giving her place" and told how one day while driving through Hanover Square he met a mob carrying "a mawkin in a chair with three footmen, and a label on the breast, inscribed 'Lady Mary.'" There are glimpses of her at Houghton playing comet with Horace and singing for him at her harpsichord. She had, he wrote Mann,

"remarkable taste and knowledge of music," but being shy she sang for
few. Her father's known partiality to her encouraged the belief that she
was a great heiress and brought noble suitors. She rejected them for
Charles Churchill, a natural son of the Marlborough family at Blenheim,
a match that Horace called "foolish," but which turned out well. The
only letter of his to Churchill that we have seen is written in his wittiest
and easiest style. A letter from Churchill to Horace that announces the
pending marriage of their daughter Mary to Lord Cadogan is at Farmington, but no more of their correspondence is known, a major loss in Walpole's history.

The first picture I ever bought was of Lady Mary Churchill, and like
so many "finds" in collecting I came on it by chance. One morning in
February 1925, while killing half an hour in the library of the University
Club in New York, I happened to look at an auction catalogue of pictures
for the first time in my life. The sale was that evening at the Anderson
Gallery. Lot 26 was described, "Lady Mary Churchill by Francis Cotes."
Webster's definition of "luck" is just right: "That which happens to one
seemingly by chance." The "seemingly" allows for the possibility of divine
intervention and extra-sensory perception, to both of which ardent collectors are susceptible. My hesitation before Hodgson's sale room in Chancery
Lane illustrates these mysterious forces, and I believe my opening the sale
catalogue in the University Club library was another intervention of the
same nature. There was, however, no luck in the speed with which I
hurried to see the picture. That was zeal fired by my resolve two months
earlier to make the finest collection of Horace Walpole in existence.

Lady Mary appears in this portrait as a plain young woman sitting at a
table with an open music book. She is looking up at us rather shyly. Her
resemblance to Horace is strong, a significant circumstance because if the
gossip about his paternity were true they would be no blood relation. I
got the picture with only one opposing bid for $175. The following
morning, after paying my bill, I bundled Lady Mary into a taxi instead
of sending her to Farmington by express. I was sailing for England in a
few days and wanted to get the picture home before I left, but the wisdom
of carrying it myself seemed doubtful when I got to the Grand Central.
It was Saturday noon. The Anderson Gallery people, after recovering
from their surprise at such an unorthodox delivery, advised me to carry
the picture unwrapped to protect it from those who might stick their
umbrellas through it unaware that it was a picture. As I walked down the
wide stairs on to the concourse with Lady Mary clasped to my bosom I was

noticeable. The porter who had my bag slumped along in front, embarrassed. One youth regarding me with awe asked, "Is that over a hundred years old?" Another asked, "Say, did that come from Athens?" A friend who was going with me to Farmington for the week-end looked at me and hurried on without speaking.

When I got to the gate of my train the gateman sprang to attention. "You can't take that thing on here," he said, and threw a chain across the entrance. I rested Lady Mary on my toes. What was I to do? The train was leaving in a few minutes. My faithless friend was already on it; there was not another train for two hours. "I have my ticket on this train," I said, and added with what I hoped was an effective blend of authority and pitifulness, "I've *got* to make it."

The gateman hesitated, then said in a low, conspiratorial voice, "Follow me." We dashed off in the direction of the Graybar Building, my porter gloomily following. Our guide stopped before a little door I had never seen before, opened it, said, "Jeez, I'd get hell for this! What would happen to the express companies if everybody carried things like that?" He accepted my dollar bill as I sped through the gate with the porter and hurried back to his post, none the worse, I hope, for circumventing the express companies.

At home I sought for the first time confirmation of a Walpolian relic in the Strawberry Hill Catalogue. I found it among the family portraits in the Great Parlour: Twenty-first Day's Sale, lot 39, "a half-length of Lady Maria Walpole, only child of Sir Robert Walpole and Maria Skerrett, and wife of Charles Churchill, only son of General Churchill. ECCARDT. She is represented in a veil, with a music-book before her, a very charming picture." Most of this was taken from Walpole's *Description of Strawberry Hill,* but Walpole did not mention that Lady Mary is wearing a large diamond brooch. He spoke of the diamond years later when defending his father against the charge of receiving expensive presents from George II. Sir Robert was given only two, Horace said, "a crystal hunting bottle" and a large diamond with a great flaw in it, "both of which he gave to Lady Mary." I believe this is the diamond she is wearing in her portrait. Eccardt is a less valued artist than Francis Cotes, whose best pictures have been attributed to Reynolds, but Walpole placed him second only to Reynolds in a list of "Principal Painters now in London" that he made in 1761 and he commissioned Eccardt to paint Walpole himself and twenty-one members of his family and friends. Walpole's "The Beauties, An Epistle to Mr Eccardt, the Painter," was "handed about," he complained,

Lady Mary Churchill by Eccardt.

until it "got into print very incorrectly," yet the text follows closely the original manuscript of the verses in his Second Common Place Book, which is described in Choice 4.

A second portrait of Lady Mary by Eccardt is at Farmington. She is with her husband and their eldest little boy in a frame designed by Walpole. It hangs next to the Grinling Gibbons frame, as it did in the Blue Bedchamber at Strawberry. Walpole tells us that it was taken "from the picture at Blenheim of Rubens, his wife and child." I owe it to Andrew Ritchie who when he was Director of the Yale Art Gallery found it at Colnaghi's in London and had it put aside for me. Such pictures bring with them the sense of life and color one has on regaining one's sight after a long interval. In this small conversation piece Lady Mary leaning towards her little son is more *grande dame* than a doting young mother and a more engaging woman than in the earlier Eccardt I carried home from New York. Walpole's fondness for her is reflected by Mme du Deffand, who found her *très aimable, ses manières sont nobles, simples, et naturelles.* She became Housekeeper at Kensington and Windsor, lucrative and not too demanding posts. Two of her sons, George and Horace, flanked their Uncle as his aides-de-camps when he, aged 76, put on a sword to receive the "Queen and eight daughters of kings" at Strawberry Hill in 1794. His correspondence with Lady Mary was lifelong, but not one of his letters to or from her has appeared. At Farmington there is a portfolio from Upton that once contained letters to him. His list of the thirty correspondents is still inside the back cover. There are also a few stubs with their names: "From my Father, Sir Robert Walpole, afterwards Earl of Orford," "From my Brother Robert Earl of Orford," "From my Nephew George 3rd Earl of Orford," "From my Brother Edward Walpole," "From Lady Mary Walpole, since married to Charles Churchill Esq. son to Genl Churchill." The gap after the stub with her name is one of the widest in the book. Later evidence of his correspondence with her appears in his "Paris Journals" in which he recorded the letters he wrote on his five journeys to Paris between 1765 and 1775. Owen Morshead, the King's Librarian at Windsor, who performed miracles of discovery for me, recommended a skilled researcher at Somerset House. He sought out the wills of the Churchills, their seven children, and their children's children who spread throughout the Empire, a search that went on for months. I had given up when I met one of the descendants whose family name had appeared during the search and in whose country house was a portrait of Lady Mary on a horse. "Oh," she said, "I know all about Horace Walpole's letters to Lady Mary Churchill. They belonged to my Uncle George who lived in Sussex." And what of him? "Uncle George went mad during the war and believed that the Germans were coming to get the letters. So he threw all of them into the fire shrieking with laughter." And that, I'm afraid, is just what happened.

Walpole learned by chance of another illegitimate daughter of his father's, Catherine Daye, who was living in great poverty with her mother. Horace told Cole that Sir Robert left her £100 a year and bought a rich living that he presented to a young clergyman with the understanding that he would marry Catherine when she came of age. The young clergyman took the living, married an heiress instead of Catherine, and went on to become Bishop of Chester and Ely. Horace brought Catherine to live at Strawberry Hill. Our only glimpse of her is from Cole who wrote that she was of "a squab, short, gummy appearance," but she died soon after she moved to Strawberry and when visitors came she perhaps had a tray in her own room. I like to think of her and her kindly younger brother visiting the Blue Bedchamber to pay their respects to their father's portrait in the Grinling Gibbons frame.

Choice 3
Walpole's Mezzotint of The Ladies Waldegrave

As I have said, the memorials at Farmington of Edward Walpole and his family are so numerous I have put them in a Choice of their own.

Edward was eleven years older than Horace. The brothers were not at all friendly as young men when they had a serious row about money. Their published correspondence begins in 1745 with a letter from Edward that works up to

your conduct to me has always . . . made it the most painful thing in the world to me to have any commerce with you. You have, I must confess, showed a great disposition to me and to my children at all times, which is agreeable to the good nature that I shall ever do you the justice to think and say you possess in a great degree. But it has been mixed with what I dare say you can't help and never meant offence by, but still what I am not obliged to bear, such a confidence and presumption of some kind of superiority, that, my sentiments not tallying with yours upon that head, it has been very unpleasant. You have assumed to yourself a preeminence, from an imaginary disparity between us in point of abilities and character that, although you are a very great man, I cannot submit to.

This letter and Horace's rejoinder, which he marked "not sent," came to Farmington from Upton. The unsent letter begins: "Brother, I am sorry you won't let me say, Dear Brother, but till you have still farther proved how impossible it is for you to have any affection for me, I will never begin my letters as you do. Sir," and Horace goes on to rebut Edward's charges for several pages. One passage is "In my mother's lifetime, you accused me of fomenting her anger against you. The instant she died, did I not bring you all my letters to her which she had kept, in never a one of which, was your name mentioned, but to persuade her to continue that love to you, which your behaviour has always laboured to extinguish in the hearts of all your relations. As to my father, I well know how ill you always used him on my account. . . . Your converting all the jealousy you used to have of Lady Mary, into a friendship with her, to prevent her loving me, is another." Hours of seething rage must have gone into the unsent reply, but Horace prudently put his letter aside and in two days answered more in sorrow than in anger, a display of self-control that must have made Edward detest him all the more. When three years later Edward planned to use Horace's house without permission for his daughter Laura who was ailing, Horace wrote Montagu, "I can conceive forgiveness; I can conceive using people ill—but how does one feel to use anybody very ill without any provocation, and then ask favours of them?" Three years later still Horace proved he was a good brother rising above ill-usage when a gang charged Edward with sodomitical assault. Horace took the stand as a witness for the defense and helped to convict the conspirators who were heavily fined, made to stand in the pillory, and were imprisoned at hard labor.

As time went on Horace and Edward's association became easier. Even in his first furious letter Edward acknowledged Horace's kindness to him and his children "at all times." Horace's summary of Edward in his *Last Journals,* which was written in 1772, shows him at his most just and charitable:

My brother Edward . . . was a man of excellent parts and numerous virtues; the first he buried in obscurity and retirement, the latter he never failed exerting. He had great natural eloquence, wit, humour even to admirable mimicry, uncommon sensibility, large generosity and charity. He drew well, but seldom, was a profound musician, and even invented a most touching instrument, which from the number of its strings, he called a *pentachord.* All these engaging qualities and talents, formed for splendour and society, were confined to inferior companions, for he neither loved the great world, nor was his temper suited to accommodate himself to it, for he was exceedingly passionate, jealous, and impatient of contradiction, though in his later years he acquired more mildness. He wrote several small pieces in prose and verse, a very few of which were printed, but never with his name, for no man had less parade. In pathetic melancholy he chiefly shone, especially in his music, and yet, though his ear was all harmony, his verse was more replete with meaning than it was sonorous.

A small collection, "Verses and drawings by my brother Sir E. Walpole, which I desire may be preserved in my family. H.W." is bound in Choice 8, the most notable of Horace's own copies of his 1774 *Description of Strawberry Hill.* There are several of Edward's verses in manuscript; two more are identified by Horace on cuttings from the *Public Advertiser.* Edward's spirited rhymed couplets show that he was one of "the mob of gentlemen who wrote with ease." Other of Edward's verses that Horace transcribed in his Book of Materials, 1759, (Choice 4) are chiefly notable for a four-letter word written out in full with a freedom only recently regained. Among Edward's pencil sketches is an excellent one of Sir Robert. Horace's extreme partiality to the productions of amateur artists and writers (which is shown in Choice 10) played a part in his improved relations with Edward.

Slaughter's portrait of Edward hung in the Refectory, or Great Parlour, at Strawbery Hill with a dozen other family portraits including the one of Lady Mary Churchill now at Farmington. The Slaughter of Edward is now at Wolterton, the Norfolk house built by "Old" Horace Walpole where his descendants still live, but a water-color of it by G. P. Harding, who copied so many pictures and objects at Strawberry, is at Farmington and shows Edward very splendid in the scarlet robes of the Bath. In 1930 I bought from Agnew in London a portrait of him in a beautiful blue-green coat. This was exhibited in the Royal Academy Exhibition of 1781, "Portrait of a Gentleman by Edward Edwards," and identified by Walpole in his copy (now in the possession of Lord Rosebery), "Sir E. Walpole." I also have a miniature of him in middle age and one in old age by Edward Edwards that was reproduced in color as the frontispiece to *The Connoisseur* of September 1915. All four portray a much more portly and rosy man than Horace, who was excessively thin and pale.

Edward had four children by his mistress, Dorothy Clement, who Horace said was "a milliner's apprentice at Durham." The children were Laura, Maria, Edward, and Charlotte. They appear together in a most attractive conversation piece by Slaughter that is now in the Minneapolis Art Museum. When they were ill Uncle Horace took them to Strawberry Hill and looked after them, an instance of his "great disposition" to Edward's children. Laura married a Keppel who became Bishop of Exeter. Maria's first husband was the second Earl Waldegrave; her second husband, whom she married secretly without her Uncle Horace's approval, was George III's younger brother, the Duke of Gloucester. Charlotte married the fifth Earl of Dysart. Walpole reported the death of the younger Edward to Horace Mann: "My brother has lost his son, and it is no misfortune, though he was but three and thirty, and had very good parts; but he was sunk into such a habit of drinking and gaming, that the first ruined his constitution, and the latter would have ruined his father."

Maria, the beauty of the family, was her Uncle Horace's favorite. He boasted to Horace Mann of how he brought about her marriage to Lord Waldegrave who was twenty-one years her senior. "A month ago," Horace wrote, "I was told that he liked her. . . . I jumbled them together, and he has already proposed. For character and credit he is the first match in England—for beauty, I think she is. She has not a fault in her face or person, and the detail is charming. A warm complexion tending to brown, fine eyes, brown hair, fine teeth, and infinite wit, and vivacity. . . . My brother has luckily been tractable, and left the whole management to me." A pastel of her, very beautiful in her coronation robes, has appeared since I wrote this chapter. It hangs in the center of the new library at Farmington next to her father. Horace's affectionate concern for Maria extended to her three Waldegrave daughters, Elizabeth Laura who married her cousin the fourth Earl Waldegrave, Charlotte Maria, Duchess of Grafton, and Anna Horatia, who married her cousin Lord Hugh Seymour Conway after the death of her first betrothed, the Duke of Ancaster. These three are "The Ladies Waldegrave" of Reynolds's conversation piece that shows them sewing at their work table. The original picture is now in the National Gallery of Scotland; Reynolds's bill for it, 300 guineas, is at Farmington and so is Walpole's copy of Valentine Green's mezzotint of it, a proof before letters. It is what I have chosen to save from all the objects relating to Edward and his family at Farmington. Walpole pasted it into his copy of the 1784 *Description of Strawberry Hill* saved in Choice 9. That copy was acquired in 1919 for £1650 by Sabin and Co. of Bond Street. They removed the mezzotint of The Ladies Waldegrave and held it for 2000 guineas because they said it is "the finest English mezzotint in existence." The book itself came to Farmington in 1927 at a greatly reduced figure. During the next eleven years I would stop in at Sabin's to pay my wistful respects to the print. Its price wilted during the Depression and I was not surprised when on the day war was declared my cabled offer of $500 was promptly accepted. The beautiful print sailed safely through the newly laid German mine fields to Farmington where it hangs beside drawings of Strawberry Hill that were formerly with it in the book. Drawings of Charlotte, Horatia, and Elizabeth Laura are also at Farmington along with a lock of the latter's hair, braided, in a gold case.

On Lord Waldegrave's death in 1763 his widow was painted by Reynolds as "The Mourning Bride"; a miniature of it is at Farmington. She was comforted by the Duke of Gloucester who married her secretly in three years. The duke is best remembered for his remark, "Another damned thick book? Always scribble, scribble, scribble, eh, Mr Gibbon?" Uncle Horace disapproved of the marriage because he foresaw Maria's unhappy situation when the king refused to accept her, but he stood by her loyally

The Ladies Waldegrave by Valentine Green after Reynolds, mezzotint.

then and after her extravagance and imperious temper estranged the duke. One of her letters at Farmington to her Aunt Jane Clement in 1777 feared for her future because she believed, correctly as it proved, that her father would leave her sister Mrs Keppel the bulk of his fortune. "I once thought myself his favourite," she wrote Aunt Jane, "but it would be ridiculous to think so any longer." Then she came to what never left her mind during the remaining twenty years of her Uncle Horace's life. "Mr Walpole must be worth some money, why am I to get nothing from my relations, he has none nearer to him than me, and now I have a son, he might entail Strawberry upon him, and having an house for shelter would be a consolation, and he must, by his own account be worth at least 10,000£, which you know would be a very great legacy, with an house attached to it—but this won't happen, and yet I believe he loves me as well as he does any body." Walpole left her £10,000 and settled Strawberry Hill on the children of her daughter, Elizabeth Laura Waldegrave, not on her son Prince William of Gloucester, who is remembered as Silly Billy. We shall come to Elizabeth Laura in Choice 4 as an overzealous censor of Walpole's notebooks.

In 1842 her grandson, the seventh Earl Waldegrave sold the contents of Strawberry Hill in a thirty-two days' sale. I regard the sale with mixed feelings, disapproval of breaking up Walpole's library and collections, and gratitude for giving me a life spent in salvaging the fragments. Walpole's three Common Place Books, his letters to Horace Mann, and his memoirs from 1751 to 1783 were kept out of the sale and remained in the family until the present Lord Waldegrave sold all of them to me except the memoirs. They are being edited properly at long last by John Brooke for the Yale Edition of Horace Walpole's Memoirs with the fullest co-operation of Lord and Lady Waldegrave, as we shall see in Choice 21.

After Dorothy Clement, the mother of Sir Edward's children, died in 1738, her younger sister Jane took her place in Edward's household and in the affection of his children. That the post of mistress to Edward was no sincecure is proved by four letters at Farmington that he wrote Jane in 1766 with the same intemperance he wrote Horace twenty years earlier: "choleric" was the word for Edward. In the first letter to Jane he informs her of "My conclusion and final resolution—First, that I will live with you no longer. Secondly, that I will never stay in a room where I find you," and so on for another unbridled page. Bishop Keppel gave Jane excellent advice: never contradict Sir Edward even in the smallest matters. Edward's better nature asserted itself in his will, which made ample provision for her. The devotion of his children to her and to her niece Ann appears in

their letters that were preserved by Ann and descended intact to Miss Eleanor Forster of Tynemouth, Northumberland, who sold some of the family
miniatures and many letters in 1958. They were bought by Miss Doris
Haydock of Newcastle who sold me the miniatures, gave me the letters,
and introduced me to Miss Forster, who sold me hundreds more of the
letters and bequeathed the remaining miniatures to me. The letters have
furnished innumerable footnotes to the Yale Edition of Horace Walpole's
Correspondence and reveal a side of Walpole's nature unknown to
Macaulay, his deep and steady concern for the welfare of his family. Both
Miss Haydock and Miss Forster came to Farmington to see their former
possessions in their final home. Among a collector's greatest rewards are
the friendships formed with strangers who join his quest in their own
houses and turn their possessions over to him with pleasure.

The runner-up in this Choice is not Edwards's portrait of Edward, but
the small oil of Dorothy Clement, the only picture known of her, which
Miss Forster bequeathed me. It shows a poised, rather sad and questioning
young woman with the good looks she gave her children. The portrait
hangs now above another of Miss Forster's bequests, a fine large miniature
of Princess Sophia of Gloucester, Maria's daughter by her second husband,
who George Cooper informs me was beloved by her first cousin, the Prince
of Wales. Not every milliner's apprentice has had a granddaughter who
might have been a queen.

The Clement collection is supplemented by dozens of letters between
Edward and his favorite daughter, Laura Keppel and her family. This
collection was given me by Miss Winifred Myers, whose London firm has
through the years provided hundreds of letters for my library. The contributions of scholarly booksellers to learning is not always recognized.
Miss Myers gave me the Keppel letters in 1973 to celebrate the fortieth
year of the Yale Walpole. The letters include dozens from Sir Edward,
Laura, her husband the Bishop, and some verses by Edward on Hope, a
virtue he held in low regard. "Mock Herald of the ever distant hour," he
called it. The correspondence of Edward and his family illustrates Walpole's pronouncement, "Nothing gives so just an idea of an age as genuine
letters; nay, history waits for its last seal from them." "Familiar letters,"
he wrote, "written by eye-witnesses, and that, without design, disclose circumstances that let us more intimately into important events, are genuine
history; and so far as they go, are more satisfactory than formal premedi-
tated narratives." When all the letters of Edward and his family are published their readers will know that family as well as they know their own.

Dorothy Clement by an unknown artist. From the original oil.

Among Miss Forster's and Miss Haydock's contributions to my library are a wax medallion of Sir Robert, the miniature of Sir Edward in middle age, one of his son Edward, very smart in his military uniform, Maria as a maid, countess, widow, and a silhouette of her as duchess (very portly) with the duke on the reverse. Earlier I got two drawings of Elizabeth Laura, as well as one of her aunt Charlotte, Lady Dysart. A copy of Walpole's epitaph for Lady Dysart was brought to Farmington as a present by the Waldegraves. It concludes,

> Pain could not sour, whom blessings had not spoiled,
> Nor death affright, whom no one a vise had soiled.

Of his three nieces one gathers she was the most admirable.

In his last letter to Lady Ossory, which was written only six weeks before he died in 1797, Walpole speaks of "about four score nephews and nieces of various ages, who are each brought me about once a year to stare at me as the Methusalem of the family." Age and illness lay heavily upon him, but he maintained his position as affectionately regarded head of his family to the end.

Choice 4

Walpole's Three "Common Place Books,"
Two "Books of Materials," "Miscellany,"
and Pocket Book

These seven manuscripts are being saved on the generous principle that permits the rescue of an entire set and not just its first volume. If the Almighty objects, "This is going *too* far!", I'll choose the earliest one, for which Walpole wrote a title-page, "Verses, Stories, Characters, Letters, etc. etc. with some particular memoirs of a certain Parcel of People. 1740."

The three vellum-bound folio Common Place Books were left by Walpole to the Waldegrave family and stayed at Strawberry Hill. They were kept out of the 1842 sale, but were sold the following year to Richard Bentley the publisher (not to be confused with Gray's and Walpole's Bentley), along with the manuscripts I talk about in Choices 1 and 17. Grandfather Bentley sold back the Common Place Books in 1861 to the widow of the seventh Earl, Frances Lady Waldegrave, who restored the splendors of Strawberry by two later brilliant marriages and her own social gusto. In 1942 when I was in London on O.S.S. business the present Lord Waldegrave sold the three Common Place Books to me. During the flight home they were in jeopardy when the wheels of my plane were locked for what seemed quite a long time over Shannon. I see the crew now in their shirts, sweating with fright despite the cold, while we circled round and round the airport and they jabbed madly with long red spanners at the entrails of the plane that had been exposed beside my seat. Fortunately, they got the wheels down and so the "Verses, Stories, Characters, Letters, etc., etc." were saved, after all.

Walpole added an epigraph to the title-page of the earliest book, "Ole, quid ad te? Mart." "Oleus, what is it to you? Martial." He was saying that what he put into his commonplace book was his own affair. He began keeping it while he and Gray were staying with Horace Mann at Florence

1740.

A Common Place Book
of Verses, Stories, Characters, Letters &c &c.
with some particular Memoirs of a certain Parcel of People.

Ohe, quid ad Te? .... Mart.

Epig. VII.10

last entry (p. 90) dated 1753 – but single additions of later date as e.g. at page 66 – 1761 . P. 86 in 1767
pagination in pencil, by me, March 1934. blank pp. numbered [except at end . 90 is last page used
    R. Tuve   writing. 42 blank sheets follow]
There are 13 intervening blank pp. inclosed in the 90 = 77 pp written on

Title-page from Horace Walpole's Common Place Book, 1740.

on their Grand Tour. Among the very miscellaneous entries are examples of the popular eighteenth-century diversion, *Sortes Virgilianae*. A man was named, Virgil was opened at random, and a phrase pinpointed that would be applied to him, a game rather beyond most of us today. The first "fates" in the book are those for the King, Prince of Wales, the Old and Young Pretenders, Sir Robert Walpole, and after several more Horace Walpole himself. His lot was *Accipe daque fidem.* "Take and give friendship," and we can see the company smiling and nodding approval because Horace Walpole was a friendly young man.

He and his closest friends at Eton loved the classics. "Why," Walpole wrote from Cambridge to Richard West at Oxford, "mayn't we hold a classical correspondence? I can never forget the many agreeable hours we have passed in reading Horace and Virgil, and I think they are topics will never grow stale." They wrote Latin verses for the fun of it and had the pleasure of seeing them printed in *Musae Etonenses* and the *Gratulatio Academiae Cantabrigiensis* on the marriage of Frederick Prince of Wales. There were some 250 volumes of classics in the Strawberry Hill library; thirteen editions of Virgil, eleven of Horace, and nine each of Ovid and Juvenal. My favorite among them is the tiny Sedani edition of Horace, 1627, in which Walpole wrote his name and "1733," the year he bought it, and added Greek and Latin quotations on its fly-leaves. Seventy-six volumes of the classics bound in red morocco were given him by the Duke of Brunswick, as we learn from the Duke's inscription to *Horatio, Roberti filio,* in the first volume, Caesar's *Commentaries,* 1713, which, by great good luck A. N. L. Munby found and kindly let me have. The Duke had suppressed a will of George I in consideration of a handsome English pension negotiated by Sir Robert's administration. One wonders if he met the twelve-year-old Horace in London or had merely heard that Sir Robert's youngest son was precocious. In any event, he must have believed that his gift would please the Prime Minister. Six others of the books have come to Farmington. They have suffered from wear and rebinding, but one can see how splendid they must have looked stretched across the fourth shelf in presses *L* and *M*.

A Strawberry book of special interest among the sixty-odd in Latin at Farmington is Herman Moll's *Geographia Antiqua Latinorum et Graecorum,* 1726. Walpole wrote "H. Walpole 1731" on the inside cover when he was aged thirteen or fourteen at Eton. Later he kept it in the Glass Closet at Strawberry Hill with his most personal books. He covered the fly-leaves and backs of many maps with notes; his fondness for genealogical charts appears on the first four pages with extra bits of information such as that Roxana, Alexander's wife, was sawn in two by order of Porisia, a biographical point not mentioned in *The Oxford Classical Dictionary*. There is no schoolboy drudgery in these notes, quite the contrary. On a rear fly-leaf below two genealogical charts is a quatrain in French:

> Ah! que Renaud me plaît!
> Qu' Armide avoit de grace!
> Le Tasse s'en scandalisait;
> Mais je suis Serviteur au Tasse.

Several of the later entries in the first Common Place Book have been printed as appendices in the Yale Edition of Horace Walpole's Correspondence. Among them are "Particular Memoirs on a Certain Parcel of People," that include "Anecdotes relating to Dr Conyers Middleton," "Some Anecdotes relating to Sir Charles Hanbury Williams and his Works," "Mr Thomas Gray," "Pieces Written by Mr Bentley, only son to Dr Bentley," "Suite of Mr Ashton." One section illustrates Walpole's lifelong enjoyment of the odd that Macaulay noted, "Instances of extraordinary Avarice and Economy," which leads off with, "Sir Robert Brown computed and found that in his life he had saved two hundred pounds by never having an orange or lemon at his table."

The manuscript title-page of the second Common Place Book is "Poems and other Pieces by Horace Walpole youngest Son of Sir Robert Walpole Earl of Orford." The first poem, of 81 lines, is addressed "To the honorable Miss Lovelace/On the Death of Lord Lovelace/Her only Brother. 1736." Walpole later added a note, "The Author's age was 18 at Cambridge." The verses end:

> So the young Phoenix, when the sickening Fire
> Of vital warmth winks in his fading Sire,
> Shakes off his "Mortal Coil," and from the tomb
> Embalmed with fragrant spices and perfume,
> (Fresh vigor bracing his eternal wings)
> Renew'd with sublimated essence springs.

A note on the opposite page tells us that "Mortal Coil," is an "expression in Hamlet."

Miss Lovelace disappeared from his life and was succeeded by other young ladies with whom he had amiable friendships, twenty-two of which he celebrated in "The Beauties." All his life he depended on women friends, concluding with the Berry sisters who were forty-odd years his junior, but he never married. It was said after his death that he offered to marry Mary Berry and when she refused him, her sister Agnes, yet he seems to have given little thought to marrying earlier. The arch references to Mme Grifoni at Florence in his correspondence with Mann and the portrait of her that he kept in his bedroom at Strawberry Hill suggest she was his mistress. Among the dozen-odd verses in these books that he did not print are two or three that escaped the vigilance of Elizabeth Laura Waldegrave. One of them, of 92 lines, is "Little Peggy/a/Prophetic Eclogue/In Imitation of Virgil's Pollio," with a note that "Peggy Lee, a whore of Lord Lincoln's, had a daughter by him whose birth was the subject of this eclogue," and is explicit enough to satisfy the most demanding connoisseurs of erotica today. Lord Edgcumbe thought that when his mistress left him she had passed into Walpole's keeping and made him trustee for her successor because, he said, Walpole had "more feeling and had given better advice about his mistresses than the rest of his acquaintance," yet Walpole wrote to Mann at the age of thirty-two that he "lay alone." Years later when Chatterton linked his name with Kitty Clive, the actress, in some verses, Walpole noted in his copy of them (Choice 19) that he had given her a house near Strawberry Hill, and that "on this foundation she was represented as his mistress, though they were both between fifty and sixty." He might have added that they appeared together in the *Town and Country Magazine* Tête à Tête series over the title "Mrs Heidelburg and Baron Otranto." Other actress friends were Mrs Abington, Mrs Pritchard, for whom he wrote an "Epilogue to Tamerlane on the Suppression of the Rebellion, spoken by Mrs Pritchard in the character of the tragic muse, Nov. 4, 1746" at Covent Garden and which he reported to Mann "succeeded to flatter me." Another actress friend whom he much admired was Eliza Farren, later Countess of Derby, whose presentation copy of his *Fugitive Pieces in Verse and Prose,* Strawberry Hill, 1758, is now at Farmington.

A charge was made some years ago that he was a homosexual on the basis of his youthful letters to Conway and Lord Lincoln; but extravagant letters written in the effusive style of the time are not proof of "overt behavior." The verses of a friend at Cambridge who described Walpole as "untossed by passion" fit him throughout his life if one means, as the writer did mean, sexual passion.

Walpole transcribed all the verses on the right-hand pages of the second

Common Place Book with glosses on the opposite pages that acknowledge their indebtedness to Dryden, Addison, Pope, Virgil, and Juvenal. The unprinted verses run to hundreds of lines. They are not in my *Horace Walpole's Fugitive Verses,* 1931, owing to a lapse of Paget Toynbee's customary generosity. I called on him at his house in Bucks whenever I was in England, taking with me my latest outstanding finds to show him. He looked at them with mixed feelings—pleasure for me, but regret that they would affect the value of his work. In 1927 we talked about my plans for an edition of Walpole's *Fugitive Verses.* "Oh," he said, "wouldn't you like to look in *there!*" and pointed to a cabinet that had, he said, his copies of the unpublished verses from the second Common Place Book. It was not until 1942 when I acquired the books that I saw how much had been kept from me. Perhaps the most notable prose piece in it is Walpole's "Speech in the House of Commons for an address to the King Jan'y 17th 1751," one of the few speeches he made during his twenty-six years in Parliament and the only one I know of in manuscript. The motion was carried 203 to 74, Prime Minister Pelham, Pitt, and Uncle Horace Walpole voting for it.

Walpole labelled his third Common Place Book "Political Papers." They were printed in the weeklies *Old England, The World, The Remembrancer, The Protester.* The "papers" are written on the right-hand pages; opposite them are voluminous notes such as, "Mr Pitt's fort [*sic*] was language. He dealt much in creation of words, such as Vicinage, Colonize, Whiggery, Desultoriness," a claim not confirmed by the *Oxford English Dictionary,* which gives earlier uses of all of them. The forthcoming Yale Edition of Walpole's memoirs will be enriched by this Common Place Book.

In 1759 and 1771 Walpole began what he called "Books of Materials" in two green vellum quartos and in 1786 a "Miscellany" in a small red morocco notebook with silver clasps. For nearly forty years he wrote up his visits to country houses, thoughts on Shakespeare, notes for a fifth volume of the *Anecdotes of Painting in England,* and much besides. The first note in 1759 is on the death of Prince George of Denmark taken from the *Secret History of England;* the final note in the Miscellany was written in the last year of Walpole's life. It records that Murphy's *Portugal,* 1795, raises the possibility that "the fine Gothic church of Batalha was built after a design by Stephen Stephenson, an Englishman"; Walpole kept his interest in "Gothic" to the end. The Miscellany's epigraph is from Cibber's *Apology* and fits all the notebooks: "Such remaining scraps—as may not perhaps be worth the reader's notice: but if they are such as tempt

Journey to Rousham, Ditchley, Blenheim, July 17th 1760.

Rousham, Sr Charles Cotterel's, was a small old indifferent house, built by a Dormer; much improved for general Dormer, by Kent, in four years; with the garden. Head of Ds of Norfolk divorced for Adultery; id by Sr Peter Lely, but finished smooth like Carlo Dolci. D. Johanna Dormer Duquessa de Feria, æt. 25. The library a good room, totally by Kent, a half kind of gothic; odd cieling, does not seem to belong to the room; chimney with ionic pillars; fine pict. of Gen. Dormer by Vanloo. good collection of books & prints. The garden of 25 acres; the best thing I have seen of Kent. Gothic buildings, Arcade from ancient baths, temples, old bridge, palladian Do. river, slender stream winding in a stone channel thro grass walks in wood, cascades overgrown with Ivy; grove of Venus of Medici: the whole, sweet. several portraits by Lely & Kneller.

Ditchley, Ld Litchfield, built by last Lord, very good house except Salon, which too small, bad carved figures, painted olive; chimney & a buffet, each in a corner. Fine Hall, basreliefs by him in marble, ornaments by Kent, cieling & side pieces by him, not so bad as his common. Head of old Sr Henry Lee, with Dog who saved his life, by Corn. Jansen. the Motto, more faithfull than favoured. He was Q. Eliz. knight for 30 yrs, by vow, & then resigned it to the Earl of Oxford. Four heads of old men, said to be his brothers — but I don't find he had any; they are good pictures. Sr Th. Kich killed at Isle of Rhee, good. Sr Chr. Hatton. Sr Hen. Lee, again, whole length; old fat man, with a stick & the garder, good. Anne Cs of Lindsey, with an urn; by Sr P. Lely, good. J. & Ds of York, types Mary & Anne, children, 3 qrs. The Duke's head & one hand by Lely, good; all the rest by some wretched scholar of his.

Blenheim. Execrable within, without, & almost all round. most of the Rubens's spoiled by the sun. a fine lively head by Holbein. Ld Strafford & Leer. a copy. a pict. called Ds of Portsm. & Nell Gwyn, is a copy of a picture at Wilton of Mrs Morton

One of Walpole's Journeys from "Book of Materials, 1759."

me to write them, why may not I hope that in this wide world there may be many an idle soul no wiser than myself who may be equally tempted to read them?" Hands across the ages.

The "Conversations with Lady Suffolk" and "Journeys to Country Houses" that Walpole wrote in the Common Place Books were edited by Paget Toynbee; the notes for contemporary painters in the Books of Materials were published by F. W. Hilles and P. B. Daghlian as the fifth volume of *Anecdotes of Painting in England;* Lars Troide has edited the entire Miscellany; I printed privately the notes on Shakespeare.

The unpublished notes include "Streets of London," which was to be the English equivalent of Saint Foix's book on the streets of Paris. Many pages headed "Miscellaneous" are extracts from Walpole's reading. A sample is:

"In Earl of Northumb's declar. ag. Hen. IV. He affirms that Richard II was starved. Parl. Hist. 2.74.
Best laws under kings of worst titles. 105.
Piked shoes tied up with chains. Act ag. them. 327.

Card. Wolsey goes to Commons to demand a subsidy. Speaker falls on his knees, abashed at the presence of so great a personage. 30."

As Walpole remembered and repeated what he read his reputation for brilliant and erudite conversation is not surprising.

My seventh notebook is small enough to be carried in a pocket. Walpole kept it from 1780 to 1783. Its notes range from *A Discourse of Husbandrie used in Brabant and Flanders,* 1650, to George Washington's Royalist ancestors. Walpole thought so highly of one of his own bon mots in it, "Man is an Aurivorous Animal," that he included it among his "Detached Pieces" in his posthumous *Works.* The history of this pocket notebook is lost until it re-emerged in the Red Cross Sale at Sotheby's in 1917. Then it passed into the R. B. Adam library in Buffalo and when that library was sold in 1926 Dr Rosenbach bought it for me. The Walpole Press at Mount Vernon, New York, brought out a facsimile of it in 1927 with notes by me that foreshadow the Yale Edition of Horace Walpole's Correspondence, which I began six years later.

The Books of Materials, 1759 and 1771, and the Miscellany, were taken by Mrs Damer as part of her share of Walpole's manuscripts. She bequeathed them to her Twickenham neighbor Sir Wathen Waller, 1st Baronet, in whose family they remained until they were sold at Sotheby's in 1921 by the then Sir Wathen Waller of Woodcote near Warwick. This was three years before I began to collect Walpole. A sale of manuscripts is like the wind that rushed into the Sibyl's cave and blew the leaves all over the world and I began getting lots from the Waller Sale far from Sotheby's. De Ricci in Paris gave me six letters to Walpole, a few had reached New York, fifty-four were owned by a plasterer in Chicago (who was kindly reported to me by Arundell Esdaile Secretary of the British Museum), two by Dr Frank Pleadwell, U.S.N. retired, in Honolulu, and two by a dealer in Dunedin, New Zealand, reported by Humphrey Milford. The "Books of Materials," Miscellany, and some letters had got to the Folger Shakespeare Library in Washington; Mr Percival Merritt of Boston acquired the "Paris Journals" and the Book of Visitors to Strawberry Hill, which he bequeathed to Harvard. I presently bought in London the "Journal of the Printing Office" (Choice 7) and a few other pieces from the Waller Sale.

In 1933 when I showed my priced copy of its catalogue with the names of the purchasers to Seymour de Ricci in Paris he saw at once that several of the alleged buyers were fictitious. The use of such names is sanctioned by British practice for lots bought in by the owner. Nearly two-fifths of the Waller sale had such names and were presumably still in the possession of Sir Wathen Waller. In reply to my letter he answered that he did own them and volunteered that they were not for sale. A year later I wrote him again and this time he asked me down to Woodcote for a night to see the manuscripts and letters he had bought in at Sotheby's. While sitting in the railway carriage at Paddington, I realized that I had come away without pajamas, a circumstance made the more awkward by its being Thursday, an "early closing day" at Leamington where I was met. Fortunately, the Waller chauffeur was a man of resource who knew how to knock on a back window of a certain draper's shop. It was a relief to think, as we swept up the drive at Woodcote, that the bootleg pajamas had completed my wardrobe. The Wallers were waiting on the terrace with visible apprehension. Lady Waller later confessed that they were braced for an elderly professor with a beard, but they were relieved by the story of the pajamas. The day was fine, just the day for an extended tour of the gardens; Walpole could wait. At tea a somewhat rustic footman appeared and asked, trying to preserve his decorum, which shoes would I wear at dinner? I had put in one evening shoe and one golf shoe, both lefts. My friendship with the Wallers had begun.

After dinner the Walpoliana were spread out on the billiard table, a ritual repeated in the following summers when my wife and I went down for visits at Woodcote. On my initial visit I said nothing about the possibility of Sir Wathen's sending the manuscripts to the British Museum to be photostated, but he willingly consented to do so the next year. He and I also began the searches in the attics and storerooms that furnish a collector's best stories when, as at Woodcote, we "found" and brought our discoveries to the billiard-room cupboard. Their history was known straight back to Mrs Damer and Walpole.

Sir Wathen died just after the war. Lady Waller sent to Christie's the new manuscripts we had found about the house as well as those bought in at the earlier sale, and I was able to get all but two of them. Later a lacquered snuff-box that had been Walpole's arrived as a present from Lady Waller. During the war it had been slightly damaged by a land mine that fell near the bank in Coventry where the Wallers had transferred various objects for safe-keeping, a circumstance that would have given its original owner, who liked to think of Strawberry's contents in the glorious future, cause for reflection.

One hundred and eighty-two of the leaves blown round the world in the 1921 Waller Sale have been swept up and brought to Farmington. Among them are the Books of Materials and Miscellany that, owing to the good offices of Joseph Q. Adams and Louis B. Wright, came to Farmington from the Folger Shakespeare Library as related in my *Collector's Progress* and Choice 13. Photostats of thirty-two manuscripts from the first Waller Sale in other hands are also at Farmington; only forty-one are still missing. Doubtless some of them will turn up sooner or later in unexpected places. I discovered this may be so when one day I opened my copy of Joseph Spence's *Polymetis*. A letter from Spence dated 27 October, 1757, slid out. It is mostly about Richard I. The address is missing and the recipient might have been any antiquary but for Spence's closing wish, "May the press at Strawberry Hill ever flourish and abound," an unpublished letter that I had forgotten Maggs bought in the first Waller Sale and sold me in 1927. Missing Walpoliana may be anywhere.

Choice 5

Richard Bentley's Drawings for Strawberry Hill

This is the book that the Almighty agreed is the most important object in my house.

The drawings are pasted in a calf-bound folio scrapbook with gray leaves. Walpole probably did the pasting himself; certainly he had the title-page printed at the Strawberry Hill Press, the sole copy known, "Drawings and Designs by Richard Bentley only son of Dr Bentley, Master of Trinity College, Cambridge." The book was sold in the 1842 auction of Strawberry's contents to a dealer and sank from sight until May 1926 when I found it in a London bookshop. The morning of the General Strike I departed for Paris on the last train and boat from England, leaving the unwieldy book behind, but in a few days I had it flown across the Channel, the first of Walpole's books, I believe, to take to the air.

It is mentioned in the first Common Place Book rescued in Choice 4. "I have a large book of [Bentley's] drawings," Walpole wrote, "and his original designs for Mr Gray's poems [Choice 6]. He drew the ceiling of the Library at Strawberry Hill, designed the lanthorn, staircase, north front, and most of the chimney-pieces there; and other ornaments." Walpole annotated many of the drawings, stating if they were not executed; Bentley initialed a few and gave some dimensions. Thirty of the drawings are for Strawberry Hill, fifty are for other buildings and objects. There are also a few landscapes of Jersey, whither Bentley fled to elude his creditors, a Temptation of St Anthony, and a Turkish Bath. The drawings were pasted in higgledy-piggledy. "Gothic chairs at Strawberry Hill taken from painted glass there by Mr Bentley" come between two designs for Lord Strafford, "a chimney piece in the style of architecture in the reign of James the First," not executed, and a Gothic building inspired by Chichester Cross that was set up in Strafford's menagerie at Wentworth Castle. "The Priory of St Hubert, a [Gothic] farm belonging to the Countess of Suffolk" and a "Gothic farmhouse for Sir Thomas

DRAWINGS

AND

DESIGNS

BY

RICH^{D.} BENTLEY,

ONLY SON

OF

Dr. BENTLEY,

MASTER OF TRINITY-COLLEGE

CAMBRIDGE.

Title-page for *Drawings and Designs* by Richard Bentley.

Seabright at Beechwood in Hertfordshire" flank "sketches for the windows in the Holbein Chamber at Strawberry Hill." Bentley was at home
in any style—a Palladian palazzo for the Duke of Cumberland at Windsor,
a Chinese temple for Henry Fox at Holland House, a Georgian Town
Hall at St Helier in Jersey, a "design for a fictitious steeple for Nicholas
Hardinge, Esq. at Kingston," which is a Gothic clocktower stuck on the
roof of a Georgian house and shows how simple it was to become a Goth
if one tried.

Walpole tells us in his *Description of Strawberry Hill* that "where the
Gothic Castle now stands was originally a small tenement" built in 1698
by the Earl of Bradford's coachman. It was let to various celebrated people until Walpole bought it in 1748, a year after he rented it. He wrote
Henry Conway that it was "the prettiest bauble you ever saw. It is set in
enamelled meadows, with filigree hedges:

> A small Euphrates through the piece is roll'd,
> And little finches wave their wings in gold.

Two delightful roads, that you would call dusty, supply me continually
with coaches and chaises: barges as solemn as barons of the Exchequer
move under my window; Richmond Hill and Ham Walks bound my
prospect; but, thank God! the Thames is between me and the Duchess of
Queensberry."

The announcement of the cottage's Gothic future is in a letter to
George Montagu of 1749: "Did I tell you," Walpole asked, "that I found
a text in Deuteronomy to authorize my future battlements? 'When thou
buildest a new house, then shalt thou make a battlement for thy roof,
that thou bring not blood upon thy house, if any man fall from thence.' "
To help him plan his "castle" he formed The Committee with Bentley
and John Chute of The Vyne in Hampshire, an older connoisseur Walpole met at Florence while on the Grand Tour. The Preface to *A Description of Strawberry Hill,* 1774, explains that the house was intended to
exhibit "specimens of Gothic architecture, as collected from standards in
cathedrals and chapel-tombs, and [to show] how they may be applied to
chimney-pieces, ceilings, windows, balustrades, loggias, etc. The general
disuse of Gothic architecture," Walpole asserted, "and the decay and
alterations so frequently made in churches, give prints a chance of being
the sole preservatives of that style." The Committee pored over the prints
in such works as Dugdale's *St Paul's* and Dart's *Westminster,* picking out
Gothic details to be "imitated," especially in the chimney-pieces. The

Description of Strawberry Hill gives their derivation: the chimney-piece
in the Little Parlor was designed by Bentley from the tomb of Thomas
Ruthall, Bishop of Durham, as shown in Dart's *Westminster;* the book-
cases in the Library were copied from the side-doors to the choir in Dugdale's *St Paul's Cathedral.* The Committee did not know how their
Gothic predecessors built, but they didn't have to know because William
Robinson, a professional architect at the Board of Works, took care of
the stresses and strains and all that and made certain that the house
wouldn't fall down as other neo-Gothic houses did. We see the Committee
at work in Walpole's copy of Sandford's *Genealogical History of the
Kings of England,* 1677, at Farmington. On the plate of the great screen
for the tomb of Prince Arthur in Worcester Cathedral are notes by Walpole and Bentley that transformed the screen into the "Gothic paper" for
Strawberry's entrance hall. The Committee saw no more impropriety in
substituting paper for stone than in converting Edward the Confessor's
tomb to the chimney-piece in the Round Drawing-Room. The fabric of
the house was lath and plaster and had to be renewed from time to time.
Twenty years before Walpole died "Gilly" Williams said, "Mr Walpole
has already outlived three sets of his battlements."

    Four of the eight Gothic chairs "taken from painted glass at Strawberry
Hill" by Bentley were sold in 1842 to the Earl of Charleville and four to
"Piggott, Richmond." Lord Charleville bought other lots that were sold
by his descendants in 1950 at an auction in Dublin of which, unfortunately, I heard nothing until it was over. When my wife and I got to
Dublin in February 1951 the leading antiquarian dealer regretted he
hadn't heard of me because he could have got all the Walpoliana for very
little. "Is there nothing left in Ireland?" I asked. "Well, yes," and he
produced a photograph of two of the Gothic chairs. They were, he said,
"in a religious house." Would there be any possibility, I wondered, of
their migrating to Farmington? They were two hundred years old and
must be rather shaky; mightn't the religious house prefer sturdy new ones
from Grand Rapids, Michigan? The dealer suggested that I leave the
matter to him and in two days the chairs were on their way to Farmington for a modest check. A year later a letter from England offered two
more of the chairs. The writer had just heard a talk about my library by
Wyndham Ketton-Cremer on the Third Programme of the BBC and
wondered if I would like two of the Gothic chairs that had been bought
at the Strawberry Hill sale by his grandfather. The writer's name was
Piggott. His chairs have now rejoined Lord Charleville's, standing against

a wall as in a water-color drawing of them in Choice 9. The four remaining chairs have also turned up, two in Ireland, two in England, where, alas, they remain.

Why do I value Bentley's drawings and designs for Strawberry Hill so highly? It is because of their primary importance in the Gothic Revival and the light they throw on Walpole himself. In the Preface to *A Description of Strawberry Hill* he states that the house was built "to please my own taste, and, in some degree, to realize my own visions." He had already written, "When by the aid of some historic vision and local circumstance, I can romance myself into pleasure I know nothing transports me so much." The sepulchral monuments in cathedrals and churches gave him this romantic pleasure. His love of "the true rust of the Barons' Wars" was heightened by patriotic pride: England's mediaeval buildings were as fine as any in Europe and should be more esteemed by Englishmen. This awareness grew after 1748 and the close of a successful war; "Gothick" became fashionable, as in this country we built "Colonial" houses after the First World War. Although the Walpoles had been Norfolk landowners for centuries, they were relatively modest compared to Horace's Conway and Townshend cousins or to his mother's relations, the Philippses of Picton Castle. One of the latter produced a chart (now at Farmington) that shows how the Phillipps family went back to Edward III and Cadwallader, the vigorous seventh-century King of North Wales. Under Walpole's joke about "the old counts of Strawberry" lay the same desire for ancient lineage that moves the descendants of the *Mayflower*'s passengers.

Among Bentley's designs for Strawberry Hill is the Gothic lanthorn. We learn from the *Description* that "In the well of the staircase by a cord of black and yellow [the colors in the Walpole arms] hangs a Gothic lanthorn of tin Japanned, designed by Mr Bentley, and filled with painted glass; the door of it has an old pane with the arms of Vere earl of Oxford." When Sir Leigh Ashton, then director of the Victoria and Albert Museum, saw this pane at Farmington he said that glass of its period "simply doesn't exist." "What is its period?" "The fifteenth century, Agincourt!" he pronounced, "1415. *That's* what it is!" "The lanthorn," Walpole wrote, "casts the most venerable gleam on the stairs that was ever seen since the days of Abelard," who was brought in because the entrance hall in which the lanthorn hung was called "the Paraclete" after the oratory Abelard founded.

How did I find the lanthorn? Apparently by luck, but I never would have found it had I not been driven to seek out unique Walpoliana. This compulsion was recognized by Max Beerbohm when late in life he wrote me that he had read my *Collector's Progress,* "with envy. To have a consuming and overwhelming passion and to be able to write about it so lightly and well is surely a most enviable state. If Orestes with the Furies ever at his heels had been, in his headlong flight, able all the while to be talking charmingly and wittily about them he would have a modern counterpart in yourself." Mr R. M. Holland-Martin, a collector as well as head of Martin's Bank, wanted to help me in my headlong flight and asked my wife and me down to his house in Worcestershire one weekend in 1935 to see the pictures from Strawberry Hill at nearby Sudeley Castle where Queen Catherine Parr lived after Henry the Eighth's death. They were bought at the sale in 1842 by John Dent, the glove king. Thirty-four of his purchases greeted us in the entrance hall of the house, the oil tracings made by George Vertue from Holbein's drawings of Henry the Eighth's Court. Walpole bought them from Vertue's widow, put them into his favorite black and gold frames, and built the Holbein Chamber to receive them. "Have you ever looked at their backs?" I asked our host, who was Dent's grandson. He hadn't, and asked why he should? "Because I think you'll find that Walpole identified the sitters." Down came the pictures and, sure enough, Walpole had written the names of each sitter on the backs.

After enjoying this success, which pleased the owner as much as the visitor, I asked if he had a list of his grandfather's purchases at the sale? He had and the last item on it was "Gothic Lanthorn." "Is that the famous Gothic lanthorn?" I asked. "I don't know whether it's the famous Gothic lanthorn" was the reply, "but it's the ugliest blasted lantern that ever was." That sounded like it and I said, truthfully, I would rather see the lanthorn than anything in England because it was the epitome of Strawberry Hill and I had the original design and later drawings of it after Walpole added the painted glass.

"I'm afraid," the owner answered, "you're too late."

"Oh!"

"My wife wouldn't have it hanging about any longer and threw it out."

"Threw it out!"

"It just may not have gone."

We hurried across a large inner court to a lumber room where on a bench stood Bentley's lanthorn, its tin cross slightly awry, but worth its weight, so far as I was concerned, in Catherine Parrs.

"Well," said the wife of the owner, who had joined us, "I won't have it back in the house. Perhaps we should give it to the Cheltenham Museum."

"Oh, *don't* do that," I burst out.

"What," I asked Mr Holland-Martin on the ride home, "can I do now?"

He was very helpful. "When you write to thank them for tea, why don't you say that if they decide to part with the lanthorn you hope they will let you know." The owner answered my letter by return post to say that he and his wife would be delighted to give me the lanthorn if I would have it taken away, and it hangs now in the East Library at Farmington.

Walpole's first mention of Bentley is in a letter to George Montagu of 23 June, 1750: "I have had another of your friends with me some time, whom I adore, Mr Bentley he has more sense, judgment, and wit, more taste, and more misfortunes, than ever met in any man." In his day Bentley was identified as the son of the great classical scholar of the same name who put Pope's translation of *Homer* in its place by saying that it was "a very pretty poem, but it must not be called Homer," a pleasantry that landed him in the *Dunciad*. Besides his drawings and designs for Strawberry Hill and Gray's Poems, the younger Bentley translated the Press's edition of Hentzner's *Journey to England in 1598* from the Latin, and drew the fleurons for the most handsome of the Press's books, Lucan's *Pharsalia* with Dr Bentley's notes. Walpole printed it for Bentley's benefit, but after several years of intimacy Bentley's improvidence and "disposition to chimerical schemes" exhausted his patron's patience, and he left never to return. According to William Cole, Bentley was "too forward in bringing his wife to Strawberry Hill." As Walpole called her "Mrs Hecate," "Mrs Tisiphone," and "Hannah Cleopatra" she probably did contribute to the breach. After it Walpole showed his continuing concern for Bentley by getting a sinecure in the Exchequer for his son. Walpole's letters to Bentley are among the best he wrote; Bentley's side, which Walpole praised highly, has never been printed and is lost. Although the *Dictionary of National Biography*'s article on Dr Bentley dismisses his son as "an accomplished but eccentric man who achieved nothing signal in life," it gave him an entry of his own as a "writer on miscellaneous subjects" whose "artistic talent was exaggerated by his contemporaries"; yet today the younger Bentley's writings are forgotten and his drawings are accorded high praise. The most interesting to us of his tracts is *Reflections on the Different Ideas of the French and English in regard to*

Cruelty, 1759, to which Walpole contributed the Dedication "To the most Humane Person alive (Whoever that is.)"

When Chute, the second "architect" of Strawberry Hill, died Walpole wrote, "He was my oracle in taste, the standard to whom I submitted my trifles, and the genius that presided over poor Strawberry!" His drawings for it are also at Farmington. Although they are stiff and finicky they show that his contribution to the house was much greater than was known before his drawings reappeared at Chewton. They were pasted in an oblong notebook, doubtless by Walpole who wrote a title-page for it, "Slight Sketches of Architecture by John Chute, Esq., of the Vine [*sic*] in Hampshire," and annotated several of the sketches. Bentley's drawing for the library was rejected because, as Walpole wrote him, "Mr Chute's design has a conventual look that yours totally wants." Severe but just as a comparison of the sketches proves. Chute also contributed the Long Gallery and Great Cloister beneath it after Bentley left. Students of Eighteenth-Century amateur architects agree that his drawings for Strawberry Hill rival Bentley's but that Bentley's are the ones to save.

The house that emerged from Bentley's and Chute's designs is the archetype of a style that spread round the world; its descendants include the Houses of Parliament at Westminster and Ottawa, the Residences of the Governors in Sydney and Singapore, the Old Library at Yale, and countless Victorian buildings from John o'Groats to Land's End and from Maine to Hawaii. Sir Nikolaus Pevsner tells us that its influence extended to France and Italy, Germany, Sweden, and Russia, as well. In the early years of this century Strawberry Hill was spoken of with amused condescension, but, as with all buildings that survive long enough, it has acquired architectural and historical respect and is studied for its influence on the Gothic Revival and the light it throws on Horace Walpole himself. At the end of his life he admitted that "Every true Goth must perceive that [Strawberry's rooms] are more the works of fancy than of imitation" because the Committee "had not studied the science," yet his early satisfaction in "implanting the gloomth of abbeys and cathedrals" on his house lingered despite his growing awareness of its architectural imperfections. Bentley's and Chute's drawings survive and Strawberry continues to resist the assaults of age which have included a German fire-bomb that crashed into the Long Gallery in 1941. Walpole left Strawberry to the descendants of his favorite niece Maria whose first husband was the second Earl Waldegrave. As I have said, the seventh earl auctioned off the contents of the house in 1842. The house itself was bought in

1888 by Lord Michelham whose family sold it in 1920 to St Mary's College, a Vincentian seminary in the University of London's Institute of Education. They consecrated the Tribune, which Walpole originally called "The Chapel." Houses now shut off the view of the river, Walpole's forty-six acres have shrunk, but more and more people are visiting Twickenham to pay their respects to Strawberry Hill and the memory of its creator.

Choice 6
Bentley's Original Designs for Gray's Poems

"Short Notes" records, "This year [1753] published a fine edition of
poems by Mr T. Gray with prints from designs by Mr R. Bentley." He
might have added that the fine edition had an "Explanation of the Prints"
by himself. A sample is:

Ode on the Death of a Favourite Cat.
Frontispiece.
The cat standing on the brim of the tub, and endeavouring to catch a gold
fish. Two cariatides of a river god stopping his ears to her cries, and Destiny
cutting the nine threads of life, are on each side. Above, is a cat's head between
two expiring lamps, and over that, two mouse-traps, between a mandarin-cat
sitting before a Chinese pagoda, and angling for gold fish into a china jar; and
another cat drawing up a net. At the bottom are mice enjoying themselves on
the prospect of the cat's death; a lyre and pallet.

Walpole published the book through Robert Dodsley in London to
help his two friends. In the absence of his correspondence with Dodsley
about the book we don't know the terms of its publication apart from
Dodsley's payment of £42 to Gray for the copyright of his poems. *Designs
of Mr R. Bentley for Six Poems by Mr T. Gray* finally appeared in 1753,
a royal quarto of thirty-six pages so cut that it looks like a small folio.
The price was high, half a guinea, the equivalent today of what—fifty
dollars? Dr Johnson in his chapter on Gray in *Lives of the Poets* annoyed
the poet and his friends by saying that the poems were printed on one
side of each leaf "that they might in some form or other make out a
book," but *Bentley's Designs* went through three editions in 1753 and
four more from 1765 to 1789. In our own day it has been hailed as a
landmark of English book illustration by Osbert Sitwell and Kenneth
Clark who called it "the most graceful monument to the Gothic Rococo."

Both Bentley's original drawings and Walpole's copy of the printed
book are at Farmington. I am saving the book of drawings. Walpole noted
in it, "These are the original drawings by Mr Bentley from which

Bentley's Frontispiece to his designs for Gray's Poems, 1753. From the original drawing.

Grignion and Müller engraved the plates. Hor. Walpole." He pasted the drawings where the prints were to be. His usual binding was plain calf, but he had this book bound in red morocco with elaborate gilt tooling, a beautiful book. William Beckford paid eight guineas for it in the Strawberry Hill sale through his bookseller, Bohn, as we know from their correspondence about the sale at Farmington. Bohn reported that the drawings are so like engravings he had to look pretty carefully to satisfy himself that they are not engravings, an uncertainty shared by all then and since. After the Beckford Sale in 1882 they went to the ardent Walpolian Laurence Currie and came to me from Maggs in 1933.

The publication of the *Designs* did not proceed smoothly. Gray objected to numbering the stanzas and the numbers were removed; he insisted that "Mr" be put before his and Bentley's names for fear that their omission would make him appear as "a classic." Walpole saw no "affectation in leaving out the *Mr* before your names; it is a barbarous addition. . . . Without ranging myself among classics, I assure you, were I to print anything with my name, it should be plain Horace Walpole: *Mr* is one of the Gothicisms I abominate," but Gray insisted on having it. Although he disliked Walpole's "Explanation of the Prints," he conceded, "If you think it necessary to print these explanations for the use of people that have no eyes, I could be glad they were a little altered." Gray, always the candid friend with Walpole, wrote that he, Gray, would "revise the press, for you know you can't." He became seriously alarmed when Dodsley, to make the book look more for its money, had Eccardt's portrait of Gray at Strawberry Hill engraved for the frontispiece. On hearing this the poet wrote Walpole, "Sure you are not out of your wits! This I know, if you suffer my head to be printed, you infallibly will put me out of mine. I conjure you immediately to put a stop to any such design. Who is at the expense of engraving it I know not, but if it be Dodsley, I will make up the loss to him. The thing as it was, I know, will make me ridiculous enough, but to appear in proper person at the head of my works, consisting of half a dozen ballads in thirty pages, would be worse than the pillory. I do assure you, if I had received such a frontispiece without any warning, I believe it would have given me a palsy." The print appears in only a few copies, including Walpole's own. He lettered "Thomas Gray" neatly on it and below the print, "Eccardt pinx, Müller Inv. In the collection of Mr H. Walpole."

With the removal of Gray's portrait the frontispiece became Bentley's illustration for the "Elegy" that shows the poet musing by the babbling

brook. There has been some speculation about the poet's identity, whether
he was Gray, Richard West, or just anybody. Comparison of Bentley's
original drawing with Müller's print of it shows that the musing figure
was originally Gray, adenoids and all, and that Müller's figure, in com-
pliance with Gray's wishes, is nobody in particular. Walpole's annotations
in his printed copy of the book point out Gray's indebtedness in the
poems to *Richard III, As You Like It,* La Bruyère, and the *Spectator.*
Walpole also noted that the Favourite Cat Drowned in a Tub of Gold
Fishes belonged to himself and that the authority for Chancellor Hatton's
dancing in "A Long Story" is found in Anthony Bacon's papers, vol. I,
p. 56. Walpole bound in an excellent sketch by Gray of Stoke House in
A Long Story opposite Bentley's drawing of it and when we put these
two drawings beside Grignion's engraving of Bentley's drawing we have
Stoke House from start to finish.

So far as we know, Gray did not thank Walpole for publishing the
book, but he did write "Stanzas to Mr Bentley":

> See, in their course, each transitory thought
>   Fix'd by his touch a lasting essence take;
> Each dream, in fancy's airy coloring wrought,
>   To local symmetry and life awake!
> The tardy rhymes that us'd to linger on,
>   To censure cold, and negligent of fame,
> In swifter measures animated run,
>   And catch a lustre from his genuine flame.
> Ah! could they catch his strength, his easy grace,
>   His quick creation, his unerring line;
> The energy of Pope they might efface,
>   And Dryden's harmony submit to mine.

The story of Gray's and Walpole's friendship begins at Eton in 1727
when Walpole was ten and Gray eleven. Their intimacy was shared with
Richard West and Thomas Ashton of the Quadruple Alliance. Bookish
school-boys are not usually well thought of by their contemporaries, but
the son of the Prime Minister protected the Quadruple Alliance. Gray's
"Eton Ode" expressed their love for the school and became in time the
"leaving book" given to each departing Etonian. Walpole wrote Montagu
from Cambridge, "I can't say I am sorry I was never quite a schoolboy;
an expedition against bargemen, or a match at cricket may be very pretty
things to recollect," but he had preferred exploring the shelves of Pote's
bookshop. He and Gray saw less of each other at Cambridge where Wal-

pole was at King's and Gray at Peterhouse and because Walpole who was
a Fellow-Commoner could come and go as he pleased and was much in
London with his dying mother. Both left Cambridge without taking a
degree, a lack that did not prevent Gray being called later "the most
learned man in Europe" and becoming Professor of History and Modern
Languages at the University.

In 1739 Walpole took him on the Grand Tour to France and Italy
where they spent a year at Florence with Walpole's distant cousin Horace
Mann, the British Minister there who was to become his chief correspondent and the central figure in Choice 15. On starting home Walpole
and Gray went to Reggio with John Chute for the fair. There they quar-
relled and Gray left Walpole for Venice with Chute. Walpole records in
"Short Notes" that he fell ill "of a kind of quinsy, and was given over
for fifteen hours, escaping with great difficulty." Fortunately, Lord Lincoln and his travelling tutor, Joseph Spence, went to Reggio for the opera.
Spence wrote his mother how

After we had been there a day or two, we heard that Mr Walpole (who we
thought was gone) was still there, but that he was ill abed. We went, you may
be sure, immediately to see him; and found him very ill, with a quinsy; and
swelled to such a degree as I never saw any one in my life.

Between three and four in the morning, Spence wrote, he

was surprised with a message that Mr Walpole was extremely worse, and desired
to speak with me immediately. I dressed as soon as I heard it; stepped into his
coach, which waited at the door, and found him scarce able to speak. I soon
found there, upon talking with his servants, that he had been all this while
without any physician; and had doctored himself. So I sent immediately for the
best physician the place could afford and dispatched an express to Florence, to
our minister there, with orders to bring a physician from thence who is a very
good one and my particular friend, Dr Cocchi; and who (which was a very
material thing in these parts) understands and talks English, like an Englishman. In about twenty hours time, Mr Walpole began to grow better; and we
left him with his Florentine doctor in a fair way of recovering soon. I was with
him perpetually till the doctor came and if he had been worse, had got leave of
Lord Lincoln to stay behind for some days to take care of him: but I thank God
all went well before my Lord went away; and we took our leaves of him with
pleasure, and hope to see him next week at Venice, whither he is bound as well
as we, and then for England. You see what luck one has sometimes in going out
of one's way; if Lord Lincoln had not wandered to Reggio, Mr Walpole (who is
one of the best natured, and most sensible, young gentlemen that England
affords) would in all probability have been now under the cold earth.

When Walpole was well enough he joined Lincoln and Spence at Venice, which couldn't have been too pleasant with the estranged Gray there, and returned to England in their company. Doubtless he described the immediate cause of the quarrel to Mann, but when he got his letters back from Mann and copied them he deleted the episode and the originals were burned. So we shall probably never know what precisely caused the rupture; it could have been anything after two years of travel with one of the travelers an outgoing young man who loved masquerades and elegance and was paying all the bills and the other a highly sensitive recluse touchily aware of his inferior position. Walpole and Gray were not the first or last friends to end their travels by separate routes; even Saints Barnabas and Paul ended theirs with "a sharp contention" and they, unlike Gray and Walpole, were never reconciled. Walpole's explanation of the break to William Mason thirty-odd years later sounds true to me as well as generous:

I am conscious that in the beginning of the differences between Gray and me, the fault was mine. I was too young, too fond of my own diversions, nay, I do not doubt, too much intoxicated by indulgence, vanity, and the insolence of my situation, as a prime Minister's son, not to have been inattentive and insensible to the feelings of one I thought below me; of one, I blush to say it, that I knew was obliged to me; of one whom presumption and folly perhaps made me deem not my superior *then* in parts, though I have since felt my infinite inferiority to him. I treated him insolently: he loved me and I did not think he did. I reproached him with the difference between us, when he acted from conviction of knowing he was my superior; I often disregarded his wishes of seeing places, which I would not quit other amusements to visit, though I offered to send him to them without me. Forgive me, if I say that his temper was not conciliating; at the same time that I will confess to you that he acted a more friendly part, had I had the sense to take advantage of it; he freely told me of my faults. I declared I did not desire to hear them, nor would correct them. You will not wonder that with the dignity of his spirit, and the obstinate carelessness of mine, the breach must have grown wider, till we became incompatible.

In a few years they were reconciled and their adult friendship continued unbroken until Gray died; yet Walpole was clear-eyed. "I agree with you most absolutely in your opinion about Gray," he wrote Montagu in 1748, "he is the worst company in the world—from a melancholy turn, from living reclusely, and from a little too much dignity, he never converses easily—all his words are measured, and chosen, and formed into sentences; his writings are admirable; he himself is not agreeable."
Bentley's Designs for Gray's Poems was inspired by Walpole's eager-

Thomas Gray by Benjamin Wilson.

ness to help his friends who he believed were geniuses. Gray's lesser regard for him is shown by his destroying most of Walpole's letters, an act understandably wounding to Walpole. Yet Gray was one of his closest friends and I was delighted not long ago to get a portrait of him by Benjamin Wilson, a version of the one at Pembroke College, Cambridge. While it was being cleaned the church at Stoke Poges emerged before the poet's glassy smile and to the cleaner's pleased surprise. Nearby in the New Library at Farmington is Gray's biographer, William Mason, gazing at Gray, pencil in hand. Not far away is an accession that has arrived from Italy since I began this chapter, an animated bust of Dr Cocchi, a welcome addition to the library that would not have been formed without his timely intercession at Reggio.

Choice 7
The Journal of the Printing Office

The Journal of the first private press in England is a small quarto bound in green vellum with gilt tooling, a very special notebook for a very special use. Walpole wrote his name and "1757" on the inside cover. Below the date he added, "Archbishop Parker kept in his house a Painter, Engraver, and Printer," and pasted a cutting from the *Craftsman* of 20 February 1731, that describes the printing press set up in St James's House for the entertainment of the Duke of Cumberland, aged ten. These were exalted precedents for his own press at Strawberry Hill, which was to become more celebrated than either of them. He also pasted before the first leaf of the journal an impression of Maittaire's *Annales Typographici,* 1719, with the portraits of Gutenberg, Faust, Coster, Aldus, and Froben engraved by Houbraken. At the end are pasted business letters and bills relating to the Press. Mrs Damer took the Journal in 1797. It was sold in the first Waller Sale in 1921, edited by Paget Toynbee, and published by the Clarendon Press in 1923. I bought it in 1933 from Maggs. Among the twenty-six choices it ranks high.

Walpole set up his press to be independent of the London bookseller-publishers: he would print what he pleased in as many copies as he pleased and dispose of them as he saw fit, giving away most of them, but selling Gray's *Odes,* Bentley's edition of Lucan, and the Rev. Mr Hoyland's *Poems* for the benefit of their authors. He also printed Joseph Spence's *Parallel* of Magliabecci and Mr Hill, a tailor of Buckingham, to raise a little sum of money for the latter poor man. Six hundred copies were sold in a fortnight, and it was reprinted in London." "I am turned printer," he wrote Mann, "and have converted a little cottage here into a printing-office—My abbey is a perfect college or academy—I keep a painter in the house and a printer—not to mention Mr Bentley who is an academy himself. I send you two copies (one for Dr Cocchi) of a very honourable opening of my press—two amazing odes of Mr Gray—They are Greek, they are Pindaric, they are sublime—consequently I

Journal of the Printing-Office at Strawberry hill
near Twickenham in Middlesex.

1757.

June 25.th The Press was erected. W.m Robinson, printer.

July 16.th Began to print. The first work was an edition of two new
Odes by mr Gray: one, on the power & progress of Poetry;
the other, on the destruction of the Welsh Bards by Edward 1.st

Aug. 3.d 1000 copies of the Odes finished.

— 8.th 2000 copies published by Dodsley. ——

... began to print Hentznerus's account of England, with a
translation by Rich. Bentley; the advertisement by H. Walpole.

18.th mr muntz printed for his first essay a sonnet written that
evening by mr Walpole on killing Time; the thought from
a French epigram. * (see on other side)

19.th Lucy Younge, Countess of Rochford, Etheldeda Viscountess Townshend
miss Bland, & James Earl Waldgrave dining at Strawberry hill,
were carried to see the printing-office, where the following lines
being ready prepared were taken off;

For Lady Townshend;
The Press speaks:-

From Me Wits and Poets their glory obtain;
Without Me their Wit & their Verses were vain:
Stop, Townshend! and let me but Print what You say;
You, the fame I on others bestow, will repay.

Lady Rochford desiring to see the manner of composing
for the press, four lines from a play were given to the,

First page of the "Journal of the Printing Office" at Strawberry Hill.

fear a little obscure—the second particularly by the confinement of the
measure and the nature of prophetic vision is mysterious; I could not
persuade him to add more notes; he says 'whatever wants to be explained,
don't deserve to be.' "

The opening of the Press was described to Chute: "On Monday next
the Officina Arbuteana opens in form. The Stationers' Company, that is
Mr Dodsley, Mr Tonson, etc. are summoned to meet here on Sunday
night. And with what do you think we open? *Cedite, Romani Impressores*
—with nothing under *Graii Carmina.* I found him in town last week: he
had brought his two Odes to be printed. I snatched them out of Dodsley's
hands, and they are to be the first-fruits of my press." Two thousand
copies of the *Odes,* "The Bard," and "Progress of Poesy," were printed
by the Press and were distributed by Dodsley who, as I have said, paid
Gray £42 for the copyright.

The Press had several printers before Thomas Kirgate arrived in 1765.
He stayed to the end, becoming Walpole's secretary as well, taking his
dictation when he couldn't write, and annotating his books in a hand so
similar to Walpole's that it has misled many since. We shall come to him
frequently.

The Press's authors range from Lucan to Hannah More, whose
"Bishop Bonner's Ghost" closed its list of books in 1789. Among its other
publications are letters of Edward VI, a translation by Bentley of Paul
Hentzner's *Journey to England in 1598,* the first appearance of Lord
Herbert of Cherbury's autobiography, Count Gramont's *Mémoires* (discussed in Choice 18), and Charles Lord Whitworth's *Account of Russia
. . . in . . . 1710.* Fourteen of the Press's thirty-four books are by Walpole himself; seven others have his Prefaces. Chief among his own books
are *A Catalogue of Royal and Noble Authors,* 2 vols, *Fugitive Pieces in
Verse and Prose, Anecdotes of Painting in England* and *A Catalogue of
Engravers,* 5 vols, in two editions, *The Mysterious Mother,* a tragedy,
and *A Description of Strawberry Hill* in two editions. Walpole's copies
of the last three are in Choices of their own.

His copy of *Fugitive Pieces* with his arms on the sides is at Farmington.
The prose pieces in it are chiefly his nine contributions to *The World*
that include essays on the new-style calendar adopted in 1752, letter-
writing, and British politeness. The manuscripts of the nine essays and
two others came to Farmington from Upton. Walpole wrote at the end
of the Dedication to Conway, "They [he and Conway] were first cousins,
their mothers, Catherine Lady Walpole and Charlotte Lady Conway,

being own sisters." He wrote this in his neatest hand and then blotted the *g* in *being*. Two centuries later we feel his annoyance as he put his little finger on the blot and drew it quickly down leaving a nasty smudge on the carefully prepared dedication page.

Fugitive Pieces starts off with "Verses in Memory of King Henry the Sixth, Founder of King's College, Cambridge. [Written February 2, 1738.]" Two lines in it were echoed by an even greater Cambridge poet in his sonnet, "Inside of King's College Chapel, Cambridge." Walpole wrote:

> Sweet strains along the vaulted roof decay,
> And liquid Hallelujahs melt away,

and Wordsworth echoed,

> .... that branching roof
> .... where music dwells
> Lingering—and wandering on as loth to die.

Henry the Sixth is followed in *Fugitive Pieces* by "An Epistle from Florence to Thomas Ashton, Esq., Tutor to the Earl of Plimouth. (Written in the year 1740.)" This is Walpole's longest poem, 380 lines, and is one of the three by him that Dodsley printed in his celebrated Collection, 1748. It was written while Walpole was idling at Florence, "Lapp'd in trifles and inglorious ease." His conscience drove him to express his fundamental seriousness. The "Epistle" decries authority, as bright young men have always been driven to do:

> The greatest curses any Age has known
> Have issued from the Temple or the Throne.

The poem was much admired, even by Gray, but when it was reprinted in Bell's *Fugitive Poetry* in 1789 Walpole found it "the worst poem in the volume." His other poems in Dodsley's *Collection* are "The Beauties" and "Epilogue to Tamerlane, on the Suppression of the Rebellion."

In "Short Notes" Walpole tells us that he wrote his *Catalogue of Royal and Noble Authors,* 2 vols, 12 mo, 1758, in less than five months, a remarkable feat. It was a pioneer work compiled largely from the authors that Walpole shelved in press *A* of the Strawberry Hill library. "Author" is a misleading epithet for such as Richard I who wrote only one poem of dubious authenticity. Walpole's uneasiness about the book appears in the Italian epigraph, "Where the devil, Sir Louis, did you find such a collection?" Walpole's Advertisement is also apologetic:

Yet are there such great names to be found in this Catalogue, as will excuse erecting a peculiar class for them: Bacon, Clarendon, Villiers Duke of Buckingham, the second Lord Shaftsbury, Lord Herbert, Lord Dorset, and others are sufficient Founders of a new Order. Some years ago nothing was more common than such divisions of Writers. How many German, Dutch, and other heralds, have marshalled authors in this manner! Balthazar Bonifacius made a collection of such as had been in love with statues: Ravisius Textor, of such as have died laughing: Vossius, of chronologers: Bartholinus, of physicians who have been poets. There are catalogues of modern Greek poets; of illustrious bastards; of translators; of Frenchmen who have studied Hebrew; of all the authors bred at Oxford, by Antony Wood; and of all British writers in general by Bale, Pitts, and Bishop Tanner. But if this collection, fortified with such grave authorities, should still be reckoned trifling by the generality; it cannot, I would hope, but be acceptable to the noble families descended from these authors. Considering what trash is thought worthy to be hoarded by Genealogists, the following List may not be a despicable addition to those repositories. Of one use it certainly may be; to assist future editors in publishing the works of any of these illustrious Personages.

The *Royal and Noble Authors,* 300 copies, appeared in 1758 and was such a success that in two weeks Walpole sold the copyright to Graham and Dodsley for two years for £200 to help Bentley. Graham and Dodsley published a second edition of 2000 copies in 1759. Walpole's corrected proof sheets of it are at Farmington. He made few changes in the text, but straightened lines that were carelessly set by the printer. Among the copies of the first edition at Farmington are those that belonged to Garrick, Lady Diana Beauclerk, Isaac Reed, Augustus Hervey Lord Bristol, "Given me by my dear Friend the Author, Mr Horace Walpole," two that Walpole sent Horace Mann, and a nineteenth-century owner, John Ruskin. The second edition was followed by two others in London, two in Dublin and two in Edinburgh, a total of eight editions during the eighteenth century. In 1786 Walpole brought out a Postscript to it of twenty-six pages with two prints. The new noble author was the third Earl of Salisbury (1350?–1400), who flourished in the reign of Richard the Second. Walpole added him, "As I should be unwilling to defraud my country of any sparkle of genius that glimmered in our ages of darkness." In his note to Richard Bull accompanying a copy of the *Postscript* (now at Farmington) he asked Bull not to speak of it because it was not meant for the public and he had printed only forty copies, "which I destine for presents and have allotted them all." The most recent edition of the whole work appeared in 1806 edited by Thomas Park and Isaac Reed in five volumes enlarged "by additional specimens of [the authors'] performances." This edition was found in every nineteenth-century gentleman's library in England along with Agnes Strickland's *Queens of England* and Creasy's *Fifteen Decisive Battles of the World.*

An ambitious project was given up almost as soon as begun. This was *Miscellaneous Antiquities,* "To be continued Occasionally," according to its title-page. It came out in 1772 with an "Advertisement, by the Editors."

The taste [Walpole wrote] for anecdotes and historic papers, for ancient letters that record affairs of state, illustrate characters of remarkable persons, or preserve the memory of former manners and customs, was never more general than at present. To indulge this disposition in the public and in themselves, the Editors of the following pages, being possessed of several original MSS and being promised the use of others, propose to publish in numbers some of the most entertaining: at the same time intending to mix with them other pieces formerly printed, now little known, and not to be met with but by accident. Nor will the numbers appear with any periodic regularity, but as it shall suit the leisure and convenience of the Gentlemen who have undertaken the work, which is in imitation of Peck's *Desiderata Curiosa,* and is solely calculated for amusement; for which reason the Editors make no promises, enter into no engagements; but shall take the liberty of continuing, varying, or dropping the plan, when and in what manner they please—a notice they think right to give, that no man may complain hereafter of being disappointed.

"The Editors" were a pleasantry to include Gray, Cole, and any other antiquary who might suggest a piece that appealed to Walpole. Number I was "An Account of some Tournaments and other martial Diversions," which were extracted from Sir William Segar's *Honor, Military and Civil,* 1602; Number II was "Life of Sir Thomas Wyat, the elder," copied by Gray from the original in the Harleian Collection in the British Museum. Walpole printed 500 copies of each on ordinary paper and twenty-five on writing-paper for presents, but the results were disappointing. "The *Miscellaneous Antiquities* have not sold above a fifth of them," he wrote Mason in 1775," so there will be no more." And there were no more until 1926 when I revived them and brought out a number almost every year for Christmas presents until 1939. Walpole's copy of the first two numbers, with his arms on the sides, two manuscript notes, and a few extra-illustrations is at Farmington, but is outshone by Bull's fully extra-illustrated copy.

The runner-up to the Journal in this Choice is Walpole's collection of

"Detached Pieces" that he pasted into a quarto notebook with marbled paper covers. Its spine has a label, one of the Press's rarest productions, "Loose Pieces Printed at Strawberry-Hill." On a fly-leaf Walpole wrote, "This book is unique as there is no other compleat Set of all the Pieces preserved. H.W.," but it lacks the title-page to Bentley's *Designs for Strawberry Hill.* Walpole showed his affection for this collection by printing a special title-page for it, "A/Collection/of all the/Loose Pieces/ printed at Strawberry Hill." This is followed by the south front of Strawberry after Paul Sandby and a print of Kirgate annotated by Walpole. I owe this supreme collection of Detached Pieces to the good offices of John Carter and John Hayward who in 1952 encouraged its then owner, the Dowager Marchioness of Crewe, who had inherited it from her father Lord Rosebery, to let the collection go to Farmington. Their petition came at a time when repairs were needed in the owner's bathroom and were effected by letting the Detached Pieces cross the Atlantic, an instance of domestic benefit conferred by a collector.

The first "piece" is a type-smudged sheet of Gray's "Progress of Poesy" that Walpole identified, "The first sheet ever printed at Strawberry hill July 16, 1757." It is followed by the finished *Odes* on which Walpole wrote, "The first book compleated at Strawberry-hill. Aug. 9. 1757." One of the earliest detached pieces was written by David Garrick to console Gray for the public's failure to understand the Odes. It begins:

> Repine not, Gray, that our weak dazzled Eyes
>   Thy daring heights and brightness shun,
> How few can track the Eagle to the skies,
>   Or like Him gaze upon the sun!

We learn from the Journal that sixty copies of Garrick's verses were printed, an entry that corrects T. F. Dibdin and others in the nineteenth century who said there were only six copies and so misled collectors and booksellers until the Journal came to light.

The Press was a novelty that Walpole loved to show visitors in its early days. On 25 August 1757, he wrote Montagu,

I must give you some account of *les amusements des eaux de Straberri.* T'other day my Lady Rochford, Lady Townshend, Miss Bland and the new Knight of the Garter dined here, and were carried into the printing-office, and were to see the man print. There were some lines ready placed, which he took off; I gave them to my Lady Townshend; here they are:

The Press speaks:

> From me wits and poets their glory obtain;
> Without me their wit and their verses were vain:
> Stop, Townshend! and let me but *print* what you say;
> You, the fame I on others bestow, will repay.

They then asked, as I foresaw, to see the man compose; I gave him four lines out of *The Fair Penitent,* which he set, but while he went to place them in the press, I made them look at something else; without their observing, and in an instant he whipped away what he had just set, and to their great surprise when they expected to see *Were ye, ye Fair,* he presented to my Lady Rochford the following lines:

> The Press speaks:
>
> In vain from your properest name you have flown,
> And exchanged lively Cupid's for Hymen's dull throne:
> By my art shall your beauties be constantly sung,
> And in spite of yourself you shall ever be Young.

You may imagine, whatever the poetry was, that the gallantry of it succeeded.

The Press never ceased producing complimentary verses. Among them were those Lord Chesterfield found on the library table when calling at Strawberry Hill. They invited him to "bless with some immortal page thy favour'd Press," but he declined to do so. That he and Walpole were not at all close appears from Walpole's letters and his 300-odd notes in Chesterfield's *Letters to his Son,* 1774, at Farmington. Among them is a derisive exclamation point beside Chesterfield's pronouncement, "Laughter is easily restrained, by a very little reflection; but, as it is generally connected with the idea of gaiety, people do not enough attend to its absurdity," and in one of his letters he spoke of having been carried "beyond my Lord Chesterfield's allowed simper."

Among the last complimentary verses were those to the Misses Berry and the Duke of Clarence (later William IV) when he at the age of twenty-five paid a visit to Strawberry Hill.

> /To/His/Royal Highness/The/Duke of Clarence.
> Sir, When you condescend to grace
> An ancient Printer's Dwelling,
> He such a Moment must embrace
> Your Virtues to be spelling:
>
> Your Naval Talents, Spirit, Zeal,
> Shall other Types record;

He but one Sentiment can feel,
   —And Gratitude's the Word.

Condemn not, Sir, the Truths he speaks,
   Tho' homely his Address;
A Prince of BRUNSWIC never checks
   The Freedom of the Press.

At Farmington are 103 presentation copies of the Press's publications that Walpole gave his friends and acquaintances among whom are some new to us, and since Walpole sent a note with the book and had a note of thanks in return the newcomers are putative correspondents. In the eighteenth century it was customary to give books in their original boards or wrappers so that the recipient could have them bound to match his or her library. The most elegant Press books at Farmington are those in red morocco that belonged to Charles Bedford, Walpole's deputy at the Exchequer, and to Richard Bull of Ongar in Essex. The spines of Bedford's books are enlivened with green panels on which are printed in gold the titles, "Strawberry Hill," and the date of publication; below are his initials entwined under his crest. Both he and Bull despoiled other books for prints to extra-illustrate their copies, a deplorable practice that adds, it must be confessed, to the interest of the embellished copies. The handsomest of Bull's Strawberry books at Farmington is his Lucan which he had bound in vellum by Edwards of Halifax in his Etruscan style. It has Bull's arms painted on the front cover, a scene from the *Pharsalia* on the back cover, Roman coins and a view of Strawberry are on the spine; there is a fore-edge drawing of its south front; all at a cost of four guineas according to the bill Bull had bound in with a long letter from Edwards about the book's care. Bull lent the book to Walpole, whose letter of thanks speaks of the "New proof of the expense I have so often (though unwittingly) put you to. What joy would Cicero, who said to his friend *Orna me,* have felt if *his* friend had been as partial and as magnificent as Mr. Bull!"

In 1938 I realized we must have a descriptive bibliography of the Press. A lot had been written on it from Walpole's day to Paget Toynbee's *Journal of the Printing Office* in 1923, but a professional bibliographer could add much more. After Allen T. Hazen, who was then teaching at Yale, embarked on his *Bibliography of the Strawberry Hill Press* I set out to get ten percent of the Press's entire output; that is, twenty copies of a book printed in 200 copies, and got them in several titles. To the uninitiated, duplicates are proof of the collector's lunacy, yet when Allen Hazen collated our duplicates leaf by leaf he found unrecorded variants, and proof that Kirgate printed unauthorized copies at the end of Walpole's life. The work reproduces title-pages, gives full collations, and the history of individual copies with the prices they have fetched at auctions and been offered in booksellers' catalogues. Five hundred copies of the bibliography were published in 1942 by the Yale University Press. As one hundred of them were torpedoed on their way to the Oxford University Press and librarians have realized the work is essential for Walpolian studies, surviving copies have reached as high as seventy pounds. Dawson's of Pall Mall reprinted it in 1973 with additions and corrections by Hazen, the additions being mostly copies of the Press that have come to Farmington since 1942.

Kirgate, as Mr Hazen showed in his bibliography, was indifferent honest. He reprinted Gray's *Odes,* Lady Temple's *Poems,* and eight or nine of the detached pieces. Most, if not all, were reprinted after Walpole died. Whether he sold his reprints in Walpole's lifetime we do not know, but we have the bills for sales of them later. He extra-illustrated copies of the 1784 *Description of Strawberry Hill* and sold them to collectors of the Press after Walpole's death. I believe that Walpole, so perceptive about the "rascally attorneys" and "rookery of harpies," who preyed upon his nephew Orford, suspected Kirgate of dishonest dealing. Proof of his dishonesty is his keeping the portions of Walpole's correspondence with Horace Mann that Walpole cut out when he and Kirgate transcribed the originals. The suppressed passages were offered in the sale of Kirgate's library the year after he died, but his daughter on learning that Walpole did not wish them transcribed or printed had them withdrawn from the sale and destroyed in the presence of Mrs Damer, an instance of regrettable virtue.

Kirgate complained loudly and bitterly of Walpole's "neglect" in leaving him only £100. His friend Silvester Harding wrote for him "The Printer's Farewell to Strawberry Hill," which according to a note by Kirgate on a copy of it at Farmington was "The Last thing Printed at" the Press. I brought out fifty copies of it in 1931 as Number Six of *Miscellaneous Antiquities.*

> Adieu! ye Groves and Gothic Tow'rs,
> Where I have spent my youthful Hours,
>   Alas! I find in vain:

Since he who could my Age protect,
By some mysterious, sad neglect,
   Has left me to complain!

For thirty Years of Labour past,
To meet such slight Reward at last,
   Has added to my Cares:
To quit the quiet Scenes of Life,
T'encounter Bus'ness, Bustle, Strife,

   Hangs heavy on my Years.
On thee, my Fellow-Lab'rour, dear,
My Press, I drop the silent Tear
   Of Pity, for thy Lot;
For thou, like me, by Time art worn,
Like me, too, thou art left forlorn,
   Neglected and forgot!

October 1797   T.K.

All very sad, but things could have been worse. Mrs Damer seems to
have been kind and generous to him and he was not forgotten by the
Press's eager collectors to whom he sold its remainders for his own benefit.
One of the best of his customers was George Baker who shortly after
Kirgate's death in 1810 printed twenty * copies of *A Catalogue of Books,
Poems, Tracts, and small Detached Pieces Printed at the Press at Strawberry Hill belonging to the Late Horace Walpole Earl of Orford*. We have
two of his bills from Kirgate for fifty-two books and detached pieces that
came to £47.12s, or the better part of Kirgate's wages for a year. The
first item on one of the bills is a *Grammont* at six pounds. In 1781 Walpole wrote Richard Bull regretting he had only his own copy of it left,
but later he sent him a copy (now at Farmington) that Bull annotated and
extra-illustrated in his sumptuous style. It has a preliminary statement
framed in a border supported by caryatids in eighteenth-century dress
recording that the copy was given him Mr Walpole; doubtless it was
supplied by Kirgate in whose posthumous sale were thirteen other copies.
An even more awkward failure to produce a Press book occurred when the
King of Poland requested a copy of the *Anecdotes of Painting in England*.
Walpole had to pay £13 for one because he had only his own copy left,
which is Choice 10. One wonders how much of the £13 went to Kirgate.
There were two other sets of the *Anecdotes* in his 1810 sale.

* In the MS of the Introduction at Farmington Baker wrote "12 copies."

Besides selling to eager collectors of the Press Kirgate held a raffle "For the Benefit of T. Kirgate. Late Printer at Strawberry Hill." The prize was a copy of the 1784 *Description* extra-illustrated by him. "Each leaf," of it, his prospectus stated, "is inlaid on a large Sheet of fine Dutch Paper; the Pages bordered with a double Line of red ink; the Title printed in three Colours, and ornamented with a Drawing of a Foliage of Strawberries. The whole Book adorned with upwards of three Hundred Drawings and Prints, illustrative of the external and internal Parts of that delightful Seat, its Furniture, Pictures, Sculptures, Antiquities, etc. etc. Several of the Prints are scarce and valuable, and most of the Drawings were made on Purpose for the Book by the Friends of T. KIRGATE, who has been Fourteen Years in forming the Collection;" that is, it was begun years before Walpole died. I don't doubt it was the finest of all the extra-illustrated copies of the *Description*. There were seventy-five chances at two guineas a chance, a total equal to almost three years of Kirgate's wages. The preliminary List of Subscribers was headed by the Duchess of Gloucester and her two royal children, the Duchesses of Devonshire, Dorset, Roxburgh, and seventeen lords and ladies. Lord Cholmondeley, Walpole's great nephew, took five chances; Richard Bull and his sister three each. One would like to know how the subscribers were solicited: they, Walpole's nearest and dearest, were being asked to mitigate his alleged injustice to an old and essential retainer. The subscribers were informed that the book would be raffled for on Wednesday the third of June, 1801, at Mr S. Harding's, No. 127 Pall Mall, near Carlton-House, from one till five o'clock in the afternoon, under the Inspection of some of the Subscribers. A second List of Subscribers issued after the sale, a copy of which was pasted by Bull in his extra-illustrated *Description*, reports the scores made by each subscriber. The winner was the Hon. Horatio Walpole, Pigwiggin's son. Unfortunately, the wonderful book has disappeared.

The eleven-days' sale of Kirgate's library was conducted by King and Lochée in London shortly after Kirgate's death in 1810. They accorded the sale the distinction of printing six copies of its catalogue on large paper; one of them at Farmington is elegantly bound in contemporary red morocco, gilt, by Hayday. Its 1279 lots included thousands of prints from admirals to butterflies and some 500 miscellaneous books such as *Isocrates*, 1638, and *Vossius*, 1556; Fleming's *Foot Pathe to Felicitie*, 1556; Holland's *Against the Pestilence*, 1603, and Sherwin's *Mathematical Tables*, 1762. They were followed by eighty-nine lots of "Earl of Orford's Works, Chiefly

Printed at Strawberry Hill," which reached a total of £155.15s. Two of Baker's purchases are now at Farmington, an *Anecdotes of Painting* with many notes by Kirgate, and one of his forged copies of Gray's *Odes*. There were not only books and prints in the sale; the tenth day had 153 lots that remind one of Walpole's collecting such as "a Curious Lock," "a Roman Lamp," "A curious Powder Horn, with a Plan of New York engraved on it," and "An old Muffet, Tippet, and Fan." The total sale brought £833.12s.9 and one likes to think of Kirgate's honest daughter receiving the present-day equivalent of many thousands of dollars.

Choices 8 and 9

Walpole's Two Chief Copies of His
Description of Strawberry Hill, Printed there in
1774 and 1784

A Description of the Villa of Horace Walpole Youngest Son of Sir Robert Walpole Earl of Orford, at Strawberry Hill near Twickenham, with an inventory of the Furniture, Pictures, Curiosities, Etc. first appeared in 1774, a small quarto in an edition of 100 copies with six more on large paper, four of which are at Farmington, with ten of the smaller size. The second edition of 200 copies was printed in 1784, a large quarto with twenty-seven plates.

The importance of the *Description* in Walpolian studies cannot be exaggerated. Choice 8 is Walpole's copiously annotated copy of the first edition. His notes are on almost every page and there are fifty additional pages of drawings and text. Most of the notes report objects acquired after 1774; nearly all of them were used in the 1784 edition. An exception tells how in the Little Library in the Cottage "three of the antique sepulchral earthen lamps and some of the vases on the mantel were broken in 1777 when an owl fell down the chimney." Besides the scores of marginal notes in Choice 8 Walpole added ten pages that he printed in the 1784 edition. They include "Explanation of the different coats of arms about the house at Strawberry Hill," "Collections [56 of them] from which were purchased many of the Curiosities at Strawberry Hill," a "List of the books printed at Strawberry Hill," and a list of "Works of Genius at Strawberry Hill by Persons of rank and Gentlemen not Artists," that will appear in Choice 11. There are also sixty-seven "Principal Curiosities"; among which were the silver bell designed by Benvenuto Cellini, "a bronze bust of Caligula with silver eyes at the beginning of his madness," "Callot's Pocket Book" which we met in Choice 3, and a clock that the *Description* tells us was of "silver gilt, richly chased, engraved, and ornamented with fleurs des lys, little

83

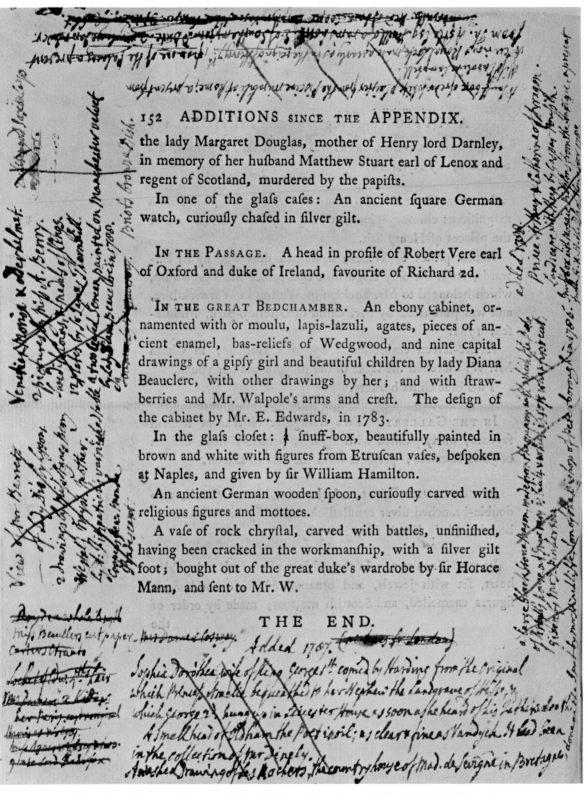

152 ADDITIONS SINCE THE APPENDIX.

the lady Margaret Douglas, mother of Henry lord Darnley, in memory of her huſband Matthew Stuart earl of Lenox and regent of Scotland, murdered by the papiſts.

In one of the glaſs caſes: An ancient ſquare German watch, curiouſly chaſed in ſilver gilt.

IN THE PASSAGE. A head in profile of Robert Vere earl of Oxford and duke of Ireland, favourite of Richard 2d.

IN THE GREAT BEDCHAMBER. An ebony cabinet, ornamented with or moulu, lapis-lazuli, agates, pieces of ancient enamel, bas-reliefs of Wedgwood, and nine capital drawings of a gipſy girl and beautiful children by lady Diana Beauclerc, with other drawings by her; and with ſtrawberries and Mr. Walpole's arms and creſt. The deſign of the cabinet by Mr. E. Edwards, in 1783.

In the glaſs cloſet: A ſnuff-box, beautifully painted in brown and white with figures from Etruſcan vaſes, beſpoken at Naples, and given by ſir William Hamilton.

An ancient German wooden ſpoon, curiouſly carved with religious figures and mottoes.

A vaſe of rock chryſtal, carved with battles, unfiniſhed, having been cracked in the workmanſhip, with a ſilver gilt foot; bought out of the great duke's wardrobe by ſir Horace Mann, and ſent to Mr. W.

THE END.

Page from '74 extra-illustrated *Description of Strawberry Hill* with Walpole's notes.

heads, etc. On the top sits a lion holding the arms of England, which are also on the sides. This was a present from Henry 8th to Anne Boleyn; and since, from Lady Elizabeth Germaine to Mr Walpole. On the weights are the initial letters of Henry and Anne, within true lovers knots; at top, *Dieu et mon Droit;* at bottom The most happy.—One of the weights, agreeably to the indelicacy of that monarch's gallantry, is in a shape very comfortable to the last motto." The clock, which is now at Windsor, has been a source of not altogether innocent merriment since 1533. The drawing I value most in Choice 8 is Walpole's own crude sketch, "Front of Strawberry hill to the garden as it was in 1747 before it was altered," the only view we have of it at that time.

The rooms contained 760 pictures and framed prints crowded with thousands of miscellaneous objects that must have wilted the best informed and keenest of visitors. Take, for example, the charming Battersea enamel in the Green Closet, "A king-fisher and ducks" now at Farmington, the gift of John and Helen Mayer of Greenwich. It had to compete with its immediate neighbors, one of Walpole's copies of Watteau mentioned in Choice 3, and "Charles 2d, young, in armour, with the Garter, oval miniature." The China Closet housed two Faenze plates on which were printed the Death of Abel and the Sacrifice of Isaac, given me by Osbert Sitwell. They were among dozens of cups and dishes from far and wide—even one from Peru—each of which had a claim to recognition. As we turn the pages of this richly annotated copy we are at Walpole's side relishing with him his vast and varied treasures.

The clutter is illustrated in the seventeen pages of the Tribune where among its 164 pictures and prints and hundreds of objects were "Two lockets in shape of hearts, with hair of Sir Robert Walpole and Catherine Shorter, set with diamonds"; "An Egyptian duck; antique cameo, on agate"; "A sleeping hermaphrodite with two satyrs"; "A small gold watch, given by George 2d when Prince of Wales to Catherine Lady Walpole," "A chrystal sceptre, set in gold enamelled, with pearls, from Lady E. Germaine's collection, and given to Mr Walpole by her niece lady Temple"; "A magnificent missal, with miniatures by Raphael and his scholars, set in gold enamelled, and adorned with rubies and turquoises; the sides are of cornelian, engraved with religious subjects; the clasp, a large garnet. This precious prayer-book belonged to Claude queen of France, wife of Francis 1st and seems to have belonged to the father of Thuanus; . . . It was purchased by Mr Walpole from the collection of doctor Mead, 1755," and is now in the John Carter Brown Library, Providence, Rhode Island.

Not far from it in the Tribune was "Henry the 8th's dagger, of Turkish work; the blade is of steel damasked with gold, the case and handle of chalcedonyx, set with diamonds and many rubies. From the collection of lady Elizabeth Germaine. The Duchess of Portland has such another set with jacinths." According to the Germaine sale catalogue the dagger was "designed by Holbein," and it is odd that Walpole failed to say so, for it was one of Strawberry's most admired curiosities; sketches and prints of it are in Richard Bull's and Kirgate's extra-illustrated copies of the '84 *Description* at Farmington.

"A small capricious house," Walpole called it. By modern standards a house of twenty-two master rooms is hardly "small," but Strawberry was small compared to Knole with 365 rooms. Everyone has agreed from Walpole's day to ours that it was "a capricious house" because of its contents as well as its design. Walpole was a passionate collector all his life. In 1740 he wrote Conway from Rome, "I am far gone in medals, lamps, idols, prints, etc. and all the small commodities to the purchase of which I can attain; I would buy the Coliseum if I could." In 1744 he bought Conyers Middleton's collection of Roman antiquities for £131, as the receipt of the purchase at Farmington shows. Forty years later he wrote Mason, "The old child's baby-house is quite full of playthings," and he went on adding them as long as he lived.

He was especially proud of his "miniatures, enamels, and portraits of remarkable persons," stating in the Preface to the *Description* that his collection of them was "the largest and finest in any country." How he annotated them is shown at Farmington by one that he endorsed, "Liotard by himself a Legacy to Mr Horace Walpole from Mrs M. Delany," George the Third's "Dear Mrs Delany," who knew that her bequest would be affectionately displayed at Strawberry Hill. Walpole might also have called attention to his collection of coins and medals that took two days to sell in 1842, thousands of Greek, Roman, Saxon and English coins in gold, silver, brass, and copper from Philip of Macedon to George III. Among them were nine silver jettons or counters made by Simon van Pass of James I and his family. They had an adventure at Farmington when a ten-year-old great-niece removed them from their exhibition case to play with on a sofa. I rescued eight of them, but the ninth was missing. "Stand up, Pinkie!" I ordered. She obeyed contritely. I gave her, an ample child with curves more than Grecian, a good shake and out from his hiding place in her inmost recesses Prince Charles slid on to the floor. He was restored to his family and our curatorial problem was solved.

Macaulay wrote of Strawberry Hill eleven years before its contents were dispersed: "Every apartment is a museum; every piece of furniture is a curiosity; there is something strange in the form of the shovel; there is a long story belonging to the bell-rope," and he singled out "Queen Mary's comb, Wolsey's red hat, the pipe which Van Tromp smoked during his last sea fight, and the spur King William struck into the flank of Sorrel" at the Battle of the Boyne. Walpole loved these "reliques" because they evoked visions, but he was not over-solemn about them. "You would laugh if you saw in the midst of what trumpery I am writing," he wrote Conway in 1758, "Two porters have just brought home my purchases from Mrs Kennon the midwife's sale. Brobdignag combs, old broken pots, pans, and pipkins, a lanthorn of scraped oyster-shells, scimitars, Turkish pipes, Chinese baskets, etc., etc. My servants think my head is turned, I hope not: it is all to be called the personal estate and movables of my great-great-grandmother. . . . P.S. I forgot, that I was outbid for Oliver Cromwell's nightcap."

The Preface of the 1784 *Description* tells us that ". . . the following account of pictures and rarities is given with a view to their future dispersion. . . . The several purchasers will find a history of their purchases; nor do virtuosos dislike to refer to such a catalogue for authentic certificates of their curiosities. The following collection was made out of the spoils of many renowned cabinets; as Dr Mead's, Lady Elizabeth Germaine's, Lord Oxford's, the Duchess of Portland's, and of about forty more of celebrity. Such well attested descent is the genealogy of the objects of virtu—not so noble as those of the peerage, but on a par with those of race-horses. In all three, especially the pedigrees of peers and rarities, the line is often continued by many insignificant names," a classic description of "provenance." Walpole's copies at Farmington of Lady Elizabeth Germaine's, Lord Oxford's, and the Duchess of Portland's sale catalogues, in which he noted his purchases and what he paid for them, illustrate the importance he gave "provenance." In the Duchess of Portland's catalogue he pasted a four-page account of her that I printed for the Grolier Club in 1934.

The fifty pages of drawings and manuscripts at the back of the '74 copy I am saving begin with Sir Edward Walpole's verses and drawings mentioned in Choice 3 and continue with sketches by Thomas Walpole, Horace's favorite Wolterton cousin. There are caricatures of the Dukes of Cumberland and Newcastle by Walpole's cousin Lord Townshend, "the father of English caricature," and sketches by Lady Diana Beauclerk (whom we come to in Choice 11), by Mrs Damer and other talented persons of quality. Finally, there is a printed title-page, the only one known, *Catalogue of Pictures and Drawings in the Holbein-chamber at Strawberry Hill,* which is followed by plans that show where the pictures hung in the room.

Another of Walpole's annotated copies of the 1774 *Description* at Farmington was bought by William Beckford in 1842. It has Walpole's arms on the covers. For a frontispiece he added the print of himself after Falconet, a portrait on which he wrote "Earl of Orford, 1791" to bring himself up to date. The manuscript additions in this copy include verses by him and Kirgate's transcript of Lady Burrell's lines "On Strawberry Hill" that gave the owner great satisfaction:

> Hail sacred Shades! by every Muse revered,
> By every Grace embellished and endeared;
> Hail, Gothic Scenes! where the astonished Sight
> Finds Art and Nature happily unite;
> Where proud Antiquity Attention gains,
> Where Science flourishes, and pleasure reigns.

A note by Walpole at the end identifies the author as "Sophia Lady Burrell, wife of Sir William and daughter of Sir Charles Raymond. They were sent to Mr Walpole anonymously in 1790 after seeing his house."

Included in most of the fourteen '74 copies at Farmington is a printed twenty-four-page Appendix of "Pictures and Curiosities added since the catalogue was printed," six pages of "Additions since the Appendix," and two "More Additions," which were printed in 1786. Walpole's second copy at Farmington extols Mrs Damer, Conway's only child and Walpole's executrix, to whom he left life-use of Strawberry Hill. What Walpole thought of her as a sculptress appears in a note on the head of Jupiter Serapis in basalts that tells us, "In 1787, Mrs Damer modelled a neck to it (as it was a mere head when brought from Rome) and had it cast in bronze, with a gilt modius, which had been lost, and she supplied in wax some lower curls that were wanting, and mounted the whole on a white marble plinth, so that it is now as perfect as ever it had been, and still more valuable from being repaired by the greatest Female Artist ever known."

The Preface to the 1784 *Description* apologizes for

the mixture of modern portraits, and French porcelaine, and Greek and Roman sculpture, [which] may seem heterogeneous. In truth, I did not mean to make my house so Gothic as to exclude convenience, and modern refinements in luxury. The designs of the inside and outside are strictly ancient, but the decorations are modern. Would our ancestors, before the reformation of architecture, not have deposited in their gloomy castles antique statues and fine pictures, beautiful vases and ornamental china, if they had possessed them?—But I do not mean to defend by argument a small capricious house. It was built to please my own taste, and in some degree to realize my own visions. I have specified what it contains; could I describe the gay but tranquil scene where it stands, and add the beauty of the landscape to the romantic cast of the mansion, it would raise more pleasing sensations than a dry list of curiosities can excite: at least the prospect would recall the good humour of those who might be disposed to condemn the fantastic fabric, and to think it a very proper habitation of, as it was the scene that inspired, the author of the *Castle of Otranto.*

Strawberry's eclecticism appears in the Gallery: its ceiling was copied from Henry VII's Chapel in Westminster Abbey, there was gold network from Chantilly over the looking-glass, and crimson Norwich damask on its settees, two of which are now at Farmington; there were Axminster and Wilton carpets and Aubusson tapestries. Walpole supplemented Bentley's Gothic furniture with "a thousand plump chairs, couches, and luxurious settees covered with linen" of blue and white stripes adorned with festoons. They are not mentioned in the *Description* or sale catalogues and were doubtless withheld for the Waldegrave's comfort. To enrich the "gloomth" Walpole sent a man to Flanders to buy painted glass, which he stuck into the Lanthorn and windows throughout the house, four hundred and fifty pieces showing "scriptural stories, stained in black and yellow . . . birds and flowers in colors, and Flemish coats of arms," which Walpole called "the achievements of the old counts of Strawberry." Many of these panes were sold in 1842; four of them are in a window at Farmington. Romantic visions, comfort, novelty, gaiety, and gloomth—all were found at Strawberry Hill.

The east end of the house was finished in 1754 with the Refectory and Library, but rooms and outbuildings were added for nearly forty years in the spirit of the chambered nautilus, "Build me more stately mansions, O my soul!" Walpole was driven by his compulsion to enlarge and adorn the architectural projection of himself. The later rooms were larger; whereas the China Closet was only about ten by twelve feet, the Gallery was "fifty-six feet long, seventeen high, and thirteen wide without the five recesses"; the second largest room, the Great Parlour, or Refectory, was over nineteen by twenty-eight feet. The drawings of it show Bentley's black

Gothic chairs against the wall, but no dining-room table; apparently one was brought in when needed. Walpole had his meals all over the house. To get to wherever he dined, the food had to be carried from the kitchen at the west end of the house through a long passage, outside into the open air, and back through the oratory and into the main entrance of the house.

As time went on, Strawberry had so many sight-seers that its creator shuddered when the bell rang at the gate. He printed rules for seeing the house and issued tickets of admission to it:

Mr Walpole is very ready to oblige any curious Persons with the Sight of his House and Collection . . . but as he refuses a Ticket to nobody that sends for one, it is but reasonable that such Persons as send, should comply with the Rules he has been obliged to lay down for showing it.

Any person, sending a Day or two before, may have a Ticket for Four Persons for a Day certain.

No Ticket will serve but on the Day for which it is given. If More than Four Persons come with a Ticket, the Housekeeper has positive Orders to admit none of them.

Every Ticket will admit the Company only between the Hours of Twelve and Three before Dinner, and only one Company will be admitted on the same Day.

The House will never be shown after Dinner; nor at all but from the First of May to the First of October. . . .

They who have Tickets are desired not to bring Children.

The ticket read,

This Ticket, on being delivered to the Housekeeper, will admit Four Persons, and no more, on [written in] Thursday Aug. 4th 1774, between Twelve and Three, to see Strawberry Hill, and will only serve for the Day specified.

N.B. The House and Garden are never shown in an Evening; and Persons are desired not to bring Children with them.

                                                              Hor. Walpole.

When strangers came Walpole kept out of the way, leaving the tour to his voluble housekeeper who expected a guinea from each guest on his departure, the equivalent today of many dollars. When Walpole took the special guests round himself he hobbled ahead on his gouty feet, talking steadily and delightfully the whole time, pausing to open a locked cabinet to place an ivory or cameo in the hand of a flattered visitor. An over-indulged little dog waddled at his heels and sat beside him on a sofa eyeing the strangers dubiously; squirrels came to the windows to be fed;

canaries sang in their cages; jars of tuberoses and heliotrope and bowls of pot-pourri were in all the rooms, and after dinner a pot of frankincense was brought in to improve the air. The tour of the house must have been exhausting. The contents of the tiny China Closet alone fill twelve pages of the '74 *Description* and Walpole's manuscript additions in Choice 8 fill another page. The visitors' eyes must have glazed as they wandered over the enamels, medals and coins, Roman lachrymatories, faience, Venetian glass, Saxon, Arabian, and Portuguese earthenware, English and French china and porcelaine, and portraits of Louis Quinze, Voltaire, and Dr Franklin in biscuit.

Choice 9, Walpole's extra-illustrated 1784 *Description* inlaid to elephant folio with his arms on the sides, was mentioned in Choice 4 because it contained the mezzotint of the Ladies Waldegrave. Choice 9 has two dozen water-color drawings of Strawberry by the "topographical" artists who are at last coming into their own, Paul Sandby, Edward Edwards, J. C. Barrow, John Dobbin, John Carter, William Pars, and J. H. Müntz. Walpole unfortunately saved money on the engravings of their drawings for the *Description of Strawberry Hill*. The prints are muddy and dull and furnish no idea of Strawberry's "gay but tranquil scene" that Walpole wished he could send Horace Mann. We see it in the water-colors: cows graze by the river, Twickenham and its church are in the distance; Richmond Hill bounds the prospect; gardeners slope along carrying watering-cans and short-handled scythes to trim the lawns; ladies and gentlemen stroll by or pause to admire the garden; we stop in the passage from the Star Chamber to the Long Gallery to look in at the Holbein Chamber. At Little Strawberry Hill, we see Mary and Agnes Berry, very smart in tilted hats and long skirts, walking through the garden up to the cottage as a gardener goes about his business with a wheelbarrow. There are views of Strawberry itself from the obelisk at the junction of the roads to Hampton Court and Teddington and, closer at hand, the entrance through "the embattled wall" that was copied from a print in Dugdale's *Warwickshire*. We look towards the Round Tower from the two-story Offices designed by James Essex in 1790 that included the stables, servants' rooms, the laundry, coach and harness rooms, coal hole, dairy, and still another library for recently published books. The offices were built in what Walpole called "Collegiate Gothic," anticipating the final phase of neo-Gothic building at Yale in our own time. We admire Po Yang in the walled garden. It was a small pool named for the great Chinese lake described in Walpole's copy of du Halde's *Voyage en Chine* at Farmington. Straw-

South front of Strawberry Hill by Paul Sandby.

berry's Po Yang was stocked with goldfish, which Walpole reported bred with him "excessively." He gave them away to friends until one night a heron came and flew off with the lot.

When I got Choice 9 from Sabin in 1926 there were eleven other water-color drawings loose in it, five of which Walpole had engraved for the '84 edition of the *Description*. Perhaps I should have pasted them back into the book, but I am glad I framed them instead, for they are a daily joy in our side hall. My delight in them was shared years ago by Ross, our Scots butler, whose favorite was by Edward Edwards of the large Chinese vase on a stand in the Oratory. "And that, Ma'am," Ross would intone with a genteel indication of his hand when showing visitors the house in our absence, "is the vase in which Mr Walpole's favorite cat was drowned, immortalized by Mr Gray." Also in the hall are Walpole's three copies of Watteau mentioned in Choice 2, three of Robert Adam's designs (not executed) for the Cottage in the Garden, McArdell's mezzotint after Reynolds's portrait of Walpole (Choice 26), Carter's entrance of the Knight into the courtyard of the Castle of Otranto, (which is discussed in Choice 15), and half a dozen prints with the Ladies Waldegrave. One print I particularly prize is of Richard Temple Lord Cobham with Walpole's transcription of Pope's tribute to him. It hung above A. Edward Newton's desk at Daylesford, Pennsylvania, until he took it down and sent it to me after the Newton's last visit to us.

There are twenty-seven copies of the '84 *Description* at Farmington. The second in importance to Choice 9 is Richard Bull's copy, which I owe to H. M. Hake who was then Director of the National Portrait Gallery. It was his friendly practice on visits to country houses for purposes of probate to report whatever he knew would interest me. Bull's copy of the *Description* with two other books from Strawberry Hill turned up in Nottinghamshire, and thanks to Hake's intervention the new owners were happy to let me have them. Many of the drawings in Bull's *Description* are finer than those in Choice 9, for Bull employed John Carter, one of the best of the topographical artists. Carter's own set of the drawings is at the Huntington; a few of them are in Choice 9. Three small sketches of Walpole by him in 1788 that are described in Choice 26 are at Farmington. Several of the subjects drawn by him are not given by other artists, such as "View of the Little Cloyster with the Chinese Jar in which the cat was drowned and on which GRAY wrote his elegant ode," Ross's favorite object at Strawberry seen from the other side. Below it Bull pasted the very rare label printed at the Press for the vase's pedestal:

> 'Twas on *this* lofty Vase's side
>   Where China's gayest Art has dy'd
> The azure Flowers, that blow;
>   Demurest of the tabby Kind,
> The pensive SELIMA reclin'd,
>   Gaz'd on the Lake below etc. GRAY.

When Walpole's great-great nephew, the improvident seventh Earl Waldegrave, sold the contents of Strawberry Hill in 1842 the auction was conducted by George Robins, "the King of Puffery," who boasted afterwards "that he gave this sale a degree of publicity that is without parelel [sic]—there is nothing upon record to approach it." Early in 1842 newspaper and magazine articles began preparing the public for the unparalleled event. Woodcuts of Walpole, of Strawberry Hill, and of its most curious objects were printed over and over. On the whole these preparatory articles were conscientious and sober, which the sale catalogue was not. Its title-page asserted that Strawberry Hill "may fearlessly be proclaimed as the Most Distinguished Gem that has ever Adorned the Annals of Auctions," and that within would be found, "a repast for the Lovers of Literature and the Fine Arts, of which bygone days furnish no previous example, and it would be in vain to contemplate it in times to come." "Prefatory Remarks" that followed were their own parody and inspired Crofton Croker to write *Gooseberry Hall, the Renowned Seat of Sir Hildebrod Gooseberry,* Alfred Crowquill to illustrate it and *The Times* to print a third parody in which it offered, "A pip and part of the stalk of the apple which Eve plucked from the Tree of Knowledge," and "The bridge of the fiddle on which Nero played while Rome was burning."

The Times was the leader of the opposition to the sale. Day after day its writer insisted that the contents of Strawberry Hill were "rubbish" and that Walpole instead of being what Robins called him, "the mighty master who planned and matured this wondrous whole," was really nothing but a fribble. Robins protested to *The Times* in vain.* Other journalists came to the defense of the sale and Walpole in equally shrill rejoinders. The writer in the *Athenaeum* said "the gorge rises with disgust or the midriff explodes with laughter, to hear and read the supercilious opinions passed upon [Horace Walpole] by persons who, comparatively, are beasts of burden

---

* The reply of the editor, Walter, is at Farmington: "I regret that anything should have occurred to give you pain, but I could not venture to interfere between an accredited agent employed by the journal, and his employers."

to an Arabian courser, droning beetles to a bird of Paradise." Robins was probably quite right in saying that there had never been so much interest in any sale before.

The private view began 28 March 1842, and lasted a week. Cards of admission were designed by Delamotte and were sent with the compliments of Robins to persons of the first quality. The implacable *Times* jeered that only three lords came on the first day—Tankerville, Cadogan, and Lilford. When the general public was admitted the crowds were so great that Twickenham and Teddington were like a fair. The neighborhood swarmed with carriages and liveries. "The Extraordinary Fast Packet, the VIVID" ran every day during the sale from Old Swan Pier at nine o'clock to Strawberry Hill for 1s.6d.; hundreds walked. To get into the grounds one had to buy a catalogue for seven shillings, but it admitted four persons and was "a passport for the entire sale." The catalogue could also be bought in London, Paris, and Leipzig. The average visitor was less interested in the books and pictures than in the armor of Francis I, the tile from William the Conqueror's kitchen, and the hair of Mary Tudor. A rival of *The Times* reported that "in spite of the inexplicable opposition that a respectable contemporary is daily offering to the spendid museum of the works of art of Horace Walpole," 18,000 persons had already gone to Strawberry Hill during the fifteen days that the public had been admitted. Eleven days later *The Times* admitted that 50,000 had been there, which meant the sale of many catalogues.

They were brought out so hurriedly and inaccurately they had to be revised and reprinted over and over. The sixth edition is the one bookmen must have because it gives all the books for the first time; the books lumped among "and others" in the earlier editions being printed in black letters. Another marked change in the sixth edition is the removal of the prints and books of prints in the Seventh and Eighth Days' sales to make a ten-days' sale in London the following month. Thus the total sale-days came to thirty-two.

The auction at Strawberry Hill was held in a temporary structure erected for the purpose between the Offices and Round Tower. At Farmington are water-color drawings showing it outside and inside with Robins in the chair. These drawings are in lavishly extra-illustrated and annotated copies of the sale catalogue with newspaper reports of each day's highlights; there are manuscripts and letters from Robins and others including the manuscript of *Gooseberry Hall* in Crofton Croker's copy. That Straw-

berry and its contents are now more in favor than ever became clear at
Sotheby's in 1975 when a sixteenth-century Sainte Porchaire ewer designed
by Giulio Romano that was bought in 1842 by Baron Anthony de Roths-
child for 19 guineas went to a West German dealer for £44,000, or nearly
£9000 more than the entire sale fetched in 1842.

Choice 10

Walpole's Copy of *Anecdotes of Painting in England*, 4 vols., Strawberry Hill 1762–71

This, the most ambitious of Walpole's works, was based on forty note-books compiled by George Vertue, the engraver and antiquary (1684–1756), with a view to writing the first history of painting in England. Walpole records in "Short Notes" and the "Journal of the Printing Office" that he bought Vertue's notebooks and drawings from Vertue's widow in 1758 for £100 and that in 1759 he "began to look over the notebooks in order to compose the lives of English painters." The result was *Anecdotes of Painting in England, with some Account of the principal Artists; And incidental Notes on other Arts; Collected by the late Mr George Vertue; And now digested and published from his original MSS, by Mr Horace Walpole*, 4 vols. 1762–71. "Mr" was no longer "a Gothic abomination" as it was in Choice 5.

Walpole's Preface states that owing to the paucity of native-born geniuses, England "has not a single volume to show on the works of its painters. This very circumstance may with reason prejudice the reader against a work, the chief business of which must be to celebrate the arts of a country which has produced so few good artists. This objection is so striking, that instead of calling it *The Lives of English Painters*, I have simply given it the title *Anecdotes of Painting in England*. The indefatigable pains of Mr Vertue left nothing unexplored that could illuminate his subject, and collaterally led him to many particularities that are at least amusing: I call them no more, nor would I advise any man, who is not fond of curious trifles to take the pains of turning over these leaves." Walpole brought his work down to the end of George II's reign in 1760. He included "other arts," "Statuaries, Carvers, Architects, and Medallists," and closed with an "Essay on Modern Gardening."

Over thirty of Vertue's notebooks have been printed *verb. et lit.* by the English Walpole Society from the originals, which are now mostly in the

Queen's Cross.

I cannot pass over the Princess Eleanor, so much celebrated by our legendary historians for sucking the poison out of her husband's wound, without mentioning the crosses erected to her memory, which Vertue with great probability supposed were built on the designs of Peter Cavalini, a Roman sculptor, and whom from various circumstances he discovered to be the architect of the shrine of Edward the Confessor.

The reader, I am persuaded, will be pleased to see how ingeniously my author traced out this hitherto unknown fact.

The original inscription on the tomb ran thus :

> Anno milleno Domini cum septuageno
> Et bis centeno, cum completo quasi deno,
> Hoc opus est factum, quod Petrus duxit in actum
> Romanus civis : Homo, causam noscere si vis,
> Rex fuit Henricus, sancti praesentis amicus.

The words *Petrus duxit in actum Romanus civis* were discernable 'till very lately. Some old authors ascribe the erection of the shrine to Henry himself, others, to Richard de Ware the Abbat, elected in 1260. It is probable that Both were concerned. The new Abbat repaired to Rome immediately on his election to receive confecration from Urban IV. At that time, says Vasari, flourished there Peter Cavalini, a painter and the inventor of Mosaic, who had performed several costly works in that city. About four years before the arrival of Abbat Ware, that is in 1256, had been erected a splendid shrine for the martyrs Simplicius and Faustina, at the expence of John James Capoccio and his wife, adorned with twisted columns and inlaid with precious marbles exactly in the taste, though not in the precise form of that of St. Edward. Nothing is more probable than that a rich Abbat, either at his own expence, or to gratify the taste of his magnificent master should

Vol. I.   E   engage

✗ The remains of this shrine with its beautifull twisted mosaic columns are now in a chapel erected for them at Strawberry hill.

British Library. The originals show that Walpole's description of them, "indigested" and "unreadable," is charitable—"chaotic" and "illiterate" would not be unjust. The *Anecdotes* show that Walpole was a superb editor who brought order and style out of Vertue's incoherence. Take, for example, Vertue's note on Rembrandt, "Rembrant van Rhine was in England liv'd at Hull in Yorkshire about sixteen or eighteen months reported by old Laroon who in his youth knew Rembrant at York where he painted several gentlemen and sea faring mens pictures, one of them is in possession of Mr. Dahl, a sea captain with the Gentlemans name. Rembrants name and York. & the year $^{62}/_{1661}$." Walpole demoted this entry to a footnote at the end of his introduction to the Reign of Charles II: "Vertue was told by old Mr Laroon, who saw him in Yorkshire, that the celebrated Rembrandt was in England in 1661, and lived 16 or 18 months at Hull, where he drew several gentlemen and seafaring persons. Mr Dahl had one of those pictures. There are two fine whole lengths at Yarmouth, which might be done at the same time. As there is no other evidence of Rembrandt being in England, it was not necessary to make a separate article for him, especially at a time when he is so well known, and his works in such repute, that his scratches, with the difference only of a black horse or a white one, sell for thirty guineas." Besides making Vertue's notes readable, Walpole added much new material and closed the gaps in Vertue's account. "From the reign of Henry III Mr Vertue could discover no records relating to the arts for several reigns," Walpole wrote. "I shall endeavour to fill this hiatus by producing an almost entire chronologic series of paintings from that time to Henry VII when Mr Vertue's notes recommence," and he did so in twenty-one pages.

The first two volumes of the *Anecdotes* appeared in 1762, the third volume and *Catalogue of Engravers* in 1763; the fourth volume was printed in 1771, but was held up until 1780 because Walpole didn't want to offend Hogarth's widow by his strictures on the artist's "Sigismonda." (We shall come to "Sigismonda" and Mrs Hogarth in Choice 23.) All five volumes were reprinted in 1825 and 1849. I hope one day that the Lewis Walpole Library will publish another edition that will make clear the contributions of both Vertue and Walpole to their pioneer history of painting in England.

Like Vertue, Walpole was an indefatigable visitor to country houses. He made extensive notes on some ninety of them in his Books of Materials, Choice 4, that were edited by Paget Toynbee for the Walpole Society. He described the houses, their situations, and their notable contents. His letters report finding masterpieces suffering from damp and neglect in passages and housekeepers' rooms and tell how he got their owners to take better care of them. He had a very good eye for artists of all schools and for sitters, but at Farmington there is a blunder: a portrait the *Description of Strawberry Hill* calls Milton turns out to be Sir William Killigrew.

Walpole's reputation as a connoisseur and authority on painting was established by his *Aedes Walpolianae, or a Description of the Collection of Pictures at Houghton Hall in Norfolk, the Seat of the Right Honourable Sir Robert Walpole Earl of Orford*, 1747. The preliminary list of the collection, which he made in 1736 in his nineteenth year, is in the Pierpont Morgan Library. In 1926 I acquired the manuscript of the *Aedes* which Walpole extra-illustrated with prints and drawings and had bound in a large folio. I had it and, unfamiliar with Walpole's early hand, let it go to the Metropolitan Museum! This is the greatest regret of my collecting life. The 1747 edition of 200 copies had many typographical errors each of which Walpole corrected in his own hand. A second edition was published in 1752, a third in 1767. The book, like so many of Walpole's publications, was a pioneer work. His object, he tells us in his Introduction, was not only to describe his father's collection, which was unrivalled in England, but to enlarge public understanding of painting. "The numerous Volumes on this art," he wrote, "have only served to perplex it. No science has had so much jargon introduced into it as painting: the bombast expression of the Italians, and the prejudices and affectation of the French, joined to the vanity of the professors and the interested mysteriousness of picture merchants, have altogether compiled a new language" that is still spoken.

Walpole's advent at an exhibition was an occasion. Mr Walpole had arrived. His catalogues of the Royal Academy exhibitions belong to Lord Rosebery; those of the Society of Artists and the Free Society are at Farmington. All are profusely annotated with identifications of the sitters and comment on the pictures. Walpole's notes identify scores of sitters among whom are two of Reynolds's portraits each described in the Royal Academy's Exhibition catalogue of 1770 merely as "Portrait of a Gentleman." Walpole identified the first in his catalogue as "Dr Goldsmith" and the second, "Dr Johnson." Doubtless this is the exhibition mentioned in his letter to Miss Berry of 26 May 1791, shortly after Boswell's *Life of Johnson* was published. "I do not think I ever was in a room with [Johnson] six times in my days. The first time I think was at the Royal Academy. Sir Joshua said, 'Let me present Dr Goldsmith to you' and he did. 'Now I will present Dr Johnson to you.'—'No,' said I, 'Sir Joshua, for Dr Goldsmith, pass—but you shall not present Dr Johnson to me,' " and he explained why: Johnson's attacks on Sir Robert Walpole and his "known brutality."

I learned in 1934 that Walpole's copy of the first edition of the *Anecdotes* and twenty-two letters to and from him about *Historic Doubts of Richard III* were at Knowsley Hall, Lord Derby's great house in Lancashire. My introduction there was managed by R. W. Chapman, the Secretary to the Delegates of the Clarendon Press at Oxford, a notable Johnsonian and the leader of the Jane Austenians (as he said they should be called). He wrote me in 1926, having heard of me from Paget Toynbee, to ask for the bibliographical explanation of the "Additional Lives" in the *Anecdotes of Painting*. I had no idea what it was and said so, but he asked me nevertheless to lunch one day the following summer at Oxford. I learned then that he and his colleague, Humphrey Milford, Publisher to the University, were sailing soon for New York and changed my passage to be with them on what proved to be the most memorable of my sixty-four crossings of the Atlantic. When he and Milford came to Farmington for a weekend shortly after we landed I was able to tell them that I had just become engaged. During the next thirty years Chapman did me countless kindnesses of which my introduction to Knowsley was one. Another was sending me Mrs Paget Toynbee's correspondence about her edition, which her husband bequeathed to the Clarendon Press for the use of the next editor of Walpole's letters. In 1929 after Chapman discovered that I keep all my letters and so am Posterity he wrote me regularly as long as he lived, a total of some 1300 letters that came every week or so. What he sent was more of a journal than letters and was written in his very difficult hand sometimes on the backs of calls to meetings, proof sheets, and his children's school exercises. Before he died he began returning my letters to him and after his death his widow sent many more to me; in all, there are about 600 of mine. Among the letters from him is my obituary that he wrote for the London *Times*. It is odd to reread one's letters years after they were written, to revive their forgotten concerns, hear dead friends, and see the person who was yourself; it is particularly strange to read your own obituary. My letters to Chapman are full of Walpolian finds, from whom I got them and for how much. My handwriting is almost as illegible as his, but the letters have brought back my visit to Knowsley in 1935 and the sale of its library nearly twenty years later.

The Knowsley Librarian was Major Henry Milner, D.S.O., who had been at Wellington with Lord Derby. I learned later that in 1888 at the age of twenty-four he had married the Dowager Duchess of Montrose, a lady forty-six years his senior who raced at Newmarket under the name of "Mr Manton." He sent the Knowsley chauffeur to pick me up at the Adelphi Hotel in Liverpool and bring me to the house at ten on a morning in July 1935. A footman showed me to a little room off the entrance hall where I found the most elegant librarian I have ever seen. After forty-odd years I can't be certain that he was wearing striped trousers, a short coat, and an Ascot, but I have a sense of them. He rose, very military, very erect, nodded briefly, and stared at me silently. "I've come to see the Walpoliana," I reminded him.

"Oh, yes, of course," he replied briskly and opened a door behind his desk into a billiard room on the table of which were placed separately the twenty-two letters to and from Walpole about his *Historic Doubts of Richard III*. I walked slowly round the table reading and admiring each letter separately. Then I asked, "You have some books from Walpole's library?"

"How did you know that?" he asked rather sharply.

"You wrote me you have."

"Oh, yes, of course." He was disconcerted; a major transformed to a rattled librarian who hadn't the faintest idea where anything was. "Norris!" he called out in alarm. Through an open door into one of the seven libraries I saw a little man on the top of a ladder. He came clattering down and entered the billiard room bowing and washing his hands deferentially. "Mr Lewis would like to see our books from Horace Walpole's library," Milner announced. Norris was delighted; no one had ever asked to see them before. He went and came, back and forth, happily bearing thirty books, including the first edition of the *Anecdotes* in which Walpole wrote "My own Copy, H.W." and which he annotated and extra-illustrated. I made a hasty list of these treasures before lunch, which Milner and I then had alone. Afterwards he took me round the house to see the fifty-seven pictures and *objets d'art* the 13th Earl had bought at the Strawberry Hill sale in 1842 under his own name, including the large Chinese "vase" in which Walpole's favorite cat, "the pensive Selima" of Gray's poem, was drowned. When the time came for me to leave for Liverpool and the "up" train to Paddington Milner joined me, as he had gone down to Knowsley solely to wait on me. The housekeeper put up supper for him in a paper box that I persuaded him to leave behind in our railway carriage and to join me at dinner. At lunch he had made it clear that he liked wine and as we worked through a bottle of Bordeaux he confided that he had had a personal crisis years ago too dreadful to describe. "And who was the first to come to my side? Edward Derby!" a loyalty expressed by Milner's appointment as "librarian" at Knowsley. When he and I reached the brandy and long Havanas I brought up the question of reproducing the letters. I assumed that Lord Derby would not part with them. "Good God, no!" said Milner, appalled. It was, I explained, very important for the Yale Walpole to be edited if possible from the originals or "roto-graphs" of them, the word then more in English use than "photostat." "And what is a roto-graph?" the Major asked. I explained it is a sort of photograph, only white on black. "Good God!" he said again. "And how does one get a roto-graph?"

"I have mine done at the British Museum. They're very reliable people," I assured him.

"I don't see why we shouldn't do this," the Major volunteered firmly.

Would he help me with my letter to Lord Derby asking for the roto-graphs and permission to reproduce them in the Yale Walpole? Yes, he would and turned over his menu, going to work at once, breathing heavily, by now the color of an eggplant. He flourished his cigar on which he had preserved a long ash in tribute to its quality. The ash fell off upon his composition and upon himself and was swept and brushed masterfully aside. By the time the letter was finished we had reached Paddington. Could I not take him home? No, he thanked me hastily, he would get there on his own, rescuing the supper the Knowsley housekeeper had put up for him. The Walpole letters went to the British Museum—registered, but not insured, his letter told me—and got back to Knowsley safely. I sent him, Lord Derby, and Norris some of my little Christmas books for which I received grateful acknowledgments. A few more friendly letters came from Milner before he died, a pleasant memory of a type that is incomprehensible to most born after 1935.

In 1953 the present Lord Derby was faced with very heavy death duties. Should he sell his horses or his books? Fortunately for me he parted with the books. Professional advice was needed to determine which should go up to Christie's, and, fortunately again for me, the architect who was to pull down two of the seven libraries turned to Chapman for help. The List of Purchasers at the Strawberry Hill sale shows that the books and manuscripts I saw at Knowsley had all been bought by Boone, the bookseller. He bought 339 volumes—some doubtless for stock and other customers, but mostly for Lord Derby. I reported his purchases to Chapman, deducting the twenty-two at Farmington and elsewhere. Chapman and Miss Dorothy Povey, the librarian at Knowsley, went through the seven libraries and found upwards of 200 volumes Boone had bought. Some of them had been rebacked or rebound and showed no signs of Walpole's ownership. What, Chapman asked, did I want to do about them? Send them all up to Christie's, I said, and I would take a chance on their being "right." How happy this decision was is shown in Choice 12. Kenneth Maggs bought for me a total of 196 titles, the largest number of books sold from the Strawberry Hill library since 1842. Among them were the letters to Walpole about his *Historic Doubts* that had been rotographed for me at the British Museum and his heavily annotated extra-illustrated set of the first edition of the *Anecdotes.* I also got his annotated copy of *A Catalogue and Description of King Charles the First's Capital Collection of Pictures, etc.* (prepared by Vertue shortly before his death) for which Walpole wrote a Preface. One book that escaped us went to the University of Liverpool, but thanks to Miss Povey and her brother Kenneth, who was its librarian, the University gave it to me. Other of my Knowsley purchases were dozens of Vertue's drawings of celebrated persons from Chaucer to Sir Robert Walpole. We already had at Farmington Vertue's copy of *A Description of the Earl of Pembroke's Pictures,* 1731, with his drawings and notes and extensive annotations by Walpole; thirty-four of Vertue's drawings of artists in the *Anecdotes,* his copies of the Harleian sale catalogues with seventeen drawings, and a folio for which Walpole made a title-page, "Original Drawings of Heads, Antiquities, Monuments, Views, etc. by George Vertue and others," and annotated fully. We also got three of Vertue's drawings for *Historic Doubts of Richard III,* which we shall come to in Choice 16.

The fourth volume of the *Anecdotes* ends, as I have said, with Walpole's essay "On Modern Gardening." It is another pioneer work that was reprinted in 1975 for the tenth time. The Walpole Printing Office of Mount Vernon, New York, brought out an edition of it in 1931 for Young Books, Inc. of New York for which my wife wrote a bibliography and I wrote a Preface. I explained the appearance of the "Essay on Modern Gardening" in the *Anecdotes* by quoting Pope's dictum, "Gardening is painting." To Walpole and his contemporaries gardening was no longer formal beds of herbs or "giants, animals, coats of arms and mottoes in yew, box and holly," but a large-scale enterprise that dealt with landscape. Woods and rocks and water were needed to "improve the view" and create the "romantic" garden on a scale commensurate with the owner's magnificence. Modern taste, Walpole pointed out, dawned with Charles Bridgman, George II's gardener, whose innovations included the destruction of walls for boundaries and the substitution of sunken ditches "that the common people called 'Ha! Ha's!' " Bridgman was followed by William Kent who, Walpole wrote, was "painter enough to taste the charms of landscape. . . . He leaped the fence and saw that all nature was a garden." The influence of the painters, especially Claude, Gaspard Poussin, and Salvator Rosa, was strong. "If we have the seed of a Claude or Gaspar amongst us," Walpole wrote, "he must come forth. If wood, water, groves, alleys, glades, can inspire poet or painter, this is the country, this is the age to inspire them." Walpole's patriotism extended to England's rocks and rills.

The Journal of the Printing Office records that in 1785 the Press began to print the translation by the duc de Nivernois of Walpole's "Essay on Modern Gardening" in an edition of 400 copies, half of which were sent to the duke. The manuscript of the translation came to Farmington from Mrs Albert E. Smith of Hollywood, whose husband was a pioneer in the movie industry. Walpole noted on the inside cover: "This beautiful Manuscript was written at Paris in 1785 by order of the Duc de Nivernois. Mr Walpole having desired to have a very accurate and legible copy of the Duke's Translation, that the printer at Strawberry Hill, who was not accustomed to print French, nor indeed understood it, might make no mistakes. From this MS the Edition was printed. H. Walpole." Among the sixteen copies of it at Farmington is one given by Nivernois to Lady Clarges and by her to Richard Bull. With Bull's many extra-illustrations is a newspaper cutting that describes the Duke lying on straw in a prison during the French Revolution. Another red morocco copy at Farmington, most beautifully tooled, was given by Walpole to his Richmond neighbor General Fitzwilliam. In it is Walpole's draft of a two-page note to page 136 with many corrections, the only such manuscript of his I know of. The book, which later belonged to Mortimer Schiff, was given to Yale by his son John for permanent deposit at Farmington. In it Fitzwilliam wrote:

Richmond Surrey October 1785.
General Fitzwilliam has often thought himself obliged to Mr Horace Walpole who has not only given to him this book of his Essay on Modern Gardening but also most of his other publications, a collection not only instructive, but very curious and entertaining.

Mr Walpole is so well known and celebrated in the learned world, that it would be needless to speak of his works; but, what would that part of it say of

him, who, like me, have been honored by his good will and attention? His
natural talents, his cheerfullness, the sallies of his imagination, the liveliness of
his manner, the unexpected impression on the ear of those who hear and listen
to him, comes on, like a shooting star, or, like Uriel, gliding on a sun beam. I
never met him, but with pleasure, and never left him but with regret.

Choice 11

Lady Diana Beauclerk's Drawings for

The Mysterious Mother

Before 1962 when I was asked, "What would you most like to find?" I answered promptly, "Lady Diana Beauclerk's drawings for *The Mysterious Mother*." After praising Gibbon's recently published *Decline and Fall,* Walpole asked Mason, "Do I know nothing superior to Mr Gibbon? Yes . . . I talk of great original genius. Lady Di Beauclerk has made seven large drawings in soot-water for scenes of my *Mysterious Mother.* Oh! such drawings! Guido's grace, Albano's children, Poussin's expression, Salvator's boldness in landscape and Andrea Sacchi's simplicity of composition might perhaps have equalled them had they wrought all together very fine." High praise, but not a bit too high for Lady Di's drawings. He wrote Mann, "Lady Di Beauclerk has drawn seven scenes of [*The Mysterious Mother*] that would be fully worthy of the best of Shakespeare's plays—such drawings that Salvator Rosa and Guido could not surpass their expression and beauty. I have built a closet on purpose for them here at Strawberry Hill. It is called the Beauclerk Closet; and whoever sees the drawings, allows that no description comes up to their merit—and then, they do not shock and disgust like their original, the tragedy." Walpole described the Beauclerk Closet in an Appendix to the '74 *Description* and bound the manuscript of it in Choice 8.

[The Closet] is a hexagon, built in 1776, and designed by Mr Essex, architect, of Cambridge, who drew the ceiling, door, window, and surbase. . . . The closet is hung with Indian blue damask, and was built on purpose to receive seven incomparable drawings of Lady Diana Beauclerk for Mr Walpole's tragedy of the *Mysterious Mother.* The beauty and grace of the figures and of the children are inimitable; the expression of the passions most masterly, particularly in the devotion of the countess with the porter, of Benedict in the scene with Martin, and the tenderness, despair, and resolution of the countess in the last scene; in which is a new stroke of double passion in Edmund, whose

One of Lady Diana Beauclerk's drawings for *The Mysterious Mother*, 1776.

right hand is clenched and ready to strike with anger, the left hand relents. In the scene of the children, some are evidently vulgar, the others children of rank; and the first child, that pretends to look down and does leer upwards, is charming.

A writing-table of "Clay's ware" in the Closet contained "the play of *The Mysterious Mother,* to explain the drawings, bound in blue leather and gilt," a modest description of a beautiful book that is now at Farmington. Walpole wrote in it, "This copy to be kept in the Beauclerc Closet to explain Lady Di Beauclerc's Drawings. H.W."

Where, I used to wonder, had these drawings got to? They were bought at the Strawberry Hill sale by Lord Portarlington, but his descendant to whom I wrote knew nothing about them. Then one morning in 1962 I walked into the back office of Pickering and Chatto's shop in London where the proprietor, Dudley Massey, an old friend from 1925, as I tell in Choice 13, was expecting me. The drawings were turned over on his desk and were switched round so that Walpole's notes on their backs were upside down. I stared at them, transfixed in the doorway, for I recognized them immediately. When I asked without moving, "What do you want for them?" Dudley dropped a land mine. To my question at lunch, "Where did I go wrong?" he answered promptly, "You asked the price too quickly," adding truthfully, "You would have given even more." One of the seven drawings is still missing, but those that Walpole described are now at Farmington.

The Mysterious Mother, A Tragedy is set in the dawn of the Reformation; the scene is a castle, of course. There are two villainous friars, a faithful friend, a faithful porter, damsels, orphans, mutes. The plot turns on a double incest. Sixteen years before the play begins its chief character, the Countess of Narbonne, took the place of a girl she knew her son was about to seduce and now sixteen years later she fails to stop him from marrying their daughter. Byron called the play "a tragedy of the highest order, and not a puling love-play," and I agree with those who rank it above *The Castle of Otranto* as a work of art. Walpole tried to forestall possible criticism; but the subject, he said, was "so truly tragic in the two essential springs of terror and pity" that he had to write it. To palliate the countess's crime, and to raise her character he bestowed upon her, he tells us, "every ornament of sense, unbigoted piety, and interesting contrition." Although he protested that the subject was too "horrid" for the stage, he hoped to see it acted; unfortunately, no one was up to playing the Countess and she has yet to be performed.

Walpole kept nearly all fifty copies of the play he printed at the Press. Those he gave away were eagerly read; five transcripts are at Farmington. In thirteen years he let Dodsley publish the play in London to forestall a pirated edition. Four more editions of it appeared before 1800, after which there was none until the Chiswick Press brought it out in 1925 with *The Castle of Otranto* and an introduction by Montague Summers. *The Mysterious Mother* is known today only to students of eighteenth-century tragedy, a small audience.

Seven copies of the Strawberry edition are at Farmington. On the most interesting one Walpole wrote, "With MSS alterations by Mr Mason." In his "Postscript to the Alterations" Mason wrote that they were "To make the foregoing scenes proper to appear upon the stage." Walpole thanked him with deepest gratitude, which he repeated years later, but what he really thought of the alterations is shown in his note written on Mason's letter to him of 8 May 1769 (now at Farmington) that accompanied Mason's alterations: "N.B. I did not adopt these alterations because they would totally have destroyed my object, which was to exhibit a character whose sincere penitence was not degraded by superstitious bigotry." Mason's copy of the play was the Walpole item bought by Maggs in the Milnes Gaskell Sale of 1924. A dozen years later I discovered the new owner who obligingly took me to Messrs Robinsons' in Pall Mall for me to see it. As he dropped me off at Brown's Hotel afterwards he said, "I don't care much about this book, but you want it so badly I think I'll keep it." When death, the ally of collectors, took him away members of his family kindly turned the book over to me. Two of my letters to their relative, written on the Yale Walpole letter-head, were inside. They show that I had not yet learned to perform sedately the English gavotte of letter-writing, a clumsiness that has frustrated countless American scholars.

In my Mellon Lectures, *Horace Walpole*, 1960, I wrote of *The Mysterious Mother*, "The twentieth century has been initiated into the mysteries of the unconscious and needs no gloss on *The Mysterious Mother*, but one point should perhaps be noted for what it may be worth. When Walpole came to arrange his works for posthumous publication he printed his 'Epitaph on Lady Walpole,' with its praise of her sensibility, charity, and unbigoted piety, immediately after *The Mysterious Mother*."

Lady Di's drawings of the *Faerie Queen* at Farmington seem to me superior to her drawings of *The Mysterious Mother*, but the runner-up in this Choice is the Lady Diana Beauclerk Cabinet. *The Description of Strawberry Hill* reads: "An ebony cabinet, ornamented with ormolu, lapis-

Lady Diana Beauclerk's Cabinet.

lazuli, agates, pieces of ancient enamel, bas-reliefs of Wedgwood, and capital drawings of a gipsy girl and beautiful children by Lady Diana Beaucler, with other drawings by her; and with strawberries and Mr Walpole's arms with crest." The Strawberry Hill sale catalogue adds that it is "on a gothic stand with gilt border," but doesn't begin to suggest its elegance or mention the four drawers on which are stuck the semi-precious stones. Walpole put a brass plaque on the inside of the door, "This cabinet was ordered by and made at the expense of Mr Horace Walpole in 1784 to receive the Drawings which were all design'd and executed by the Right Honourable Lady Diana Beauclerc." Beneath this in very small letters is "The cabinet was designed by Mr. E. Edwards." It was sold in 1842 to a dealer for fifty guineas and bought by Sir Robert Peel. I heard of the 1938 owner from Kenneth Clark, whose first book was the admirable *Gothic Revival* and who had most generously given me a book from Walpole's library for which Walpole wrote a title-page: "Six views in Italy drawn and etched by William Marlow, Scholar of Samuel Scott." Lord Clark kindly took me to the 1938 owner's house in Belgrave Square to see the cabinet where it stood, very elegant, in the drawing-room. The owner said she would sell it for a thousand pounds to buy a twenty-sixth Augustus John, whose pictures she greatly admired. As Clark and I walked away I asked what he thought the cabinet was worth. "Oh, £300," he said, and that is what I offered the owner by cable the day war was declared in 1939. The cabinet, like the Ladies Waldegrave, sailed safely through the German mine fields and is now one of the joys of the New Library at Farmington where it has been visited by the Wedgwood Society on pilgrim feet to honor its unique bas-reliefs by Lady Di.

A daughter of the second Duke of Marlborough, she married the second Viscount Bolingbroke in 1757 and was Lady of the Bedchamber to Queen Charlotte from 1762 to 1768. Bolingbroke divorced her in 1768 for *crim. con.* with Dr Johnson's friend Topham Beauclerk. Taking her side against Dr Johnson, Boswell stated that Bolingbroke "had behaved brutally to her, and that she could not continue to live with him without having her delicacy contaminated" and so on. Johnson replied, "My dear Sir, never accustom your mind to mingle virtue and vice. The woman's a whore, and there's an end on't." Two days after her divorce she married Beauclerk, with whom she was even worse off. Lady Louisa Stuart said that in his personal habits Beauclerk was "what the French call *cynique* beyond what one would have thought possible in anyone but a beggar or a gypsy. He and Lady Di, made part of a great Christmas party at Blenheim, where soon after the company were all met, they all found themselves as strangely annoyed as the Court of Pharaoh were of old by certain visitants—*"in all their quarters,"*—It was in the days of powder and pomatum, when stiff frizzing and curling, with hot irons and black pins made the entrance of combs extremely difficult—in short, the distress became unspeakable. Its origin being clearly traced to Mr Beauclerk, one of the gentlemen undertook to remonstrate with him, and began delicately hinting how much the ladies were inconvenienced—'What!' said Beauclerk. 'Are they so nice as that comes to? Why, I have enough to stock a parish . . . ' In the latter part of Beauclerk's life," Lady Louisa went on, "the man of pleasure grew morose and savage, and Lady Di had much to suffer from his temper; so had his children, to whom he was a selfish tyrant, without indulgence or affection." Neither Lady Louisa nor the *DNB* mentions that he built a library of some 30,000 volumes that Walpole wrote Lady Ossory reached half way from Great Russell Street to Highgate to "put the Museum's nose quite out of joint."

After death mercifully carried Beauclerk off in 1780 Lady Di moved to Twickenham and added much to Walpole's pleasure. In our print room hang two water-colors of her house, Little Marble Hill, that Walpole commissioned Edward Edwards to draw. Thither he hurried to comfort her when her daughter Mary eloped with her married half-brother Lord Bolingbroke, by whom she already had two children. The couple stayed abroad and ultimately she married Graf von Jenison zu Walworth and he married a Baroness Hospesch. A copy by Powel of Reynolds's portrait of Lady Di hung in the Beauclerk Closet; G. P. Hardings's water-color of it is at Farmington. Reynolds, who praised Lady Di's drawings, had her holding a portfolio of them in her left hand and a crayon in her right, according to his pleasant use of accessories to show the occupations and interests of his sitters.

Although Lady Di was easily first among Walpole's talented ladies, Margaret Smith Lady Bingham, afterwards Lady Lucan, should be mentioned among them. A recent arrival at Farmington is her portrait in water-color on the back of which Walpole wrote in his most elegant hand: "Margaret Smith/Wife/of Sir Charles Bingham/an excellent Paintress;/by/[Hugh Douglas] Hamilton, 1774.

> Without a Rival long on Painting's throne
> Urbino's modest Artist sat alone.
> At last a British Fair's unerring eyes

In five short moons contests the glorious prize.
Raphael by Genius nurs'd by labour gained it;
Bingham but saw perfection and attained it.

Walpole transcribed the above in his copy of the 1774 *Description of Strawberry Hill* at Farmington "with the prices of such pieces as I can recollect. H.W." and printed it in the 1784 edition. He wrote Lady Ossory in 1773,

Lady Bingham is, I assure you, another miracle. She began painting in miniature within these two years. I have this summer lent her several of my finest heads; in five days she copied them, and so amazingly well, that she has excelled a charming head of Lord Falkland by Hoskins. She allows me to point out her faults, and if her impetuosity will allow her patience to reflect and study, she will certainly very soon equal anything that ever was done in watercolours. They are amazingly bold, high-coloured and finished, she draws them herself, and so far from being assisted, no painter in England could execute them in half the time. It is still more surprising that she copies from oil full as well, and her only fault is giving more strength than the originals have.

Talented amateurs of the arts and letters found a teacher in Walpole as well as a patron. Chief among his poetesses was Lady Temple whose *Poems by Anna Chambers Countess Temple* he printed in 1764 in a hundred copies. He wrote introductory verses for them that begin "Long had been lost enchanting Sappho's Lyre" until it was discovered and played upon ravishingly by Lady Temple. In Walpole's copy of her *Poems* at Farmington he pasted a contemporary engraving of Sappho singing to her lyre and identified several of the ladies mentioned by Lady Temple.

Walpole's "Book of Materials, 1759," has many notes for a fifth volume of the *Anecdotes of Painting,* which was published by F. W. Hilles and P. B. Daghlian in 1937. Chapter VIII is called, "Ladies and Gentlemen Distinguished by Their Artistic Talents." In Choice 9 I mentioned Walpole's "Works of Genius at Strawberry Hill by Persons of rank and Gentlemen not Artists." Works of the artists marked *F.* are at Farmington.

> Catherine Lady Walpole, paintings in watercolours.
> Richard Lord Edgcumbe, Ditto.
> Lady Diana Beauclerc, Drawings and bas reliefs in wax. *F.*
> Caroline countess of Ailesbury. Needleworks.
> Anne Mrs Damer, her daughter, works in terra cotta and wax, and marble.
> Margaret Lady Lucan, paintings in watercolours. *F.*
> Lavinia Countess Spencer, her daughter, drawing in bister.

Mrs Harcourt, wife of General Harcourt. Do.
Mrs Delany's flowers in paper-mosaic.
Miss Jennings, Do.
Richard Bentley Esq. drawings. *F.*
John Chute Esq. Drawings of Architecture. *F.*
Rev'd Mr Gilpin, washed Drawing.
Volume of Engravings by various persons of quality. *F.*
Henry Bunbury Esq. a large Drawing, and Etchings by him. *F.*
Lady Hamilton, wife of Sr William, cuttings in paper and card. *F.*
Paintings in watercolours by Miss Agnes Berry. *F.*
Drawing by W. Lock Junr. for the box that contains D. Julio Clovio's prayerbox.

The work I prize most among them is the "Volume of Engravings by various persons of quality." It has four title-pages printed at the Press, the first of which is "A collection of Prints, Engraved by Various Persons of Quality." Separate title-pages introduce the work of Lady Carlisle, Lady Louisa Greville, and Lord Nuneham (later Lord Harcourt). Walpole described this volume to Mason: "I have just made a *new book,* which costs me only money, which I don't value, and time which I love to employ. It is a volume of etchings by *noble authors.* They are bound in robes of crimson and gold; the titles are printed at my own press, and the pasting is *by my own hand.*" His arms are stamped on the covers in elegant gilt cartouches. It is, I think, the most sumptuous book I have ever seen. A second volume bound after 1842 is labelled merely "Etchings by Amateur Artists." Walpole ranked Lord Harcourt first among them, going so far as to say that Harcourt's views of the ruins at Stanton Harcourt "are the richest etchings I ever saw," and to write Harcourt that he was "the best engraver in England."

The discovery of talent in persons of quality whose gifts were generally unrecognized gave Walpole, the champion of the neglected, great pleasure. His gallery of well-born geniuses was assembled to do justice to their talents. At its head was Lady Di who had suffered so cruelly and had borne her lot with such fortitude and dignity.

Choice 12

Walpole's Copy of Lysons, *Environs of London*, 1792–96

Fortunately, I realized from the first that I should collect the books Walpole owned as well as those he wrote and printed. I knew nothing about his library, but I knew that every library is a projection of the person who makes it. I also liked handling and reading the books that Walpole cared enough about to buy and annotate as he had annotated the first of his books that I saw. It was Lord Baltimore's *Coelestes et Inferi,* Venice, 1771, not a tale which holdeth children from play and old men from the chimney corner. It was with the Strawberry Hill detached pieces at Scribner's that started my collection in 1924 and has Walpole's note on the half-title, "It is very questionable, whether the original Work of which the following is called a republication ever existed. At least such a poem is utterly unknown in England; nor is any book written by the last Lord Baltimore known, but a silly account of his Travels in prose. H.W." I wanted it, but felt that its price, $350, was beyond me. Happily, it reappeared at Sotheby's in 1938 and was bought by Maggs for me at £12. The Depression had its compensations for collectors.

The first book I bought from Walpole's library came to me in December 1924 from Gabriel Wells. It is a strong candidate for this Choice, but I am making it Choice 13 for reasons I explain there. The book is an octavo in calf with Walpole's arms on the sides. The elegant spine reads, "Poems of Geo. 3." Walpole wrote on the inside of the front cover, "List of Pieces in this volume

> Rodondo, in two Cantos.
> Patriotism, a Mock Heroic.
> Bettenham's Poems.
> The New Bath Guide."

and added the authors' names on the title pages, "Mr Dalrymple," "Richard Bentley," "Mr Christopher Anstey." On the title of Bentley's

Horace Walpole's library, showing the arrangement of books.

Patriotism he added below the year 1765, "March 19th." In 1924 I didn't know how important Bentley was in Walpole's life, and that by 1765 they had parted company, but I enjoyed one of Walpole's marginal notes, "Ld Wilmington said the D. of Newcastle lost an hour every morning and ran after it the rest of the day." When I re-read this now after more than half a century there return the witty Lord Wilmington, the fussy Duke of Newcastle, and Horace Walpole recording Wilmington's *bon mot* for us.

He could afford to buy whatever he wanted. Space was no problem for him; when he ran out of it he built another room. His was not a large collection of books by country house standards, only some 7200 volumes as compared with Topham Beauclerk's 30,000, but Walpole bought his books to read, as his letters and his marginalia in perhaps a third of them show. The first books we hear of, which he asked his Mamma to get for him at the age of eight, are "the Yearl of Essex" and "Jan Shore." Pote's bookshop at Eton was where his library got its real start in company with Gray, West, and Ashton. An appendix in Hazen's *Catalogue of Horace Walpole's Library* lists the books he had at Eton and Cambridge. Over half, 79 out of 147 volumes, are at Farmington; all have his name and the date when he bought them. Among them are textbooks, Palairet's French grammar, Moll's *Maps of the Ancient World,* Webster's *Arithmetic* over which the owner shed unmanly tears; there are the classical authors one would expect, Homer, Zenophon, Virgil, Horace, and Ovid; an unexpurgated *Satyricon* was added when he was thirteen. Earlier he was given the seventy-six volumes of the classics by the Duke of Brunswick who had received from Sir Robert Walpole's government £100,000 in exchange for the copy of George I's will that allegedly disinherited George II.

My introduction to Walpole's library as a whole was the 1842 sale catalogue. The first eight of its twenty-four-days' sale were the books, but there was so much complaint by the public of the cataloguing of the seventh and eighth days' sales, the prints and books of prints in the Round Tower, that they were removed and recatalogued in a ten-days' sale in London a month later; that is, it took sixteen days to sell the library. The eight issues of the sale catalogue with their inaccuracies were first discriminated in 1915 by Percival Merritt in a handsome catalogue designed by Bruce Rogers.

My knowledge of the library was greatly increased in 1931 when Wyndham Ketton-Cremer took my wife and me to call on his neighbors, the Walpoles of Wolterton, and I saw the manuscript "Catalogue of Mr Horace Walpole's Library at Strawberry Hill, 1763" that was compiled,

I think, by one of Walpole's government clerks. Walpole kept it up him-self until 1768; later it was added to by Kirgate. I am eternally grateful to the Walpoles for letting me have the catalogue photostated because the Strawberry library could not have been reconstructed without it.

We now know every book that Walpole owned and on which shelf it stood in the three libraries at Strawberry Hill. The main library was 28 by 17½ and 15 feet high. The *Description* tells us that the books were "ranged within Gothic arches of pierced work, taken from a side-door case to the choir in Dugdale's *St Paul's.*" Each of its cases, or "presses," had a predominant subject: royal and noble authors in A, coins and medals and the fine arts in B, fine arts and prints in C and D, topography in E, French literature (800 volumes) in F and G, English history and literature in H, I, and K, the classics and Italian literature in L and M. There was a very special press in the corner between D and E, the locked Glass Closet, in which Walpole kept the books he did not want everyone to handle. Of its 211 books 61 are at Farmington and the British Library has 12. The unlocated Glass Closet books will doubtless reappear in time because most of them probably have notes by Walpole that more and more people now recognize. The library in the Round Tower at the west end of the house, which was 22 feet in diameter with 41 feet of shelving, 4¾ feet high, had presses A to Y chiefly for prints and books of prints. The still smaller library in the Offices, whose presses ran from N to V, housed contemporary books arranged by subjects much as in the main library.

"The Library system" in England and her colonies during the eighteenth century was what modern librarians call, disapprovingly, "fixed location." The cases, or presses, of the books at Strawberry and Yale were given capital letters, as I have said. The letters were followed by two digits. The first digit in libraries that descended from Cambridge, as did Straw-berry and Yale, was the lowest shelf in the press; the second digit was the place of the book on the shelf. The first digit in books that followed Ox-ford practice was the top-most shelf. In time Walpole and Kirgate dropped the second digit because they and others put the books back on the shelves out of order. The pressmarks are proof of Walpole's ownership, which his bookplates are not, for old-time booksellers told me that before I came along eager to buy any book from Strawberry Hill they would soak off the bookplate in a then worthless book and sell it for half-a-crown or stick it into another book and so create a "ghost." The covers with their precious pressmarks went into the office fire to save a little coal and the book itself was thrown into a sack, which when filled was sold for a pittance as waste-paper. How many books were so destroyed we don't know, but fifty years ago Walpole's bookplate was relatively common and I bought several of the ghosts before I knew about the Strawberry press-marks.

Their importance is illustrated by one of the books without any sign of Walpole's ownership that Chapman sent up to Christie's from Knowsley, as described in Choice 10. The book was Norden, *Description of Middlesex and Hartfordshire*, 1723, which had been rebacked after 1842 and given nineteenth-century endpapers on which was pasted Lord Derby's bookplate. Walpole's Manuscript Catalogue shows that Norden's Strawberry pressmark was E.3.34, which I wrote on the fly-leaf opposite the front cover after the book reached Farmington. When its nineteenth-century endpaper was removed, there was Walpole's bookplate in its proper place and above it, just where it should be, E.3.34. Another example of the press-marks' value is in Walpole's copy of Prior, *Poems on Several Occasions*, 1718, a large folio that was bought for Lord Derby in 1842 by Boone. Chapman and Miss Povey, the new Knowsley librarian, found a superb copy of the book, but it lacked all signs of Walpole's ownership, his notes, bookplate, and the Strawberry pressmarks, L.1.1. Chapman and Miss Povey looked long and hard for L.1.1. without success. Shortly after the final session of the Derby sale a stranger in Darkest Maryland reported a book that had belonged to Walpole's mother. It was not for sale, but the owner would part with it for a set of the *Encyclopaedia Britannica*. The book proved to be Prior's *Poems on Several Occasions*, 1718, with its covers hanging by a few threads. On a front fly-leaf was written, "Catherine Walpole her book." Walpole's bookplate was missing, but above where it had been was L.1.1. When I hurried off my *Britannica* to the owner I asked him where he found the book. He turned out to be a collector of firearms who was stationed near Phenix City, Alabama, during the War. On his first week-end from camp he found in a Phenix City junkshop a brace of dueling pistols that he simply had to have. The price was exorbitant, but the junkman finally offered to throw in "an old book." The old book was L.1.1. Lord Derby had made it even more forlorn by entering the Knowsley pressmark upside down on the back endpaper. How had the book got from Knowsley Hall in Lancashire to a junkshop in Phenix City, Alabama? My guess is that Lord Derby, who had a fine copy of the book, told his librarian to dispose of the shabby duplicate in Liverpool even though it had been Walpole's; after all, he had dozens of Walpole's books. Liverpool and Alabama before our Civil War were drawn together by the cotton trade. I suggest that this large heavy book sailed from Liverpool to Alabama in a tall ship as ballast.

By 1938 I realized we must have a catalogue of Walpole's library with not only its authors, titles, places of publication, sizes, and dates, but the history of each copy in so far as we could recover it from auction records, booksellers' catalogues, bookplates, and signatures of former owners. The use Walpole made of his books in his letters and works should also be given. I began by collating the books in the 1842 Sale and Manuscript Catalogues. This was routine for many of the books, but an expert was needed to deal with the rest and I turned to Allen Hazen for help. He spent several years making the catalogue, chiefly in the summers, and when the Yale Press published his *Catalogue of Horace Walpole's Library* in 1969 in three substantial volumes it became a landmark in bibliographical studies. It is in daily use at Farmington and the Walpole room at Yale and John Brooke, who is editing the Yale Edition of Horace Walpole's Memoirs in London, reports frequent use by him. Serious Walpolian studies are impossible without Hazen's three contributions to them.

In May 1957 I gave the Sandars Lectures on Bibliography at Cambridge. A liberal definition of "Bibliography" was necessary to make me eligible to be a Sandars Reader, but I felt safe in my subject, *Horace Walpole's Library*. I spent six months on each of the three lectures: the books and their arrangement at Strawberry Hill, the use Walpole made of them, and their dispersal in 1842 and partial recovery since. The lectures were given on successive afternoons following tea, the ideal hour for lectures in England when the audience is cheered but not inebriated. I asked the University Librarian about how much of an audience I might expect, reminding him of the visiting lecturer at Cambridge who had gone gallantly forward with an audience of only one. At the end of an hour the lecturer paused and asked his auditor if he might take five more minutes of his time to clear up a final point. "Take all the time you want, governor," the man replied with a wave of his hand. "I'm your taxi waiting to take you to the station." "I know," I said to the unsmiling Librarian, "I'll have more than one. There will be my wife and *you*" and I named eight Cambridge friends. "Will there be anyone else?" "Oh, yes," the Librarian replied promptly and paused, "at least for the first lecture because they want to see what you look like." In the event, old friends came from far and wide and the audience got to nearly sixty each day; very good, the Librarian assured me, for a Sandars Lecture. Mine were handsomely printed by the Cambridge University Press in an edition of 750 copies, and were reprinted in Hazen's *Catalogue of Horace Walpole's Library.*

The book I am rescuing from Strawberry Hill is Lysons, *Environs of London,* 4 vols, 4to, 1792–96. I considered seriously saving Pope's copy of Homer's *Works,* Amsterdam, 1707, in which Pope wrote his name three times and gave the date when he finished his translation of Homer; he also drew Twickenham Church from his garden on a fly-leaf. After his death the book came into Walpole's possession probably through a book-seller. Walpole noted below Pope's statement about his translation that the drawing of Twickenham Church was made by the poet himself. In the second volume Pope wrote his Epitaph to Mrs Corbet in pencil. Our other Popeiana include Walpole's set of his *Works,* 1741–43, with identification of people and quotations from other poets on whom Pope drew, a fine portrait of him in later life by Vanloo, and drawings of him and his mother by Richardson that belonged to Walpole. We also have a "portrait" of Pope's villa that Walpole commissioned his neighbor Samuel Scott, the English Canaletto, to paint, but I put Pope aside because he was not one of Walpole's favorite authors and because the objects are for me examples of casual collecting made as occasion offered rather than planned. The library has many other candidates for rescue, but I think Walpole would be pleased by my saving Lysons because he loved the histories of counties, towns, cathedrals, and great houses. "I am sorry I have such predilection for histories of particular counties and towns," he wrote in 1780, "there certainly does not exist a worse class of reading." Some years earlier he said, "I do not see why books of antiquities should not be made as amusing as writings on any other subject," and he went on collecting, annotating, and writing about them until he died.

The *Environs of London* was dedicated to him. He extra-illustrated it and bound the four royal quartos handsomely in red morocco. Into each of the first three volumes he pasted four pages of "notes on Mr Lysons' Environs." His first note tells us: "This work is one of the most authentic books of antiquities ever published, the Author having with indefatigable Industry personally visited every Parish and every Office of Record from which the extracts were made; and having by the amiableness of his Character been favoured by the Possessors with the sight of many original Deeds, that State the Tenures and Descents of several considerable Mansions and lands described in the Account." Lysons displeased Walpole in the chapter on Twickenham by mentioning several of Strawberry's chief treasures. "I must tell you," Walpole wrote him, "that as I foresaw, they are a source of grievance to me, by specifying so many articles of my collection, and several that are never shown to miscellaneous customers. Nay, last week one company brought the volume with them, and besides wanting to see various invisible particulars, it made them loiter so long by referring to your text, that I thought the housekeeper with her own additional clack, would never have rid the house of them." This was a little hard on Lysons because most of his account of Strawberry came from the *Description,* but Walpole's defense would doubtless have been that he kept nearly all copies of it out of public hands. Lysons appears on the title-page of the *Environs* as "Chaplain to the Right Honourable the Earl of Orford," an instance of peers still having "domestick" chaplains. Earls were entitled to four, but Walpole seems to have been content with two. The warrant of his second, Benjamin Suckling, issued by the Archbishop of Canterbury's Office of Faculties, is at Farmington, signed "Orford," with Kirgate's signature as a witness. Private Chaplaincies were handed out by peers to help youthful clergymen gain higher preferment. Lysons was an agreeable young antiquary and so a congenial appendage to Walpole's life. His *Environs* has a special place in my library because it was given me by my wife on the day we became engaged.

The runner-up to Lysons in this Choice is "Arms of the Knights of the Garter," which Walpole shelved in the Glass Closet. It was blazoned on vellum for Queen Elizabeth in 1573 by Sir Gilbert Dethick, Garter-King-of-Arms, and bound in red velvet. Later the monogram of Charles I was stamped on the rear cover. The book belonged in the eighteenth century to Walter Robertson, Mayor of King's Lynn, for which Walpole sat at the end of his parliamentary career. Below Robertson's signature Walpole wrote, "This book was given to me by Mr Walter Robertson Mayor of Lynn, 1762. Horace Walpole."

The Glass Closet books were miscellaneous. Among ours from it are the second Shakespeare Folio, 1632, an exchange from the Folger Shakespeare Library, and two excessively rare books of swan marks that came from Knowsley. The marks were branded on the birds' bills to identify their owners. The handsomer of the two books begins with a declaration of an Edward IV statute that "No person may have a swan mark except he have lands to the yearly value of five marks, and unless it be by grant of the King or his officers lawfully authorized or by Prescription." The Glass Closet removed from the casual visitor the two books in the library that would be classed today as "erotica," illustrations of the Spintrian Medals of Tiberius, for which Walpole wrote a title-page and noted he bought it "at the sale of Sir Clement Cotterel's Library, 1764," and Richard Payne Knight's *Account of the Worship of Priapus,* 1786, for the Dilettanti Society. The latter is a magnificent copy that was presented to Walpole by Sir Joseph Banks on behalf of the Society, of which Walpole was not a member. He wrote on the fly-leaf that "this copy was sent to me for having permitted Mr Knight the author to make a Drawing of my bronze of Ceres, which is engraved in Table viii. H.W." He was shocked by the book even though his copy lacks the more explicit prints found in other copies.

Half the books that were at Strawberry Hill are still missing. Eighty percent of those recovered, some 2400 titles, are at Farmington. In the thirties and forties I got one (and a letter to or from Walpole) on the average of one every four or five days; now I do well to get four or five a year. Since their market value has increased enormously it is odd more don't appear. We know, as I have said, that some of the books were destroyed by booksellers, but hundreds more have lost their identities through rebinding and are sitting unrecognized on learned shelves. Until quite recently most librarians lacked Walpole's regard for provenance and discarded the bookplates and marks of earlier ownership when re-backing and rebinding their books. One of Allen Hazen's students found over forty of Walpole's books in the British Library that had not been identified as his. Lars Troide, a young colleague in the Yale Walpole, found the first volume of Walpole's copy of Egerton Brydges' *Topographical Miscellanies,* 1792, in the Yale stacks. It was rebound after 1842, Walpole's bookplate and the Strawberry pressmarks were discarded, but his annotations brought it swiftly to Farmington in accordance with the generous practice begun by Andrew Keogh, the Yale Librarian, forty years earlier.

Walpole wrote his memoirs and letters in the library, the walls of which were lined from floor to ceiling with books. His copies at Farmington are shelved in the same order as at Strawberry. In our North Library Press A is on the right of the door as you face it from the inside; Press M is on the left, with the books from the Round Tower and Offices between it and the door. Over the door is a water-color of the main library flanked by drawings of the river and garden. Near the books formerly in the Glass Closet and Press E is a drawing of Walpole showing him seated by them. Few are insensitive to his presence as they stand amidst his books.

Choice 13
"Tracts of the Reign of George 3"

That is the title Walpole gave these 59 volumes. By "tract" he meant the second definition of the word in the *OED,* "A book or written work treating of some particular topic; a treatise." He collected 335 of them for this collection; 224 in fifty-four octavo volumes, five with 111 tracts in quarto. All are bound in calf with Walpole's arms on the sides and elaborately tooled spines labelled "Tracts of Geo. 3." The earlier volumes have title-pages printed at the Strawberry Hill Press, "A Collection of the most remarkable TRACTS/Published/in the REIGN/of/King George the third," and all have a "List of Pieces in this Volume" written on the inside of the front covers in Walpole's clearest hand. He frequently added the month below the year on the title-page and the names of anonymous authors; throughout are his crosses, short dashes, exclamation points, and, rarely, an asterisk. I bought the collection from the estate of Sir Leicester Harmsworth in 1938.

Its variety appears in volume 39:

Williams, John. *An Account of some remarkable ancient ruins, lately discovered in the Highlands,* 1777.

Junius, pseud. *A serious letter to the public, on the late transaction between Lord North and the Duke of Gordon,* 1778.

Burke, Edmund. *Two letters from Mr Burke to gentlemen in the city of Bristol,* 1778. Dated "May" by Walpole and with one identification by him.

Burgoyne, General John. *The substance of General Burgoyne's speeches,* 1778. A few marginal markings by Walpole.

[Tickell, Richard]. *Anticipation: containing the substance of His M----y's most gracious speech,* 1778. Among Walpole's many notes is, "Ch. Fox said 'he has anticipated many things I have intended to say, but I shall say them never-the-less.' "

[Bryant, Jacob]. *A farther illustration of the Analysis [of Mythology],* 1778. Author identified by Walpole and numerous marginal markings by him.

7

List of pieces in this Volume.

Account of ruins in the highlands.
Prospect from Barrow-hill.
Transaction between D. North & D. of Gordon.
Two letters from Mr Burke.
On the abuse of unrestrained power.
Substance of General Burgoyne's Speeches.
Anticipation. by Mr Tickell.
Mr Bryant's Answer, on his Analysis.
Three Letters from Sr J. Dalrymple to D Barrington.
Mr Gibbon's Vindication of the 15th & 16th Chapters.
Considerations on the State of affairs.
Baretti's Introduction to the Carmen Seculare.
Mr Walpole's letter on Chatterton.

"Tracts of the Reign of George 3," page from v. 39, "List of pieces in this Volume."

[Gibbon, Edward]. *A vindication of some passages in the fifteenth and sixteenth chapters of the History,* 1779. Dated "Jan. 14" by Walpole with one note and numerous markings by him.

[Walpole, Horace]. *A letter to the editor of the Miscellanies of Thomas Chatterton,* Strawberry Hill, 1779. One correction in manuscript by Walpole. Above the "List of Pieces" in volume 39 he inked a large asterisk to mark the volume's special interest. This is the volume of the "Tracts of Geo. 3" I am taking if the Almighty says I can't have the entire collection.

Also at Farmington is the collection of earlier tracts from 1613 to 1760 that Walpole began to collect about 1740. There are 662 pieces in 88 volumes, 8vo. Walpole listed the pieces in each volume, but made only a few marginalia. A disappointing lapse is his failure to identify himself as the son referred to in Ranby's *Narrative of the Last Illness of the Right Honourable the Earl of Orford,* 1745, where Ranby states, "The ensuing Journal was kept with all imaginable exactness by one of his own sons, as well as by myself." The son was undoubtedly Horace, though he did not identify himself in any of his three known copies of Ranby's *Narrative,* as I noted in Choice 2. His failure to do so is odd, but neither of his brothers was with their father constantly during his last illness, nor did they keep meticulous journals. Allen Hazen was certainly right, I think, to include Ranby's *Narrative* in Horace's "Editorial Contributions."

The pre-1760 tracts were bought at the Strawberry Hill sale in 1842 for the Buckingham Palace Library—I like to believe that Prince Albert encouraged their purchase—and migrated subsequently to Windsor. The story told in the nineteen-thirties of how they left Windsor was that Sir John Fortescue, the King's Librarian, asked his employer for extra money to buy something he thought the library should have. George V, a keen philatelist but no bookman, turned him down. "Sir," the story went, "would you mind if I disposed of some books I think are less important to us and use the money for this purchase?" The King told Fortescue to do as he pleased and the earlier tracts went to Sir Leicester Harmsworth by private treaty through Quaritch who subsequently bought the George 3 volumes for Harmsworth at Sotheby's in 1920, making a total of 1037 tracts in 147 volumes. I heard from William A. Jackson that they were in the Harmsworth library at Bexhill in Kent. When my wife and I lunched with the Harmsworths at Bexhill a year later all the volumes were laid out on tables for our inspection. The owner was asking ten times what he paid for them, a figure that seemed excessive to me at the time. However, our visit was not in vain because in 1938 after Harmsworth died his trustees sold all the tracts to me through Quaritch for a fifth of the asking price, which was still twice what the late owner had paid for them. Bookselling. Collecting.

Walpole made three other collections of pieces printed from 1760 to 1796: "The Chronicle of Geo. 3," "Poems of Geo. 3," and "Theatre of Geo. 3." All are similarly bound in full calf with his arms on the sides. "The Chronicle of Geo. 3" in 36 volumes is a set of the *London Chronicle* from 1760 to 1796 that came to Farmington from Lord Derby's sale. It is disappointing because it has no marginalia; doubtless Walpole had another set that he annotated and cut up. Next to it at Strawberry stood "Poems of Geo. 3" in 22 volumes containing 244 pieces with special title-pages printed at the Strawberry Hill Press for the earliest volumes. This collection was given to Harvard in 1924, a most enviable gift.

My acquaintance with "The Theatre of Geo. 3" began in March 1925 when I walked into Pickering and Chatto's for the first time and asked if they had any books from Walpole's library. The man who greeted me was Mr Charles Massey, a survivor of the old-time bookseller. "We have," he said, "Many plays from Walpole's library," and then, when he saw the effect of his words, he called out: "Dudley, Watson! Fetch up two or three of the Walpole plays," and they did so.

The first of the young men summoned I learned later was Massey's son. Watson made out the invoices for the firm in a beautiful copper-plate hand because Pickering and Chatto had not yet acquired one of these new-fangled typewriters. Dudley and Watson sat at small tables, their faces to the wall, their backs to the light, in accordance with the discipline that required junior clerks to be as inconspicuous and uncomfortable as possible while ready for instant action. Mr Massey explained to me that it would take time to "look out" all the plays and suggested that I come back in a week. When I returned there were 130 of the plays waiting for me on a long table. They had been bought by Maggs at Sotheby's in 1914, Mr Massey explained to me. Maggs offered them in two or three catalogues and then broke them up, having Rivière rebind the plays by Sheridan and Goldsmith and putting a few other plays back into their original Walpolian bindings. They sold the rest, over 500 plays, to Pickering and Chatto, who put each play into a brown manila wrapper with acid, I was to discover years later, that defaced the title-pages. Mr Massey stood deferentially beside me while I went through the collection, play by play. Walpole had written the month the play appeared below the year on the title-page and occasionally pasted in a newspaper cutting.

Dudley and Watson also brought up twenty-four of the tattered remains of the original covers that were hanging from them. The spines were lettered, "Theatre of Geo. 3." Walpole wrote "List of Pieces in this Volume" inside the front cover of each. It occurred to me—or possibly to Mr Massey—that it would be a pious act of restitution to put the plays back as nearly as possible into the original covers. There had been 59 volumes when the set was sold in 1914, but only 40 of the original covers remained; the rest had been sold off by Maggs with single plays. Accordingly, some of the 130 plays had to go into different covers. This sorting and arranging went on for days, while Mr Massey, who suffered cruelly from asthma, stood by my side and talked about books and book-collecting. It was one of the pleasantest experiences of my collecting life.

There was a notable interruption the morning Dr Rosenbach strolled casually into the shop with his blank stare. He had been making history by buying up most of the Britwell Court books at Sotheby's with bidding so unconventional and successful that he had earned the hearty dislike of the Trade. Instead of sitting at the long table with the other booksellers and indicating his bids silently, he stood up by the pulpit in which the auctioneer sat and called out his bids in a loud voice. I went to see him bid one day. A lot was put up and advanced by five-shilling stages from one to three pounds. Rosenbach, who was chatting to a friend, turned to the auctioneer, Charles Des Graz, and said, "*Seven* pounds!" The bidding resumed its canonical course until it reached ten pounds. Then Rosenbach turned again and pronounced, "*Twenty* pounds!" From there on the Trade carried the bidding by pound jumps, all silently conveyed, to thirty pounds. At that point Rosenbach had had enough. "*Seventy* pounds!" he shouted. "Seventy pounds," repeated Des Graz blandly. He looked round the room. "Seventy pounds?" Then he brought down his hammer. "Seventy pounds."

"Excuse me, sir," said Mr Massey when the greatest bookseller of all time appeared on that March morning, "but I'm afraid I must attend to him." Mr Chatto, who sat behind a glass partition at the back of the shop, hurried out to take Mr Massey's place beside me; he did not look at the visitor, but stood with his back to him as he bent solicitously over me. "Please don't bother about me," I said to him. Mr Chatto shook his head briefly and assumed an air of absorption in the table before us. I did not feel that his concern in our transaction was fully engaged. The room was so cold I kept my winter overcoat on, but I noticed that Mr Chatto, who of course was not wearing an overcoat, was perspiring freely.

"Have you any Folios?" Rosenbach asked quietly, referring to the Four

Folios of Shakespeare. A First Folio had recently sold for £12,000. In a
few minutes he left, having bought a Third Folio for thirty times what
I was to spend on the collection of plays, the sale of which took days.
Mr Chatto bowed to me and returned to his office, mopping his brow. Mr
Massey hurried back full of apologies. "Very sorry, sir," he said in a low
voice, "but I had to wait on him."

Having at last got the plays into twenty-four of Walpole's original
covers, we sent them off to Bayntun of Bath and had them re-bound.
This seemed the thing to do at the time, but it was a mistake, as I found
out four years later when more of the plays turned up in New York at the
Brick Row Bookshop. All the plays I looked at in the Brick Row had a
note in Walpole's hand on the title-page or cuttings from newspapers that
he dated and pasted on the fly-leaves, but when I went through this new
collection at Farmington I found that only about thirty of the plays in it
had been so marked. Many were printed before 1760 and so could never
have been part of the "Theatre of Geo. 3," but others, printed after 1760,
began to glow with significance. They, too, had been ripped untimely
from bound volumes and remnants of their former bindings clung to
their spines. Fortunately, Mr Massey had prevailed upon me in 1928 to
buy the broken covers of the original set. These now proved that the plays
before me printed from 1760 on had come from the "Theatre of Geo. 3."
Bits and pieces of their bindings matched the elaborate tooling on the
Walpolian spines that were virtually intact. This discovery supplied
thirty more plays and showed that Walpole did not annotate every one.
Since Dudley and Watson had brought up only plays with notes in Walpole's hand, there were doubtless unannotated plays from the "Theatre of
Geo. 3" still in Pickering and Chatto's cellar. "How," I wrote Dudley,
who was now in command of the firm, "are we to identify them? Maggs
were wicked to break up the set, but haven't you by cleaning off the
spines and covering them with your manila wrappers removed the last
proof that they were Walpole's?" There was a further proof, he replied,
the staining on the edges. Eighteenth-century binders used a red, brown,
green, or blue stain on the edges of their books, applying it with a plain,
marbled, or sprinkled effect. No two volumes had precisely the same stain,
but of course the staining on all plays in each volume was the same.
Dudley suggested that I send him the titles I lacked from the Lists of
Pieces in each volume and that I match their copies with mine. This
we did. One hundred and fifty of the missing plays arrived from Pickering's cellar and sixty-five proved to be Walpole's.

Further identification of the plays was provided by the angle test. Since the back of a book is slightly rounded in the binding, the front becomes concave; therefore, the fore-edges of the plays first mentioned should slant inward and those last mentioned should slant outward, while those in the middle should be straight. The angle test, which R. W. Chapman called "the Farthest North in Bibliography," was a success: all the "right" plays slanted exactly as they ought to do. When I was convinced that the play had been in the "Theatre of Geo. 3" I pulled off the manila wrapper and found that the stitching coincided precisely with the stitching in the other plays originally in the volume, and that, final proof, faint remains of the original binding still clung to the plays' narrow spines.

Shortly after the Brick Row cache appeared, I wrote to Pickering & Chatto for a list of the plays they had sold before I appeared in 1925. Their list (in Watson's fine hand) contains 64 plays, 37 of which I marked with an H. At the top of the list I wrote: "H-Hopeless." These were plays that had been sold to American libraries, the Folger Shakespeare Library in Washington, and the University of Michigan, chiefly. Of these 37 "hopeless" plays, 33 are now at Farmington.

The first of the "hopeless" plays to arrive were two from Yale. Mr Andrew Keogh, the then Librarian, handed them over to me, knowing that one day they would return to Yale with the rest of my collection. When I asked him if he thought Michigan might follow suit, he wrote to the Librarian, W. W. Bishop, on my behalf. The request was unusual, but after consultation with the Michigan authorities Mr Bishop agreed to let me have them. I returned duplicates and (since Walpole's copies were worth more than ordinary copies) paid the original bill. When after several years I was unable to find duplicates of some of the plays, Mr Bishop generously allowed me to substitute photostats of the missing plays for the duplicate copies I had contracted to supply. In all, twenty-two plays have come to Farmington from Ann Arbor. Later a similar arrangement was concluded for two plays at the University of Illinois. All of these copies had one or more of Walpole's notes in them. Doubtless there are others of his copies without his notes in these libraries.

The Folger Library offered a more difficult problem, which took twelve years to solve. J. Q. Adams, its Director, became convinced that it was in the best interests of all concerned that I should have the plays, but the terms of Folger's will made it difficult to dispose of any books in his library. Several years later I got the corrected proof sheets of Steevens's and Reed's folio edition of Shakespeare, 1791–1802. They "belonged" to the Folger as much as its copies of Walpole's plays (all of which it had in other copies) "belonged" to me. This was clear to everyone. So, the trustees concurring, my Shakespeare proof sheets went to the Folger Library and its plays came to me; and then, for good measure, Adams let me have Walpole's copy of Sheridan's *Critic* from his own library.

I always called on him when in Washington. He was a scholar who was a humanist; a bookman who read books; a librarian who had bought for his library one of the finest collections of printed books (the Harmsworth library of English books to 1641) ever brought to this country. My call on Adams in April 1939, after the exchange of the proof sheets and plays was completed, was a particularly pleasant one. Then, when I rejoined my wife in the exhibition gallery outside his office, she pointed silently to a book in a case, another play, not included in the just-completed trans-action, Walpole's copy of *Timon of Athens*, 1771, restored to its original Strawberry Hill covers—which meant that it contained another "List of Pieces in this Volume" in Walpole's hand. I prevailed upon the guard to let me show the book to Adams. "Heaven knows how many more of Wal-pole's plays we have!" he said rather wildly. "We shan't finish our cata-logue for years. Have you ever been down in the stacks?" I hadn't, and he asked Giles Dawson to take me there. We walked along the central aisle between bays of plays bound in manila wrappers until I paused, turned into one of the bays, looked along a shelf of identically bound plays, took one down, opened it, and there on the title-page was a note in Walpole's hand.

When the Library was finally catalogued, additional plays from the "Theater of Geo. 3" and some two dozen volumes from Strawberry Hill, including Walpole's copy of the Second Folio had been found. I had run out of Shakespearean proof sheets and had nothing worthy of the Folger. Would they sell its books from Walpole's library if they were duplicates? The question was put to the chairman of the Library's board, Chief Justice Harlan Stone, who approved the transfer just a week before he died. With the money it received for the duplicates, the Library was able to buy a picture of Shakespeare made for Edmond Malone before the original was retouched. "In my judgment," wrote Adams, "this is far more valuable to students than the Chandos portrait as it now is. And the price we paid was almost exactly the same represented by your check. Thanks!"

There are now 390 of the 553 plays in the "Theatre of Geo. 3" at Farmington and 35 known elsewhere (20 at Harvard); 135 are still untraced. Forty-eight of the fifty-nine covers are at Farmington, six at Harvard, three are untraced. The plays at Farmington have been shelved by my librarian, Mrs Catherine Jestin. Most of the Bayntun bindings had to be taken apart to restore the plays to their original order. Eight of the volumes are complete and at the end of the set is volume 59, the Prologues and Epilogues given me by Mrs Percival Merritt in memory of her husband. The plays stand above the unbroken collection of 220 pre-1760 plays in nineteen volumes that came from Lord Derby at Knowsley in 1954. Somehow, the broken "Theatre of Geo. 3," which is held together by red string, does not suffer by comparison. The hard covers put on by Yale, Michigan, and the Library of Congress preserve the plays' history. It is the corner of the library where I enjoy sitting most; the plays are at my right, the tracts are at my back, and across the room to the left are the 36 volumes of the *London Chronicle* standing next to the books from the Glass Closet. About eighty percent of Walpole's collections of plays, tracts, and poems that he made from 1760 to 1796 have been reunited at Farmington for the benefit of scholars as long as the collection survives.

Choice 14

Walpole's Chattertoniana

Coming back on the *Olympic* in 1925 I met Dr Edward Clark Streeter, to whom I later dedicated my *Collector's Progress*. He had been at Yale twenty years ahead of me, had formed a fine library of medical history, and was then making his notable collection of weights. After I had held forth on Walpole he looked at me quizzically and asked, "But what about the Marvellous Boy?" He was quoting Wordsworth,

> "Chatterton, the marvellous boy,
> The sleepless soul that perished in his pride,"

This was the youthful genius, Thomas Chatterton, who committed suicide in his eighteenth year, a victim of opium as well as of pride and whose brief life fills twenty columns in the *Dictionary of National Biography*, as compared to Boswell's sixteen and Walpole's eleven. While we walked the decks of the *Olympic* I explained to Ned Streeter that I couldn't collect Walpole if I wasn't convinced he was innocent of Chatterton's death and Ned accepted his innocence when I finished.

The Choice in this chapter is Walpole's collection in four volumes of sixteen pieces dealing with Chatterton. To appreciate them one must know the boy's story and how he, a precocious adolescent in Bristol, the son of a poor schoolmaster, secured a special place in English literature.

In 1776 Chatterton, aged sixteen, sent Walpole "The Ryse of Peyncteynge yn Englande, wroten bie T. Rowleie, 1469, for Mastre Canynge." Rowley was a fifteenth-century monk of Bristol invented by Chatterton who allegedly composed a treatise on "peyncteynge," that might, Chatterton wrote Walpole, be "of service to you in any future edition of your truly entertaining *Anecdotes of Painting*." He added ten explanatory notes to "The Ryse of Peyncteynge." The first of them was on Rowley whose "Merit as a biographer, historiographer, is great, as a poet still greater . . . and the person under whose patronage [his pieces] may appear to the world, will lay the Englishman, the antiquary, and the poet

under an eternal obligation." This was a hook well baited for Horace
Walpole who sent Chatterton "a thousand thanks" for his "very curious
and kind letter" and went so far as to say he would "not be sorry to print"
a specimen of Rowley's poems. What pleased Walpole most in Chatterton's letter was the confirmation of the conjecture in *Anecdotes of Painting* that "oil painting was known here much earlier than had been supposed," but before long Walpole began to suspect, with the aid of Mason
and Gray, that the examples of the fifteenth-century manuscripts that
Chatterton had sent him were forgeries. It *was* odd that Rowley wrote in
eighteenth-century rhymed couplets.

Meanwhile, Chatterton disclosed to Walpole his age and condition in
life. The letter in which he did so has been almost entirely cut away.
Walpole's recollection of it nine years later was that Chatterton described
himself in it as "a clerk or apprentice to an attorney, [that he] had a
taste and turn for more elegant studies," and hoped Walpole would
assist him with his "interest in emerging out of so dull a profession." The
learned antiquary turned out to be an ambitious youth. Walpole sent
him an avuncular letter to which Chatterton returned, according to Walpole, "a rather peevish answer" in which he said "he could not contest
with a person of my learning (a compliment by no means due to me,
and which I certainly had not assumed, having consulted abler judges),
maintained the genuineness of the poems, and demanded to have them
returned, as they were the property of another gentleman. . . ."

When I received this letter I was going to Paris in a day or two, and either
forgot his request of the poems, or perhaps not having time to have them
copied, deferred complying till my return, which was to be in six weeks. . . .

Soon after my return from France, I received another letter from Chatterton,
the style of which was singularly impertinent. He demanded his poems
roughly; and added, that I should not have *dared* to use him so ill, if he had
not acquainted me with the narrowness of his circumstances.

My heart did not accuse me of insolence to him. I wrote an answer ex-
postulating with him on his injustice, and renewing good advice—but upon
second thoughts, reflecting that so wrong-headed a young man, of whom I knew
nothing, and whom I had never seen, might be absurd enough to print my
letter, I flung it into the fire; and wrapping up both his poems and letters,
without taking a copy of either, for which I am now sorry, I returned all to
him, and thought no more of him or them, till about a year and half after,
when [a gap in all printed versions].

Dining at the Royal Academy, Dr Goldsmith drew the attention of the
company with an account of a marvellous treasure of ancient poems lately

discovered at Bristol, and expressed enthusiastic belief in them, for which he
was laughed at by Dr Johnson, who was present. I soon found this was the
trouvaille of my friend Chatterton; and I told Dr Goldsmith that this novelty
was none to me, who might, if I had pleased, have had the honour of ushering
the great discovery to the learned world. You may imagine, Sir, we did not at
all agree in the measure of our faith; but though his credulity diverted me, my
mirth was soon dashed, for on asking about Chatterton, he told me he had been
in London, and had destroyed himself. I heartily wished then that I had been
the dupe of all the poor young man had written to me, for who would not have
his understanding imposed on to save a fellow being from the utmost wretchedness, despair and suicide!—and a poor young man not eighteen—and of such
miraculous talents—for, dear Sir, if I wanted credulity on one hand, it is ample
on the other.

Seven years after Chatterton's death an article on him in the *Monthly
Review* for April 1777 stated that he had applied to Walpole, but "met
with no encouragement from that learned and ingenious gentleman, who
suspected his veracity." A month later in the same magazine George
Catcott of Bristol went a step further. Chatterton, said Catcott, "applied
. . . to that learned antiquary, Mr Horace Walpole, but met with little
or no encouragement from him; soon after which, in a fit of despair, as it
is supposed, he put an end to his unhappy life." "This," comments
E. H. W. Meyerstein, in his *Life of Chatterton,* 1930, "was a perfectly
monstrous accusation, considering that Walpole never saw Chatterton,
whose application to him was made over a year before he came to London,
and seventeen months before his death." The accusation was repeated a
year later by the editor of Chatterton's *Miscellanies in Prose and Verse.*
These statements fastened the responsibility for Chatterton's death on
Walpole in many minds. His Twickenham neighbour, Miss Letitia
Hawkins, wrote that he "began to go down in public favour from the time
when he resisted the imposition of Chatterton." Coleridge wrote of "the
bleak freezings of neglect," in his "Monody on the Death of Chatterton."
"Oh, ye who honour the name of man," he cried, "rejoice that Walpole is
called a lord!"—a remark that has been frequently quoted and was echoed
by the youthful Browning. An extreme Walpole-hater has written: "To
blame Walpole for not assisting the youth to put the Rowley romance
before the public is absurd; but for the man's cowardly, mean, untruthful
attack upon Chatterton's reputation, after the lad's death, all fair-minded
persons must hold him in contempt." This writer objected to Walpole's
saying to various correspondents that Chatterton was a liar, a forger, and

a rascal (all of which Chatterton was), as well as the genius that Walpole repeatedly called him. Critics of Walpole have been outraged by the passages in his *Letter to the Editor of the Miscellanies of Thomas Chatterton,* 1779: "All of the house of forgery are relations"; and "[Chatterton's] ingenuity in counterfeiting styles, and, I believe, hands, might easily have led him to those more facile imitations of prose, promissory notes," a remark that was certainly injudicious.

Walpole has not been without defenders from his own day on, notably Lort, Malone, Sir Walter Scott, and Saintsbury. The *Life* of Chatterton that will probably never be superseded, Mr Meyerstein's, puts Chatterton's connection with Walpole as fairly as possible: "Chatterton's attempt to make Walpole his patron has always been a favourite theme with the poet's apologists" who "have strained the facts to meet their theory of an inexperienced plebeian's encounter with a heartless man of the world; but Chatterton's action in this matter was for the most part less that of a distressed poet than a bold, presumptuous decoy duck, on his mettle, and Walpole is to be pitied rather than blamed, at any rate up to 1789, when the problem, such as it is, emerges; before that date there are few historic doubts of importance."

In 1789 William Barrett's *History of Bristol* appeared. It contained Chatterton's letters to Walpole of 25 and 30 March 1769. Walpole wrote Lort 27 July 1789, "I do assure you upon my honor and veracity that I never received such letters," and permitted Lort to pass this assurance on to George Steevens and his friends at Cambridge. He also wrote Hannah More a similar denial in September 1789. "Nothing," notes Mr Meyerstein, "has prejudiced Walpole more severely than this denial, as it has been interpreted as taking a despicable advantage of Chatterton when he was in his grave; and this is the only real problem in his relations with the poet."

The explanation of Walpole's misstatements in 1789 is not, I think, a bad conscience or a black heart. He was not a liar; he did not take "despicable advantage" of the dead or living. The explanation, I think, is the merciful instinct that expels the unpleasant from one's mind. Ten years earlier Walpole had spoken of the two letters five times in his *Letter to the Editor of the Miscellanies.* Anyone over fifty knows that his memory is not what it once was. And how many readers of this page under fifty can be certain they remember every circumstance of a distressing incident that took place twenty-one years earlier? An incident, moreover, that for nine years appeared to be closed. What is remarkable in Walpole's relations with Chatterton is not this one lapse of memory, but that he recollected so much so accurately about an unknown antiquary who was scraping acquaintance with him as the author of the *Anecdotes of Painting.*

Chatterton's letters to Walpole show as much genius as his other fabrications. They have been the cause of as much controversy as the authorship of Rowley's poems, and will be of more, because Chatterton's forging of Rowley's poems has been accepted for generations, whereas Walpole's brief part in his life will perhaps be twisted by those who hate the rich. As Walpole himself was always attracted to the causes of underdogs his relations with Chatterton are ironical; if he had given Chatterton as little encouragement as James Dodsley apparently gave him he would have avoided the opprobrium that fell upon him. Had he been the sort of person his critics said he was—heartless, purse-proud, a trifler—he would not have given Chatterton a thought. Walpole was seduced by his love of antiquities and suffered for the virtues his critics have denied him.

Walpole feared that "the Chattertonians" would produce forged letters after his death to blacken his reputation, as he wrote Lady Ossory. He urged her to preserve his letters on the subject. His best defense appears in his letter to her of 11 August 1778.

Somebody [he wrote] has published the poems of Chatterton the Bristol boy, and in the preface intimates that I was the cause of his despair and poisoning himself, and a little more openly is of opinion that I ought to be stoned. This most groundless accusation has driven me to write the whole story—and yet now I have done it in a pamphlet of near thirty pages of larger paper than this, I think I shall not bring myself to publish it. My story is as clear as daylight, I am as innocent as of the death of Julius Caesar, I never saw the lad with my eyes, and he was the victim of his own extravagance two years after all correspondence had ceased between him and me—and yet I hate to be the talk of the town, and am more inclined to bear this aspersion, than to come again upon the stage. . . . It is impossible to have a moment's doubt on this case. The whole foundation of the accusation is reduced to this—If I had been imposed upon, my countenance might have saved the poor lad from poisoning himself for want, which he brought on himself by his excesses. Those few words are a full acquittal, and would indeed be sufficient—but the story in itself is so marvellous, that I could not help going into the whole account of such a prodigy as Chatterton was. You will pity him, as I do; it was a deep tragedy, but interests one chiefly from his extreme youth, for it was his youth that made his talents and achievements so miraculous. I doubt, neither his genius nor his heart would have interested one, had he lived twenty years more. You will be amazed at what he was capable of before eighteen, the period of his existence—yet I had rather anybody else were employed to tell the story.

This was among Walpole's fifty letters to Lady Ossory that came to light in 1936 and so was not seen by earlier commentators.

In 1933 I found out that sixteen pieces of Walpole's collection of Chattertoniana bound in four volumes were in the Mercantile Library in New York; a seventeenth piece was (and is) in the British Museum. The Mercantile Library, a lending library of contemporary books, acquired the four volumes in 1868. I of course hurried to see them. Only the first volume was in its Strawberry covers with Walpole's arms on the sides, but all the pieces had his notes and formed a major Walpolian recovery. The first volume has a title-page written by Walpole on a fly-leaf: "Collection/of/Pieces/relating to/Rowley/and/Chatterton;/ containing,/ the supposed poems/of Rowley; the acknowledged works/of/Chatterton; and/Mr Walpole's letter/ to the Editor/ of the Latter;/ with notes to it/ by/ Mr Walpole himself./" The first piece is *"Poems, supposed to have been written at Bristol by Thomas Rowley, and others in the fifteenth century The Greatest Part Now First Published From the Most Authentic Copies, with An Engraved Specimen of One of The MSS to Which are added A Preface An Introductory Account of The Several Pieces and A Glossary,"* 1777. Beneath this Walpole wrote "By Mr Tyrwhitt," Thomas Tyrwhitt, 1730–86, a classical commentator, who played a big part in exposing Chatterton. The second piece in this volume is *Miscellanies in Prose and Verse; by Thomas Chatterton, the supposed author of the poems published under the names of Rowley, Canning, etc.* In his Preface to it the editor wrote, "One of his first efforts, to emerge from a situation so irksome to him, was an application to a gentleman well known in the republic of letters; which unfortunately for the public, and himself met with a very cold reception." Walpole identified the gentleman in the margin, "Mr H. Walpole." The third piece in the first volume is Walpole's *Letter to the Editor of the Miscellanies of Thomas Chatterton,* Strawberry Hill, 1779. After "Letter" he wrote, "From Mr Horace Walpole." He made a dozen annotations in ink, and pasted in relevant newspaper cuttings and a romantic view of "Monument to the Memory of Chatterton." If the Almighty allows me to rescue only one of the four volumes this is the one I shall choose without hesitation.

When I asked the Librarian of the Mercantile Library if she thought there was any possibility of the trustees selling me the four Walpole volumes she thought that they might. I urged her to have Dr Rosenbach appraise them, which he did at $600. This enabled the Library to buy many recently published books of more interest to its subscribers.

We printed Walpole's extensive annotations of his Chatterton collec-

Haveynge whilomme yn dyscourse prooved or soughte to prove the Deeitie of
Chryste byn hys Workes Names and Attrybutes, I wal seeke to prove the Deitie of
Holie Spryte. Manne moste be supplied with holie Spryte to have commensynge
ryghtfullie of thynges whyche boo of God. Seyncte Paule praieth the holie Spryte
to assyst hys Flocke ynne dhise Wordes The holie Sprytis Communione be wyth you. Lette
us dhere desyer of hym to ayde us. I in emplystynge and you yn onderstondeynge hys
Deeyttye let us saie wyth Seyncte Cyprian Adeste sancte Spiritus & paracleum tuam
expectantibus illabere coeltus, sanctifica templum corporis nostri, et consecra
in habitaculum tuum. Seyncte Paule sayeth Ye are the Temple of God for the Spryte
of Godde dwelleth ynne you. Gif yee are the Temple of Godde alleyn bie the dwellynge of
the Spryte, wote yee not that the Spryte is Godde, and folaine proofe of the personne
and Gloris of thynde personne. The person, Gyftes Operations, Glorie, and Deitie are al measured
in Holie Spryte as boo prooved fro dyffaunte Textes of Scrypteure. Beynge as
Sptie sayethe of the same Essentyalle matter as the Fadre ande Sonne who are Godde the
holie Spryte moste undubitablie boo Godde. The Spryte or divine Wylle of Godde mooved upon
the Water at creatynge of the Worlde. this meaneth the Deitie. I sayde yn mie laste
dyscourse, the promyse of Chryste who wythe Godde the Fadre wolde dwelle yn the Soughte
of his Dyscyples. howe coulde heye see botte bye missyon of holie Spryghte? yis mee
thynckethe prooveth no alleyne the personallitie of holie Spryghte botte the veris Foundaine
and Ground Warcke of the Trynitie ytselfe. The holie Spryghte cannotte boo the Godde thynges
and Vyrtues of a Mannis Mynde sythence by hym wee boo to facte hoop you
gode thynges; gif wee are boo to hope a Vertue bie yat Vertue ytteselfe meethynckethe
the Custos boo not fytted to the Change. The Spryte or Godde is the Auctaure of you
gode thynges ande bie hye obeisaunce thie mote alleyn bo hold : I maie not bo
dollysh no hereticalle, to saie whatte we calls Conveyonce, is the haythen warninge
                                      evylle
of the Spryte to forsake our Waye bifore he dothe wolelie leave our stonied Soulfre

Collection of MSS and letters that belonged to Thomas Tyrwhitt, among them six pages in Chatterton's hand,
including his poem "Happiness."

tion in the Yale Walpole. One note I particularly like is where Chatterton refers to "the redoubted baron Otranto." Walpole explained quietly in the margin, "Mr H.W. author of the *Castle of Otranto*," but he has no comment on Chatterton's wittiest sally, the reference to "Horace Trefoil."

The second volume is Jacob Bryant's *Observations upon the Poems of Thomas Rowley in which the Authenticity of Those Poems is Ascertained,* 1781. With it, annotated spiritedly by Walpole, is a 'Recapitulation.' Of the remaining eleven pieces in volumes 3 and 4 the most interesting is Thomas James Mathias's *Essay on the Evidence, External and Internal Relating to the Poems Attributed to Thomas Rowley, etc.* 1783, in which Walpole's notes are more critical than those in the other pieces.

The runner-up in this Choice is a collection of manuscripts and letters that belonged to Thomas Tyrwhitt. Among them are six pages in Chatterton's hand, including his poem "Happiness" and several drawings and inscriptions inspired by the documents and monuments in St Mary Redcliff, Bristol. "Happiness" concludes:

> Content is happiness, as sages say-
> But what's content? The trifle of a day.
> Then, friend, let inclination be thy guide,
> Nor be by superstition led aside.
> The saint and sinner, fool and wise attain
> An equal share of easiness and pain.

Chatterton's handwriting is so mature it is easy to see why it was mistaken for that of an older man. As his manuscripts are chiefly in the British Museum and the Bristol Library, we are fortunate at Farmington to have these pages that bring us into the most vexed chapter of Walpole's life.

Choice 15
Walpole's Transcripts of His Letters to Sir Horace Mann

The Mann correspondence is the great Andean range of the Walpolian continent, stretching from 1740 to Mann's death in 1786. Eight hundred and forty-eight of the letters are from Walpole, eight hundred and eighty-seven from Mann, a total of 1735 letters, nearly forty a year, many of them running to a dozen pages. As I have said, Walpole stayed with Mann in Florence for a year while on the Grand Tour, but the two men never met after Walpole returned to England in 1741.

In my Introduction to these letters in the Yale Walpole I pointed out that "For sweep and variety and the procession of great events they are unrivalled in Walpole's correspondence." I might have gone further, I think, and said they are unrivalled in those respects by any other correspondence of the time. Walpole was aware of their historic value. As early as 1744 he wrote Mann that being "entirely out of all the little circumstances of each other's society, which are the soul of letters, we are forced to correspond as Guicciardini and Clarendon." Years later he exclaimed, "What scenes my letters to you have touched on for eight and thirty years!"; and a few years later still, "A correspondence of near half a century is, I suppose, not to be paralleled in the annals of the Post Office!" Towards the end he repeated that he was forced to write to posterity. "One cannot say, 'I dined with such a person yesterday,' when the letter is to be a fortnight on the road—still less, when you know nothing of my Lord or Mr Such-an-one, whom I should mention." He had moments of realistic disillusion with us: "If our letters remain, posterity will read the catastrophes of St James's and the Palace Pitti with equal indifference."

Walpole began getting his letters back in 1749 and thereafter they were brought him by friends every few years. He started transcribing them in 1754 to remove passages he didn't want us to see, such as the account of his quarrel with Gray at Reggio and the strictures on his one-time intimate friend, Henry Fox. After a few years he let Kirgate do the copying, but resumed it for the last three years. The originals and copies were kept in separate houses and were left to different people. In a memorandum dated 21 March 1790 Walpole wrote: "I desire my executors to deliver to Sir Horace Mann the younger all my original letters to his uncle Sir Horace Mann the elder returned to me by the latter, and which letters are in the japan cabinet in the Blue Room on the first floor in my house in Berkeley Square; but the copies of those letters in six volumes which are in one of the cupboards in the Green Closet at Strawberry Hill, may be locked up in my library and remain there and devolve to those on whom I have entailed the house. But I desire they will never suffer them to be transcribed or printed." This memorandum is one of the manuscripts Sir Wathen Waller and I found in the attic at Woodcote. It was sold in the second Waller Sale in 1947 and is now at Farmington.

Why did Walpole and Mann go on writing to each other for forty-six years? Mann said that he "cherished" Walpole's letters and read and re-read them, for they were "necessary to my tranquillity." Although Walpole was the younger by eleven years one feels that he was the dominant partner in their friendship. His letters kept Mann informed of what was going on behind the scenes at home; he was a friend who was protecting Mann's interests with each succeeding Secretary of State and who helped him to proceed from resident to envoy extraordinary and plenipotentiary, to become a baronet and a Knight of the Bath. This last honor was particularly welcome to Mann because its red ribbon was a constant rejoinder to the Italians who said he was of low degree. Mann's letters brought Walpole the latest foreign news; he liked quoting them and giving friends letters of introduction to the dean of the diplomatic corps in Florence, knowing his friends would receive a royal welcome. Mann was celebrated for his entertainments and hospitality, as visiting Englishmen and foreigners, including Casanova, bore witness. He also proved his ability in affairs by the skill with which he followed the activities of the Jacobites in Rome and the advice he gave the English naval officers in the Mediterranean.

Instead of sending the originals of Walpole's letters to the younger Mann as Walpole directed, Mrs Damer kept them and bequeathed them to her Twickenham neighbor, Sir Wathen Waller, the first baronet. We know Waller had them in 1833, but not what became of them later, apart from the first sixteen that got separated from the rest and are now mine.

The simplest explanation for the disappearance of family papers is that they were burnt and it may well be that Waller, a conscientious man, fearful that the originals might one day be printed contrary to Walpole's expressed wishes, did burn them. That Walpole really wanted the originals destroyed may be questioned since he did not destroy them himself, as his earlier editors thought he had done. He was of two minds about their fate, hoping for future readers yet shrinking from them. This illustrates the "inconsequence" that Miss Berry said marked his old age.

Mrs Damer followed Walpole's instructions about the ultimate disposition of the transcripts and turned them over to the Waldegrave family where they remained until the present Lord Waldegrave sold them to me in 1948. Lord Dover used them, not the originals, for his edition of Walpole's letters to Mann, which was published by Bentley in 1833. The original worn bindings of the six volumes were removed and Paget Toynbee told me with pride that he got the ninth Earl Waldegrave to have the letters rebound in their present red morocco. I would like, of course, to save all six volumes, but if the Almighty says "NO!" I'll rescue the first volume, which has 150 letters from 1741 to 1746 transcribed and annotated by Walpole throughout.

That he had future readers of his letters in mind is clear from the Advertisement he prefixed to the first volume of the transcripts and by the epigraph he added to its title-page, "Posteris an aliqua cura, nescio! Plin. Epist," *"Whether there will be any concern about us on the part of posterity I do not know."* Pliny, *Letters*. The late Professor Clarence Mendell of Yale kindly sent me a translation of Pliny's letter to Tacitus in which the epigraph appears, pointing out that Walpole omitted *nostri* between *cura* and *nescio*. This epigraph is less confident than the one already quoted in Choice 4 from Cibber's *Apology*. We can be certain, I think, of his satisfaction if he could have known that in the twentieth century his letters to and from Mann would be published in America in eleven substantial volumes with tens of thousands of footnotes and an index of over 100,000 entries to guide an ever-increasing number of delighted readers. The English friend who saw Walpole most clearly, "Gilly" Williams, wrote to George Selwyn, "I can figure no being happier than Horry, *Monstrari digito praetereuntium* [to be pointed out by those passing by] has been his whole aim. For this he has wrote, printed, and built." For this he wrote and kept his letters.

Here is his Advertisement to the transcripts.

A
Collection
of
Letters
from
Horace Walpole
Youngest Son of Sr Robert Walpole
Earl of Orford
to
Horace Mann
Resident at Florence
from
King George the Second:
transcribed from the Originals.
Vol: 1st

Posteris an aliqua cura, nescio!
Plin. epist.

Title-page of first volume of the Mann letters, from 1741–46, with advertisement prefixed and epigraph added.

The following collection of letters, written very carelessly by a young man, had been preserved by the person to whom they were addressed. The author, some years after the date of the first, borrowed them, on account of some anecdotes interspersed. On the perusal, among many trifling relations and stories which were only of consequence or amusing to the two persons concerned in the correspondence, he found some facts, characters and news, which, though below the dignity of history, might prove entertaining to many other people: and knowing how much pleasure, not only himself, but many other persons have often found in a series of private and familiar letters, he thought it worth his while to preserve these, as they contain something of the customs, fashions, politics, diversions and private history of several years; which, if worthy of any existence, can be properly transmitted to posterity, only in this manner.

The reader will find a few pieces of intelligence which did not prove true, but which are retained here as the author heard and related them, lest correction should spoil the simple air of the narrative. When the letters were written, they were never intended for public inspection; and now they are far from being thought correct, or more authentic than the general turn of epistolary correspondence admits. The author would sooner have burnt them, than have taken the trouble to correct such errant trifles which are here presented to the reader, with scarce any variation or omissions, but what private friendships and private history, or the great haste with which the letters were written, made indispensably necessary, as will plainly appear, not only by the unavoidable chasms, where the originals were worn out or torn away, but by many idle relations and injudicious remarks and prejudices of a young man; for which the only excuse the author can pretend to make, is, that as some future reader may possibly be as young as he was, when he first wrote, he hopes they may be amused, with what graver people (if into such hands they should fall) will very justly despise. Whoever has patience to peruse the series, will find perhaps, that as the author grew older, some of his faults became less striking.

Mann's letters to Walpole remained at Strawberry Hill until 1843 when they were acquired from Lord Waldegrave by Richard Bentley, the publisher whose grandson sold them to me with four of their original red morocco bindings from which the letters had been cut. Each volume still has a title-page in Walpole's hand, "Letters/From Horatio Mann/Resident at Florence/From King George the Second/To/Horatio Walpole/youngest Son/of/Sir Robert Walpole/afterwards/Earl of Orford/" and the numbers of the volumes. John Doran wrote a book for Bentley, drawn from Mann's letters in 1876, *Mann and Manners at the Court of Florence, 1740–1786,* a work as trifling as its title.

Mann sent lavish presents to Walpole despite Walpole's protests. Among

them were the bronze bust of Caligula with silver eyes at the beginning of
his madness, a small ebony trunk for perfumes with bas-reliefs in silver by
Benvenuto Cellini representing the Judgment of Paris, a marble head
in alto relievo of John the Baptist by Donatello, and a portrait by Vasari
of Bianca Cappello, mistress and wife of Francesco de Medici Grand
Duke of Tuscany. This last particularly delighted Walpole. "The head,"
he wrote Mann,

is painted equal to Titian, and though done, I suppose, after the clock had
struck five and thirty, yet she retains a great share of beauty. I have bespoken
a frame for her, with the grand ducal coronet at top, her story on a label at
bottom, which Gray is to compose in Latin as short and expressive as Tacitus
(one is lucky when one can bespeak and have executed such an inscription!)
the Medici arms on one side, and the Cappello's on the other. I must tell you
a critical discovery of mine *à propos:* in an old book of Venetian arms, there
are two coats of Capello, who from their *name* bear a *hat,* on one of them is
added a flower-de-luce on a blue ball, which I am persuaded was given to the
family by the Great Duke, in consideration of this alliance; the Medicis you
know bore such a badge at the top of their own arms; this discovery I made by
a talisman, which Mr Chute calls the *sortes Walpolianae,* by which I find everything I want *à point nommé* wherever I dip for it. This discovery indeed is almost of that kind which I call *serendipity,* a very expressive word, which as I
have nothing better to tell you, I shall endeavour to explain to you: you will
understand it better by the derivation than by the definition. I once read a silly
fairy tale, called *The Three Princes of Serendip:* as their highnesses travelled,
they were always making discoveries, by accidents and sagacity, of things which
they were not in quest of: for instance, one of them discovered that a mule
blind of the right eye had travelled the same road lately, because the grass was
eaten only on the left side, where it was worse than on the right—now do you
understand *serendipity?*

The "old book of Venetian arms" is now at Farmington, given me by
E. P. Goldschmidt, the London bookseller, from his own library. Walpole
pencilled a small cross opposite the significant crest. How far "Serendipity" has entered into our language may be gauged by the menu of a
Farmington coffee shop whose *specialité de la maison* is a "Serendipity
sandwich."

Mann is seen at Farmington through the eyes of Thomas Patch who
spent the last twenty-seven years of his life at Florence painting visiting
Englishmen and romantic landscapes for grand tourists. Our collection of
him started in 1939 when William Randolph Hearst began selling his

vast collections that were stored in two New York warehouses, each of
which covered a city block. Perhaps a tenth of one percent of them was
offered by Parish, Watson and Co. of 57th Street. When I asked them if
Hearst had anything from Strawberry Hill they said they had no idea
and invited me to come and see for myself. I wandered through six floors
crowded with Spanish choir stalls, porphyry jars and Etruscan vases,
French cabinets and English chests. I was ready to give up on the sixth
floor, but my guide urged me on for one more, which was the attic.
Against its walls leaned a fragment of a Tiepolo ceiling, a Meissonier
battle scene, and Frederic Remington cowboys. Among them was a large
conversation piece with "Hogarth" on its ample frame. Thanks to Francis
Watson, the expert on Thomas Patch, I knew better. I was certain that
the chief figure in the picture before me was Mann from its resemblance
to a small portrait of him by John Astley that Mann sent Walpole and
that was reproduced in Cunningham's edition of Walpole's letters. He
was older in the Hearst picture, more rugose, but with the same broken
nose and air of a capable esthete. The case for the figure being Mann was
settled by his vice-regal chair with the royal crown and supporters. I
urged my guide to send a photograph of it to Francis Watson at the
Wallace Collection in London for his opinion and after Francis confirmed Patch as the artist a zero was chopped off the Hogarth price, the
remainder was divided by five, and the picture was the first of five Patches
to come to Farmington. A year later Astley's portrait of Mann emerged
from hiding and arrived with the companion portrait of his twin brother
Galfridus that Mann had also sent Walpole. When "dear Gal" died Walpole had Bentley design his tomb, the drawing for which is at Farmington.

Mann appears in two of the other Patches at Farmington, the very
large conversation piece that we shall come to in our Print Room and another that was painted for Lord Beauchamp, Lord Hertford's heir and
Walpole's first cousin once removed. Walpole saw and admired the picture. Mann is seated at the right listening to a comical Dutch singer
whom he is trying out for one of his musical entertainments. The Dutch-
man is singing eagerly while Patch himself bursts into the room from the
left bowed under a basket filled with the *Vocabulario della Crusca* and
distracting nearly all of the auditors. Beauchamp, very tall and elegant
in the center of the picture, has turned to regard the disturbance with
amused superiority. We shall come to the fourth Patch at Farmington
when we get to Henry Bunbury and Hogarth. A fifth one is a riverscape
that I got to show the sort of thing Patch painted for the Grand Tourist

Astley's portrait of Horace Mann.

trade. An ancient round tower looms beyond a bridge over which peasants and an ox-cart are passing; a shepherd and his modest flock are resting on the bank; in the distance are blue mountains. It is a scene to bring back smiling Italy to northern travellers at home. Walpole asked Mann to send him two Patches of the Arno and Florence, which he kept in his town house and bequeathed to his great-nephew, Lord Cholmondeley at Houghton, where they still are, a lovely pair. One marvels at Patch's versatility, for he was also an engraver, the author of a sumptuous folio with twenty-six engravings after Masaccio that he dedicated to Mann and of twenty-four prints after Fra Bartolommeo that he "dedicated to the Honorable HORACE WALPOLE, an intelligent promoter of the Arts," an honor no doubt inspired by Mann. It is pleasant to have the two friends brought together in this way by Patch, whose pictures, like Mann's letters to Walpole are now held in higher esteem than ever before.

When on 15 January 1777 Walpole asked Mann to return his letters, he added, "I should like to have them all together, for they are a kind of history." Readers of the *Memoirs* will be especially grateful to them because they add "the touches of nature" that the *Memoirs* lack.

Choice 16
Tonton's Snuff-Box

Walpole escaped to Paris in November 1765 after the most mortifying disappointment of his life, the failure of his friends, especially of Conway, to offer him a place in the first Rockingham Ministry which he had helped to form. He would not have accepted a place, but his pride would have been satisfied by refusing it. "Falsehood, interest, and ingratitude, the attendants of friendship, are familiar to me," he wrote Mann bitterly; but no Englishman ever went to Paris with more friendly letters of introduction to its great world or enjoyed more of a success when he got there. He wrote Gray, "Like Queen Eleanor in the Ballad, I sunk at Charing Cross, and have risen in the Faubourg Saint Germain" where he was drawn speedily into Madame du Deffand's circle. She, whom he described to Conway as "an old blind débauchée of wit," became infatuated with him although twenty years his senior. Forty years earlier she had been a mistress of the Regent Orléans and that gave her a certain panache even though the connection had lasted only two weeks. To her Walpole was a radiant newcomer who exorcised the devil ennui that possessed her. Before long they were meeting daily. His delight in her company and his pride in having made a Platonic conquest of the wittiest woman in Paris fused with his indignation at the "barbarity and injustice" of those who ate her suppers when they could not go to a more fashionable house, who laughed at her, abused her, and tried to convert her nominal friends into enemies in what she called their "société infernale."

Walpole kept a journal of his five visits to Paris from 1765 to 1775. It records what he did every day, whom he saw and where. This was one of the great prizes in the first Waller Sale when it was bought by Maggs, sold to Percival Merritt of Boston, and bequeathed by him to Harvard. It has been edited in an appendix to the du Deffand correspondence in the Yale Walpole. Two typical entries are: "30th March 1766: To Mme du Deffand. Mr [Adam] Smith came. With Sir H. Echlin to Lady Macclesfield. To Madame de Mirepoix. To Mme de Rochefort, Duchesse de

Choiseul, Mme de Gacé and others there. Supped at Mme du Deffand's with Mmes d'Aiguillon, Forcalquier and Crussol, Messrs de Sceaux, d'Ussé, d'Ambreville, Damas, and M. and Mme de Broglie." On the following day, "Mr Buckner came. To Mme d'Aiguillon, young duchess there and an old Lord Alford. Made visits to take leave. To Mme Geoffrin. To Baron d'Holbach. Played at cavagnole and supped at Madame du Deffand's, with Mesdames de Ségur, Maurevel, St-Maur, Flavacourt, Valbelle, Mlle de Courson, Contesse Czernieski, and M. Fervantcour." Such was life in the Faubourg Saint Germain in 1766. The final entry in Mme du Deffand's last journal, which she left Walpole and which is now at Farmington, shows that she carried on until she died at the age of 83: "10th September 1780," she wrote, "Sunday. Supped at home with the usual people. M. de Choiseul arrived. The Briennes left after supper for Brienne. M. de Toulouse has returned."

Walpole's initial success grew even greater after his contribution to the *société infernale*. This was a pretended letter from the King of Prussia to Rousseau in which the King offered Rousseau asylum to be as unhappy as he pleased. Copies of the letter were handed about Paris; Walpole himself sent several to England where one got into the *St. James's Chronicle* and helped destroy the friendship between Rousseau and Hume, his English benefactor.

When Walpole returned to England in 1766 he and Mme du Deffand began the correspondence which went on until she died fourteen years later, some 850 very long letters on each side. Walpole got her to return his letters and presumably directed Mary Berry, his literary executrix, to make extracts from them as footnotes to a posthumous edition of Mme du Deffand's letters to him, after which Miss Berry was to destroy his side of the correspondence. One reason for doing so was that he was uneasy about his French although Mme du Deffand assured him that "no one, but no one, expresses himself better than you" and continued to say so over and over again to reassure him. His reputation as a person has suffered from our knowing little of what he actually wrote; only seven of his letters to her (they are at Farmington) have survived. Her letters to him are emotional and demanding; she clamored on about love and coldness; she flung herself into luxurious analyses of him and of herself, all of which he found embarrassing, especially when he learned that their letters were being opened at the post office. He begged her to stick to proper names. She was hurt, angrily defended herself, and obeyed for a while. Then she burst out again in a fresh flood of emotion, and the pattern was repeated. We have both sides of the conversation for only the month of January 1775, but in it the cycle is complete. It shows her exaggerated reaction to his mild expostulations, and how mistaken it is to condemn him as an unfeeling scold from her letters alone. He made four laborious trips to see and entertain her and to bring her what comfort and pleasure he could until war was declared between France and England. When her income was cut he offered to make up the loss from his own pocket, but she would not let him do it. Although she wanted to leave him all she had, he accepted only her manuscripts and her little black spaniel, Tonton, who was not house-broken and who bit people. She included the gold snuff-box made by the king's jeweller with Tonton's portrait in wax by Gosset that a friend gave her as a New Year's present in 1778. The Chevalier Boufflers wrote verses on Voltaire and Tonton that Mme du Deffand sent to Walpole.

> Vous les trouvez tous deux charmants,
> Nous les trouvons tous deux mordants;
>   Voilà la ressemblance:
> L'un ne mord que ses ennemis,
> Et l'autre mord tous vos amis,
>   Voilà la différence.

The manuscripts were kept in a cedar chest in the library at Strawberry until sold in 1842 to Thorpe the bookseller for £156.10s. Sir Frederick Madden of the British Museum recorded that "directly after the conclusion of the sale the chest was purchased by Dyce-Sombre who came down in a carriage and four accompanied by his wife, and the latter taking a fancy to these letters her wealthy husband gave Thorpe 20 guineas additional for them and carried them off." The lady bequeathed them to her nephew, W. R. Parker-Jervis of Staffordshire. They were resold through Sotheby's in 1920, just four years before I began collecting Walpole. Paget Toynbee bought Mme du Deffand's letters to Walpole for £20 and gave them to the Bodleian; Seymour de Ricci bought her letters to Voltaire and gave them to the Bibliothèque Nationale. Most of the rest went to Maggs, who in December 1933 let me have them for £50 to make me, as they said, "A Christmas present." In 1938 they retrieved for me the most interesting book in the collection, which had been bought by another dealer in 1920. This was Mme du Deffand's "Recueil de divers ouvrages," over 270 pages, 4to, with 45 "portraits" of her friends magnificently bound in red morocco. Walpole wrote inside

Tonton's Snuff-Box.

the front cover that the book had been bequeathed to him by Mme du Deffand with her other manuscripts and he pasted in seven and a half pages of notes that included his "portrait" of her, which is in English.

Portrait de Madame la Marquise du Deffand, 1766,
                    Where do Wit and Memory dwell?
                    Where is Fancy's favourite cell?
                    Where does Judgment hold her court,

and continues for 27 lines of conventional compliment until the close:

                    Together all these Virtues dwell:
                    St Joseph's convent is her cell:
                    Their sanctuary Du Deffand's mind—
                    Censure, be dumb! She's old and blind.

Far from being wounded by the last line Mme du Deffand was flattered because it proved, she said, the sincerity of what went before.

Her "Portrait" of Walpole, which he asked her to write, is the most important summary of him ever written. This translation of it is by Catherine Jestin, Librarian of the Lewis Walpole Library.

No, no, I cannot do your portrait. No one knows you less than I do. You appear sometimes as I wish you were, sometimes as I fear you may not be, and perhaps never as you really are. It is obvious you are very intelligent in many ways. Everyone knows this as well as I, and you should be aware of it more than anyone.

It is your character that should be portrayed, and that is why I cannot be a good judge: indifference, or at least impartiality, is essential. Yet I can vouch for your integrity. You are principled and courageous and pride yourself on firmness of purpose, so that when you make a decision, for better or worse, nothing can make you change your mind, often to the point of obstinacy. Your friendship is warm and steadfast, but neither tender nor yielding. Fear of weakness hardens you; you try not to be ruled by emotions: you cannot refuse friends in dire need, you sacrifice your interests to theirs, but you deny them smallest favours; you are kind to everyone, and to those to whom you are indifferent, yet for your friends, even where trifles are concerned, you hardly bother to exert yourself.

Your disposition is very pleasing although not too equable. Your manner is noble, easy and natural; your desire to please is without affectation. Knowledge and experience of the world have made you scorn humanity and yet you have learned to adjust; you know that outward expressions are merely insincerities;

you respond with deference and good manners so that all those who do not care in the least whether you like them or not have a good opinion of you.

I do not know if you have much feeling; if you do, you fight it, for you think it a weakness; you allow yourself only the loftier kind. You are thoughtful, you have absolutely no vanity although plenty of self-esteem, but your self-esteem does not blind you: it leads you to exaggerate your faults rather than to hide them. You give a good opinion of yourself only if forced to do so when comparing yourself with others. You have discernment and tact, perfect taste and faultless manners. You would have been part of the most fashionable society in centuries past; you are so now in this, and would be in those of the future. Your character derives much from your country, but your manners are equally correct everywhere.

You have one weakness which is inexcusable: fear of ridicule. You sacrifice your better feelings to it and let it regulate your conduct. It makes you harken to fools who give you false impressions that your friends cannot rectify. You are easily influenced, a tendency you recognize and which you remedy by adhering too strictly to principle; your determination never to give in is occasionally excessive, and at times when it is hardly worth the effort.

You are noble and generous, you do good for the pleasure of doing so, without ostentation, without hope of reward: in short your soul is beautiful and good.

Addition to the Portrait, 30 November 1766.

Only truth and simplicity please you; you distrust subtleties, you hate metaphysics; large ideas bore you, and you don't much enjoy deep reflection, you think it of little use; your philosophy teaches you that it is better to suppress your emotions than to fight them. You want to do so by diversions, you mock everything and, new Democritus, the world is nothing for you but a stage whose actors you hiss; your bent is irony, you excel in fields that demand much wit, grace, and lightness. You are naturally light-hearted, but you are too sensitive and sensibility often hinders gaiety. To remedy this you seek out-of-the-ordinary ways to occupy and amuse yourself. You build exotic houses, you raise monuments to a king of brigands, you pretend to have forbearance, etc. etc. Lastly, you seem a little mad in your eccentricities which are, however, the product of reason.

I cannot say anything about your dislike of friendship; it is apparently founded on some deep sorrow, but as you are only vague about this, one is led to believe that you are afraid, or else wish to establish a rule of conduct, as little without foundation as all your rules which you do not follow despite your eloquence, because your precepts are not backed up by your practice.

You have friends, you are entirely devoted to them, their interests are yours; all your talk and all your reasoning against friendship fail to convince them that you are not, of all people in the world, the most capable of it.

Mme du Deffand was afraid Walpole was unhappy about his portrait and a week after she sent it ordered him to make certain amendments, but we don't know what he really thought of it.

Another runner-up to Tonton's snuff-box is Walpole's copy of Gramont's *Mémoires*, 1746, the copy he used when editing and printing the Strawberry *Grammont* in 1772. He made an index for this copy and added notes throughout it, all of which he used in the Strawberry edition, his copy of which is also at Farmington, annotated and extra-illustrated by him. He dedicated it "A Madame——. L'Editeur vous consacre cette Edition, comme un monument de son Amitié, de son Admiration, & de son Respect; à Vous, dont les Graces, l'Esprit, & le Goût retracent au siecle present le siecle de Louis quatorze & les agremens de l'Auteur de ces Memoires." In his copy he wrote Mme du Deffand's name after the blank her modesty insisted upon and added two charming little engravings; the upper one of three putti crowning a book with laurel, the lower of a monument embowered with flowering shrubs. No collector ever enjoyed adorning his books more than Walpole. Of the hundred copies he printed of the *Grammont,* twelve are at Farmington; they include presentation copies to the Duchess of Bedford, Lord Nuneham, George Montagu, Mrs Damer, and Richard Bull, who extra-illustrated his copy lavishly, as usual.

The single object at Farmington that brings the two friends most strongly together is not the dedication copy of the *Grammont* or "Recueil de divers ouvrages," but the very beautiful circular gold snuff-box made by Roucel, the king's jeweler, that gives us Tonton in his plump latter days sitting on a cushion with his right front paw uplifted appealingly. Inside the lid, his master had inscribed, "This box with the portrait of her dog Tonton was bequeathed by Madame la Marquise du Deffand to Mr Horace Walpole, 1780," but before I talk about Tonton I should speak of his predecessors.

Walpole's devotion to dogs appears in his first letter to his Mamma and never ceased from Tory to Tonton. Tory was a little King Charles spaniel that Walpole took on the Grand Tour, "the prettiest, fattest, dearest creature! I had let it out of the chaise for the air, and it was waddling along close to the head of the horses, on the top of one of the highest Alps, by the side of a wood of firs. There darted out a young wolf, seized poor dear Tory by the throat, and before we could possibly prevent it, sprung up the side of the rock and carried him off."

Tory's successor was Patapan, which Walpole got in Rome and took to England. He was a small white spaniel trimmed in a manner unfamiliar

Index of Remarkable Persons.

A.
Anne of Austria, 91.
Arlington (Earl of) 169.
Arran (Earl of) 106. 180. 203.

B.
Bagot (mrs) 265. 270.
Ballenden (mrs) 253.
Bardou (Mademoiselle) 264. Barbara? mrs 203.
Blagg (mrs) 132. 265.
Boineau (mrs) 305.
Brice (Don Gregorio) 171.
Brisacier (Mons. De) 133.
Brisac (Duc De) 241.
Brinon. 12-15.
Bristol (Earl of) 199.
Brook (mrs) 199. 227.
Browker (Lord) 323.
Bucks (D. of) 106. 136. 157. 341. 374.

C.
Cameron (Comedy) 26.
Castlemaine (Countess of) 109. 121. 169. 310. 371. 392.
Catharine (Queen) 105. 162. 336. 378.
Charles (King) 102. 276. 310.
Chesterfield (Earl of) 189.
Chesterfield (Countess of) 161. 203. 205.
Chin...s. 376. Chiffinch
Churchill (mrs) 377. 364.

Churchill (D. of Marlbro) 392.
Clarendon (Earl of) 105. 107.
Condé (Prince of) 72. 76. 174. — Cleveland v. Castlemaine
Cornwallis (Lord) 262.
Cromwell (Oliver) 100.

376. 392.

D.
Denham (Sr John) 200. 227.
Dorset (Earl of) 393.
Duncan, 142. 266.

F.
Falmouth (Earl of) 106. 165. 187.
Feversham (Earl of) 67.
Flamarin (Marquis de) 245.
Fox (Sr Stephen) 252.
Francisque, 203. 224.

G.
Garde (Mr De la) 264.
Grammont (Marechale) 171. 366.
Gwyn (Nell) 393. 357.

H.
Hall (Jacob) 124. 310.
Hamilton (George) 106. 161. 183. 205. 224. 332. 384.
Hamilton (mrs) 129. 246.
Hobart (mrs) 265. 260. 278. 345.
Howard (mlle R) 369.
Howard (Thomas) 125.
Hurneges (Marechal de) 77.   Hughes (mrs) 337
Hyde (D. of York) 104. 161. 186. 342.
Hyde (mrs) 123.

Walpole's copy of Gramont's *Mémoires*, 1746. Index made by Walpole.

to the rustics of Norfolk whither his master brought him after Sir Robert's downfall. Walpole passed the summer of 1742 at Houghton writing *Patapan or the Little White Dog, a Tale imitated from Fontaine,* a work he mentioned in his "Short Notes," adding "it was never printed." His manuscript of it is in the Second Common Place Book at Farmington and runs to fourteen folio pages, half in verse. It turns out to be a satire on Arthur Onslow, the Speaker of the House of Commons with whom Walpole had an altercation in the House. It has disappointingly little about Patapan, but there is much about him in the Mann correspondence and both Chute and Walpole addressed verses to him. Patapan was succeeded in due course by Rosette, a black and tan spaniel, which Walpole believed saved his life by warning him of a chimney fire. In August 1773 he wrote Lady Ossory, "My poor Rosette is dying. She relapsed into her fits the last night of my stay at Nuneham; and has suffered exquisitely ever since. You may believe I have too—I have been out of bed twenty times every night, have had no sleep, and sat up with her till three this morning—but I am only making you laugh at me: I cannot help it, I think of nothing else. Without weaknesses I should not be I, and I may as well tell them, as have them tell themselves." When Rosette died he sent Lord Nuneham her epitaph; "it has no merit," Walpole wrote, "for it is an imitation, but in coming from the heart, if ever epitaph did, and therefore your dogmanity will not dislike it.

> Sweetest roses of the year
> Strew around my Rose's bier.
> Calmly may the dust repose
> Of my pretty faithful Rose!
> And if, yon cloud-topp'd hill behind,
> This frame dissolved, this breath resign'd,
> Some happier isle, some humbler heaven
> Be to my trembling wishes given,
> Admitted to that equal sky,
> May sweet Rose bear me company!"

Mme du Deffand's first of 69 references to Tonton was when he, aged four months, was sitting on her shoulder while she dictated her letter. A year later she asked Walpole, even before Walpole had seen him, to take him after her death. Tonton was very pretty, she said, and Walpole would love him, but she did not add that he wasn't house-broken and bit people. Thomas Walpole proved his friendship by bringing Tonton to England when his mistress died, a kindness that must have added much to the hardship of those four exhausting days of travel. Walpole doted on Tonton. "You will find that I have gotten a new idol," he wrote Mason,

in a word, a successor to Rosette and almost as great a favourite, nor is this a breach of vows and constancy, but an act of piety. In a word, my poor dear old friend Madame du Deffand had a little dog of which she was extremely fond, and the last time I saw her she made me promise if I should survive her to take charge of it. I did. It is arrived and I was going to say, it is incredible how fond I am of it, but I have no occasion to brag of my dogmanity. I dined at Richmond House t'other day, and mentioning whither I was going, the Duke said, "Own the truth, shall not you call at home first and see Tonton?" He guessed rightly. He is now sitting on my paper as I write—not the Duke, but Tonton.

At just this time Walpole wrote in his pocket notebook mentioned in Choice 4,

"Charade on my dog Tonton
The first part is thine, the second belongs only to people of fashion; but the whole, tho doubly thine, belongs only to me."

When Tonton died Walpole wrote Lady Ossory that his death was merciful, for

he was grown stone deaf, and very near equally blind, and so weak that the two last days he could not walk upstairs. Happily he had not suffered, and died close by my side without a pang or a groan. I have had the satisfaction for my dear old friend's sake and his own, of having nursed him up by constant attention to the age of sixteen, yet always afraid of his surviving me, as it was scarce possible he could meet a third person who would study his happiness equally. I sent him to Strawberry and went thither on Sunday to see him buried behind the Chapel near Rosette.

Choice 17

Walpole's Last Letter to Lady Ossory

Walpole's first letter to Lady Ossory that has survived is dated Sept. 12, 1761, just before the coronation of George III when she was still the Duchess of Grafton. "If anything could make me amends, Madam, for not seeing the finest figure in the world walk at the Coronation," Walpole wrote, "it would be the letter and the *découpure* that I have received from your Grace: I will carry the latter to that ceremony, to prevent the handsomest peeresses from gaining any advantage in my eyes by an absence that I fear they are all wicked enough to enjoy." The *découpure* of herself and her Grafton baby daughter, who is tossing up a chubby arm behind her, is at Farmington. It was cut by Huber of Geneva, according to Walpole's note on it, and is the runner-up in this Choice to Walpole's last letter to her, which he dictated to Kirgate 15 January 1797, six weeks before he died.

The letter that went through the post is not at Farmington; what I am saving is Kirgate's copy of it on which Walpole wrote the date, the last line, and his signature, "O."

Jan. 15, 1797

My dear madam,

You distress me infinitely by showing my idle notes, which I cannot conceive can amuse anybody. My old-fashioned breeding impels me every now and then to reply to the letters you honour me with writing, but in truth very unwillingly, for I seldom can have anything particular to say; I scarce go out of my own house, and then only to two or three very private places, where I see nobody that really knows anything, and what I learn comes from newspapers, that collect intelligence from coffee-houses; consequently what I neither believe nor report. At home I see only a few charitable elders, except about fourscore nephews and nieces of various ages, who are each brought to me about once a year, to stare at me as the Methusalem of the family, and they can only speak of their own contemporaries, which interest me no more than if they talked of their dolls, or bats and balls. Must not the result of all this, Madam, make me a very entertaining correspondent? And can such letters be worth showing?

Duchess of Grafton, *découpure* of herself and her baby daughter.

My Dear Mm To Lady ———   Jan. 1797

You distress me infinitely by shewing my idle Notes about, which I cannot conceive can amuse any body. My old fashioned Breeding impels me every now & then to reply to the Letters you honour me with writing, but in truth very unwillingly, for I seldom can have anything particular to say; I scarce go out of my own House, and then only to two or three very private Places, where I see nobody that really knows any thing, and what I learn comes from Newspapers, that collect Intelligence from Coffee-houses, consequently, what I neither believe nor report. At Home I see only a few charitable Elders, except about Fourscore Nephews and Nieces of various Ages, who are each brought to me about once a Year, to stare at me as the Methusalem of the Family, and they can only speak of their own Cotemporaries, which interest me no more than if they talked of their Dolls, or Bats and Balls. Must not the Result of all This, Madam, make me a very entertaining Correspondent? and can such Letters be worth shewing? or can I have any Spirit when reduced to dictate? Oh, my good Madam, dispense with me from such a Task, and think how it must add to it to apprehend such Letters being shewn. Pray send me no more such Laurels, which I desire no more than their Leaves when decked with a Scrap of Tinsel, and stuck on Twelfth Cakes that lye on the Shop boards of Pastry Cooks at Christmas: I shall be quite content with a Sprig of Rosemary thrown after me, when the Parson of the Parish commits my Dust to Dust * till then pray, Madm accept the respect of your ...

Lord Orford died in six weeks after the date of this Letter.

It was the last Letter Lord Orford wrote & the last line is alone written by him. There in this Volume will be found the first Letter & the last Letter he ever wrote. J.W. Waller Aug. 1832

This note was written by Miss Berry the Editor of the Letters by permission of the Hon. Anne Seymour Damer ...... J.W. Waller

Horace Walpole to Lady Ossory, 15 January 1797.

or can I have any spirit when so old and reduced to dictate? Oh, my good Madam, dispense with me from such a task, and think how it must add to it to apprehend such letters being shown. Pray send me no more such laurels, which I desire no more than their leaves when decked with a scrap of tinsel, and stuck on Twelfth-cakes that lie on the shop-boards of pastry-cooks at Christmas: I shall be quite content with a sprig of rosemary thrown after me, when the parson of the parish commits my dust to dust. Till then, pray, Madam, accept the resignation of

Your ancient servant,
O.

Walpole's letters to Lady Ossory outnumber all others except those to Mann. There are 450 of them and they are the best, I think, he ever wrote. She was for him the ideal correspondent because, buried in the country with her kind but dull husband, she longed for news of the great world she had lost when divorced by Grafton for *crim. con.* with Ossory, and Walpole compassionately sent her the news in his most carefully composed and humourous style. If he kept her letters, they were returned to her on his death, as his will directed letters from living persons should be, but Vernon Smith couldn't find them in 1848 when he brought out his edition of Walpole's letters to her and I have found only one. While trying to identify Walpole's letters at Farmington to and from unknown correspondents, I discovered one of a few lines in a large flowery hand that had been at Upton. Walpole (a paper-saver) wrote some notes for his *Memoirs* on the back of it and I filed it with them. That it was from Lady Ossory is proved by comparison with a letter of hers to George Selwyn in the Society of Antiquaries. Walpole's use of her letter as scrap paper suggests that he did not keep her letters and that their destruction occurred more than a century before the fire in the muniment room at Euston, the Duke of Grafton's house, where her letters would have gone on her death had they survived.

Anne Liddell was the only child of the first Lord Ravensworth. In 1756 at the age of eighteen she married the third Duke of Grafton, by whom she had a daughter and a son. It was not a model marriage, for she had "a violent itch for play" and he had sixteen illegitimate children, a total in excess of the most tolerant marriage counsellor's allowance. Among his mistresses was Nancy Parsons whose history, according to Lady Louisa Stuart in one of her notes on the Selwyn correspondence, "almost rivals that of Ninon l'Enclos." The Graftons tried a trip abroad to rescue their marriage. "I announce her Grace of Grafton, a passion of mine,"

Walpole wrote Mann in 1761 before the Graftons set out for Florence. She was, Walpole said, "not a regular beauty, but one of the finest women you ever saw, and with more dignity and address. She is one of our first great ladies." Not only did the Graftons travel together, they had another son; but they separated in 1765.

The following year Walpole commended to the Duchess's attention the second Earl of Upper Ossory, whom he had met in Paris and found "one of the properest and most amiable young men I ever knew. . . . If you don't like [him] much, I shall wonder, Madam." No letter of recommendation was ever more successful, for within three years the Duchess bore Lord Ossory a daughter. There is little about this in Walpole's letters. He called it "an event I am very sorry for, as I wish well to both sides," but when the Duke of Grafton turned against General Conway, Walpole turned against him and wrote the phrase that has become the Duke's epitaph: "The Duke of Grafton, like an apprentice, thinking the world should be postponed to a whore and a horse-race."

Two months before her baby was born the Duchess retired to Richmond where the divorce proceedings show she saw only her parents and Lord Ossory. The depositions of the witnesses (who were mostly servants) fill 199 pages. Everyone testified that Lord Ossory was frequently with the Duchess. Robert Falgate, one of her footmen, recalled how some months before the baby was born he saw the Earl of Euston [then aged seven] "pushing and thumping at his mother's door. He called several times to her Grace and said, 'Mamma let me in.' " Robert Falgate "heard Mrs Duparg, her Grace's maid, call out and say 'My Lord Euston, your Mamma is not within,' and his Lordship said she was within: and the deponent . . . said that her Grace was then at home, and Lord Ossory was with her." There is a good deal about not ringing for candles when Lord Ossory was in the house, but the account was written with decorum.

Three days after the Duchess was divorced she married Ossory. After they returned from a trip abroad, it was not to the glory Lady Ossory had known as the Duchess of Grafton. Divorced women were banished from the Court of George III, and although the smart world did not enjoy going to Court, it was humiliating to be excluded. To make matters worse, her former husband had become Prime Minister, so secure in public life that he carried his latest mistress to the opera even before the Queen. Lady Ossory's first child by Ossory was Lady Anne Fitzpatrick, and Walpole's letters are, as one would expect, full of affectionate references to her.

Lady Ossory took her amiable young husband (he was eight years her junior) to Ampthill, his Bedfordshire estate, where she remained, except for rare excursions to town, until she died in 1804. When the Duke of Queensberry visited them in the first year of their marriage he reported to George Selwyn that the Ossorys "live but a dull life, and there must be a great deal of love on both sides not to tire." As time went on Lady Ossory withdrew her husband from politics and had him give up his regiment. She permitted him to continue his racing, but he was miserable at Newmarket without her. Buried in the country with him she depended upon her London friends for the news of the world in which she had once been so shining a figure. She corresponded with Horace Walpole, George Selwyn, and her sister-in-law, Lady Holland, apologizing to all for being a dull correspondent. "I can write to you about nothing but the first notes of the blackbirds, and the first opening of the buds, which are very interesting to me, but not very amusing at second hand." She had two more daughters by Ossory and adored them; the country with her children was preferable to London with its censoriousness, yet she counted on her friends in the great world to keep her informed of everything that went on.

Walpole sent her all the latest chit-chat, who was in, who out, who was marrying whom and how much was being settled on the young people, who was giving balls, who was dying. He amused her with accounts of the new books and plays, of Mr Herschel's new planet, Captain Cook's new islands, and Sir Joseph Banks's new birds and beasts. He wrote verses for her and her youngest Ossory daughters. It can be imagined what Walpole's letters meant to her. She showed them about and praised them to the skies. He scolded her for it; she would spoil everything by making him self-conscious. "You distress me infinitely by showing my idle notes," his last letter to her began, and there is no doubt he meant it. Posterity was in the back of his mind, but he didn't want her talking about it. I think he was more in love with her than with any other woman in his life. In one of his early letters to her he might be thinking of her as a successor to the Grifona who had contributed to his education as a young man in Florence.

Where, I wondered, were the originals of his letters? They were first printed in 1848, by Vernon Smith, Lord Lyveden, after which they vanished. When Mrs Toynbee was preparing her edition in 1900 she corresponded with Lord Castletown, who was then the head of the Fitzpatrick family as Lord Ossory had been in his day. "Lord Castletown has succeeded in finding out where the letters are," he wrote Mrs Toynbee, "but as they are in Stranger's hands it may be some time before he gets them." Three years later his agent closed the correspondence with "there is some doubt if they are still in existence." This suggested that Stranger had put the letters into the fire, but to edit so large and important a correspondence from a nineteenth-century text would be deplorable. I had to hunt for the originals.

My first move was a failure. The current Lord Lyveden, the great-grandson of the letters' first editor, was the most obvious person to approach, but no one, not even the *Peerage,* knew what had become of him. His sister did not answer my letter. The *Peerage* showed several collaterals and there was always Somerset House and its wills, but I had become skeptical of wills and collaterals as a means of finding missing family papers. Then English friends persuaded me to use the "Agony Column" of the *Times.* I had heard that its "Personals," "Come home. I love you, Alice," really meant, "It is safe to land the opium at Hull on Tuesday," and believed that it was not the place for the Yale Walpole; but, No, I was assured, "everybody" used the Personal Column.

R. W. Chapman and Dudley Massey helped me with my advertisement: "HORACE WALPOLE. Mr W. S. Lewis, Brown's Hotel, Dover Street, W.1., is anxious to secure information of the whereabouts of letters to and from Horace Walpole for use in the Yale Edition of Horace Walpole's Correspondence." This appeared for three consecutive days with prompt results. I heard from owners of old laces and second-hand Rolls-Royces; two young women offered their companionship. A lady in Belgrave Square wrote that she had hundreds of Walpole's letters, but they turned out to be the printed volumes of the 1848 edition. I was about to cross off the Agony Column as another failure when this letter arrived:

> Bishop's Lydeard House
> Taunton
>
> Aug. 4, 1935
>
> Dear Sir,
>
> I notice an advertisement in The Times for correspondence of Horace Walpole. I have thirty years between him and his cousin Lady Ossory—these were all published by my grandfather the Rt Honble Vernon Smith, the first Lord Lyveden: so it is possible they may be of no use to you.
>
> Yrs faithfully,
> R. Vernon

Lady Ossory was not Walpole's cousin, but that was a small error. I called Mr Vernon on the telephone because we were sailing soon and there was no time for the gavotte of correspondence. Were these the originals of Walpole's letters, I asked with the Belgrave Square lady in mind, or was he referring to the edition of them his grandfather published in 1848? These were the manuscripts, Vernon replied; at least they were written in ink on paper. That sounded like manuscript, all right. Might I go down that afternoon to see them? No, he was just about to leave for a week's yachting at Cowes.

"Look here," he said suddenly, "I don't know anything about you, but you are staying at Brown's, so you must be all right. I'll send them up to you." This seemed too hazardous and there is the axiom: a house that has one fine thing will have others. It was left that we should call at Bishop's Lydeard House Monday-week after lunch.

It proved to be a lovely Queen Anne house protected from the road by a high brick wall. It was in confusion because the Vernons, fresh from Cowes, had not yet put away their bags, the drawing-room was being done up, and the cook had just left. When Vernon let us in, the slight awkwardness of the occasion was heightened by his wearing a suit identical to mine. Later we found we had a London tailor in common who thought it quite safe to sell the same pattern to customers who lived as far apart as Bishop's Lydeard in Somerset, and Farmington, Connecticut.

Vernon led us into a small library on the left. "Well, there they are!" and he waved at a pile of letters on a shelf.

There they were, the letters allegedly destroyed in Ireland a generation earlier, one of the most brilliant collections of letters ever written.

"But," I said, "there aren't four hundred letters here."

"How do you know there should be four hundred?" Vernon asked quickly.

When I said I thought he would find there were exactly 400 in his grandfather's edition he looked it up and found that the last letter, the famous "Pray send me no more such laurels," was numbered four hundred.

"Shouldn't we count them?" I asked.

Vernon got out an aged card table; we put on our spectacles and went to work, releasing the letters from the corset strings that had cut cruelly into their edges. There were only 279 out of the 400, but Vernon found four more when he went to have a look at the place where they were kept. At this juncture his wife burst into the room, flourishing a beautiful tortoise-shell ear trumpet and full of apologies for not being on hand when we arrived, but she was trying to get a new cook from Taunton.

"Mr Lewis says there should be more letters, darling. Have you any idea where they could be?"

Mrs Vernon disappeared and returned almost at once with another batch that she tossed on the table and hurried off; a cook was about to telephone. The new letters came to about a hundred. After we had counted them Mrs Vernon made a third entrance.

"Sorry, dear, Mr Lewis says there must be more still."

"Was there ever such a man!" she said and left abruptly, returning at once with still another batch and departing again.

I wanted to find the letters, my advertisement said, "for use in the Yale Edition of Horace Walpole's Correspondence," as I now reminded Vernon, and I added one must, if possible, edit from the originals.

Mrs Vernon swept into the room for the fourth time as I said this.

"You are not wanting to carry off the family papers to *America?*" she asked, her ear trumpet at the ready. (She pronounced "America" with the inflection of extreme distaste that some Britons used at the time.) Since carrying the letters to America was just what I was hoping to do and since Vernon did not seem averse, I was less valiant than I should have been under the power of Mrs Vernon's gaze, voice, and ear trumpet. I can't recall what I faltered out in my abasement, but I was thankful when she bore me away to her bedroom to admire the drawing of Lady Ossory by William Hamilton that was given to Walpole in 1773.

At tea Mrs Vernon asked where we were spending the night.

"At Dunster," I replied.

"At the inn?"

"No."

"At the *Castle?*"

"Yes."

This changed everything, for it introduced a common friend, Geoffrey Luttrell, whose family acquired Dunster Castle in 1365, and who had asked us to stay with him whenever we were in his neighborhood. I told the Vernons that I would like to buy the letters, but if they didn't want to sell them, couldn't I, please, have them photostated? The British Museum would do it, but many of the letters had been cut into by the corset strings and I said that we would repair them well at home. The Vernons promised to let me have their decision in the morning. During the evening they prudently called the Castle to make certain we really were there. When we stopped at Bishop's Lydeard House on our way home the letters were ready for me to make what use I would of them for a year.

On landing in New York I took them to the Public Library where its friendly Librarian, Harry Lydenberg, put the manuscript repairing section at my disposal. The letters were mended and the worst damaged were put on silk. Then the whole collection was photostated and sent to Farmington where I found that fifty of the letters were unpublished. Were there still fifty more at Bishop's Lydeard? The day before we got there in 1936 Mrs Vernon found them in the attic.

How had Vernon happened to answer my advertisement? He read it, he told me later, on the first morning it appeared while he and his wife were on their way to Scotland and he had nothing else to read. "I think I'll answer this fellow," he said to his wife. She urged him not to, but on the return journey two days later he noticed my third appearance in the Agony Column and said, "I *will* write him." Before our arrival Mrs Vernon prudently took out half the letters, as she later confessed.

On Lady Ossory's death the letters went to her son by the Duke of Grafton, the little boy who pounded on her door and called for his mamma while she was with Lord Ossory. His son, the 5th Duke, turned them over to Vernon Smith, who published 400 of them. A generation later when his house in Eaton Square was broken up, Robert Vernon saw the letters lying about unwanted in the library and took them. They had been copied by a clerk at Bentley's for £16 (Mrs Vernon kindly gave me the Account of Publication and Sale of the book). The clerk's heart was not in his work, for he overlooked fifty letters. Thirty of them were written in 1778 when Walpole was at the height of his epistolary powers. We read of Dr Franklin and General Washington and the hatefulness of a war in which Englishmen fought Englishmen, but world events remain where they belong in an intimate correspondence, in the background. Of more concern to Walpole and Lady Ossory was the news brought to him one day when, as he was about to set off on a visit, the postman handed him a letter that told of the imminent death of Lord Ossory's sister, Lady Holland. "It was," Walpole wrote Lady Ossory, "one of those moments in which nothing is left to us but resignation and silence. . . . Life seems to me as if we were dancing on a sunny plain on the edge of a gloomy forest when we pass in a moment from glare to gloom and darkness."

And a month later:

I have fallen into a taste that I never had in my life, that of music. The swan, you know, Madam, is drawing towards its end, when it thinks of warbling. . . . I am quite enchanted with Mr Gammon, the Duke of Grafton's brother-in-law. It is the most melodious voice I ever heard. . . . I was strolling in the gardens [of Hampton Court] in the evening with my nieces, who joined Lady Schaub and Lady Fitzroy, and the former asked Mr Gammon to sing. His taste is equal to his voice, and his deep notes, the part I prefer, are calculated for the solemnity of Purcell's music, and for what I love particularly, his mad songs and the songs of sailors. It was moonlight and late, and very hot, and the lofty façade of the palace, and the trimmed yews and canal, made me fancy myself of a party in Grammont's time—so you don't wonder that by the help of imagination I never passed an evening more deliciously. When by the aid of some historic vision and local circumstance I can romance myself into pleasure, I know nothing transports me so much. . . . I sometimes dream, that one day or other somebody will stroll about poor Strawberry and talk of Lady Ossory—but alas! I am no poet, and my castle is of paper, and my castle and my attachments and I, shall soon vanish and be forgotten together!

Choice 18
Mary Berry's Sketch Book

Walpole wrote Lady Ossory, 11 October 1788:

If I have picked up no recent anecdotes on our common, I have made a much more, to me, precious acquisition. It is the acquaintance of two young ladies of the name of Berry, whom I first saw last winter, and who accidentally took a house here with their father for this season. Their story is singular enough to entertain you. The grandfather, a Scot, had a large estate in his own country; £5000 a year, it is said; and a circumstance I shall tell you, makes it probable. The eldest son married for love a woman with no fortune. The old man was enraged and would not see him. The wife died and left these two young ladies. Their grandfather wished for an heir male, and pressed the widower to re-marry, but could not prevail—the son declaring he would consecrate himself to his daughters and their education. The old man did not break with him again, but much worse, totally disinherited him, and left all to his second son, who very handsomely gave up £800 a year to his elder brother. Mr Berry has since carried his daughters for two or three years to France and Italy, and they are returned the best informed and the most perfect creatures I ever saw at their age. They are exceedingly sensible, entirely natural and unaffected, frank, and being qualified to talk on any subject, nothing is so easy and agreeable as their conversation, nor more apposite than their answers and observations. The eldest, I discovered by chance, understands Latin, and is a perfect French-woman in her language. The younger draws charmingly, and has copied admirably Lady Di's gypsies, which I lent her, though the first time of her attempting colours.

They are of pleasing figures; Mary, the eldest, sweet, with fine dark eyes, that are very lively when she speaks, with a symmetry of face that is the more interesting from being pale. Agnes, the younger, has an agreeable sensible countenance, hardly to be called handsome, but almost. She is less animated than Mary but seems out of deference to her sister to speak seldomer, for they dote on each other, and Mary is always praising her sister's talents. I must even tell you, Madam, that they dress *within* the bounds of fashion, though fashionably; but without the excrescences and balconies with which modern hoydens overwhelm and barricado their persons. In short, good sense, information, simplicity and ease characterize the Berrys—and this is not particularly mine, who am apt to be prejudiced, but the universal voice of all that know them. The first night I met them, I would not be acquainted with them, having heard so much in their praise, that I concluded they would be all pretensions. The second time, in a very small company, I sat next to Mary, and found her an angel, inside and out. Now, I don't know which I like best, except Mary's face, which is formed for a sentimental novel but is ten times fitter for a fifty times better thing, genteel comedy.

This delightful family comes to me almost every Sunday evening, as our region is too *proclamatory* to play at cards on the seventh day—I do not care a straw for cards, but I do disapprove of this partiality to the youngest child of the week, while the other poor six days are treated as if they had no souls to be saved.

I forgot to tell you that Mr Berry is a little merry man with a round face, and you would not suspect him of so much feeling and attachment. I make no excuse for such minute details, for if your Ladyship insists on hearing the humours of my district, you must for once indulge me in sending you two pearls that I found in my path.

The Berrys were aged twenty-four and twenty-three when they met Walpole. He was seventy. Pinkerton reports a rumour, which Macaulay, Thackeray, and Cunningham later spread, that before his death Walpole offered marriage to both Berrys in succession; but what actually took place is made clear by Charles Fulke Greville in his *Journal of the Reign of Queen Victoria, 1832–1852.* He called on Miss Berry one day in 1843 "and found her in great indignation at [T. Crofton] Croker's recent article in the 'Quarterly' upon the series just published of Lord Orford's letters to Mann, angry on his account and on her own. Croker says, what has been often reported, that Lord Orford offered to marry Mary Berry, and on her refusal, to marry Agnes. She says it is altogether false. Walpole never thought of marrying Agnes, and what passed with regard to herself was this: The Duchess of Gloucester was very jealous of his intimacy with the Berrys, though she treated them with civility. At last her natural impetuosity broke out, and she said to him, 'Do you mean to marry Miss Berry or do you not?' To which he replied, 'That is as Miss Berry herself pleases'; and that, as I understood her, is all that passed about it." "Let me repeat to both," Walpole wrote 26 February 1791, "that distance of place and time can make no alteration in my friendship: It grew from esteem for your characters and understandings and tempers, and became affection from your good-natured attentions to me, where there is so vast a disproportion in our ages." It was a thoroughly commonsensical relationship on both sides. Walpole and the Berrys delighted in each other's company, and that was that.

"I write to you two just as I should talk, the only comfortable kind of letters." This is proved in the letters where he couldn't write further because of the gout and dictated the remainder to Kirgate in the same tone and manner. The subjects he wrote about to the Berrys are much the same as those in his other intimate correspondences—great names and events and entertaining trivialities—but to the Berrys there is more neighbourhood gossip and more of his own hopes and fears. The reports of world events come less and less from the actors themselves and more and more from newspapers, which Walpole abused while he quoted them. We get occasional glimpses of the actors, as on the night he met Mme du Barry at Queensberry House just before she returned to France and the guillotine, and he discussed with her, in a postscript to his French visits her overthrow of his friends the Choiseuls twenty years earlier, but there is more in the letters of Twickenham and Richmond and Hampton Court. The Pepyses' little boy Harry, who is one day to become the Bishop of Sodor and Man, falls from a chaise and breaks his arm; partridges have arrived from Houghton and will be given to Lady Cecilia Johnston; the Berrys' Tonton has been clipped and his nose is an ell long. Later, however, Walpole reports that "Tonton's nose is not, I believe, grown longer, but only come to light by being clipped. When his beard is recovered, I dare say he will be as comely as my Jupiter Serapis. In his taste he is much improved, for he eats strawberries, and is fond of them, and yet they never were so insipid from want of sun and constant rain."

"As delightful as ever," we think when reading Walpole's letters to the Berrys although his distress over their Channel crossing and Mary's bumping her nose in Pisa is excessive. Mrs Damer speaks of "his grand fusses." They naturally increased as he got older and his concern for the Berrys grew. We are reminded of Mme du Deffand's promises to stop fretting and scolding and how she broke them before she finished her letter.

When the Berrys returned from their long European sojourn in 1791, they moved into Little Strawberry Hill and were the old man's constant companions until he died six years later. This ideal arrangement for both sides developed a somewhat disturbed undercurrent. The young women were not free from restlessness and Mary had to conduct her furtive love-affair with General O'Hara, which came to naught, in fear of Walpole's discovering it. I acquired four of Mrs Damer's small notebooks, 1791–97, in the second Waller Sale. They are addressed to Mary Berry although not by name. The sort of thing Mrs Damer wrote is,

I love your dignity as much as my own and enter into every word you said about him this morn—you understand me—You looked so low, so uncomfortable and so tired tonight, that tho' it is late I cannot go to bed in peace without telling you how much I felt and regretted it—for tho' I can seldom have the comfort of relieving, I must ever share your disquiets—perhaps, nay very likely, it proceeded from nothing particular, I know too well the numberless, nameless things that smart, and agonize a mind "too painfully alive all o'er." I know that there is but one relief, which is the sympathizing bosom of some kindred being—that being exists both to you and to me, and tho' not alwas mutually within our reach—let us bless God . . . suffer, and be thankful.

Twenty years earlier Mrs Damer had been the subject of "A Sapphick Epistle" that made her partiality to her own sex clear. Strephon was perfectly safe with her, but Chloe was not.

The biographies of her by Percy Noble, 1908, and in the *DNB* are patterns of nineteenth-century decorum without a hint of her self-centeredness. The end of her marriage to John Damer, the eldest son of Lord Milton, is described by Walpole in a letter to Horace Mann of 20 August 1776. "On Thursday Mr Damer supped at the Bedford Arms in Covent Garden, with four common women, a blind fiddler and no other man. At three in the morning he dismissed his seraglio, bidding each receive her guinea at the bar, and ordering Orpheus to come up again in half an hour. When he returned, he found a dead silence and smelt gunpowder. He called, the master of the house came up, and found Mr Damer sitting in his chair, dead, with a pistol by him, and another in his pocket. The ball had not gone through his head, nor made any report. On the table lay a scrap of paper with these words, 'The people of the house are not to blame for what has happened which was my own act.' This was the sole tribute he paid to justice and decency!" Mrs Damer's attitude towards Walpole, who loved her as a child of his own, is seen in a letter from her to Miss Berry after Walpole had been ill. She wrote, "I am sure when I think of *what* his dinners are, and *how* he eats them, I wonder he and his cat are not sick together every day for their dessert." Walpole made Mrs Damer his executrix, left her £4000, the life use of Strawberry Hill with £2000 to maintain it, and in the end the residue of his estate, some £40,000. Her final return for the affection he gave her from her birth was to have all his letters to her destroyed after her death.

Then there is the shadowy figure of Lady Mary Churchill, "sa chère soeur," as Mrs Damer called her. Walpole had stood godfather to her children and grandchildren, had written her hundreds of letters now lost, and loved her best of his brothers and sisters. She eyed the younger women jealously as she hovered about Strawberry and they banded against her. Finally, there is Walpole's favorite niece, the Duchess of Gloucester, whose jealousy of the Berrys did not escape him. All her life she turned to him for the counsel and support she did not get from her father. Had she followed his advice not to marry the duke she would have been a happier woman, but she was not one to listen to others; a handsome, unlovable, person, whose portrait by Hoare has been, I am happy to say, brought to the New Library at Farmington since I began this chapter.

The object I am saving in this Choice is a modest one, Mary Berry's sketch book. We have at Farmington only two other objects that belonged to her, a black lace parasol that came from her relations the Munro Ferguson family of Raith and a beautiful gold repeating watch that was made for Walpole in 1741 and given by him to her, as is noted on its back. We also have a miniature of her when young that I keep with them, but they are not as close to her as her rather shabby sketch book. It is oblong, covered with striped Italian paper in green, red, and yellow, and on it she wrote

MB

1790

Pisa

Inside is her bookticket, a cluster of strawberry blossoms, leaves, and fruit between her name and *Inter Folia Fructus*. I bought it from Sotheran in 1925. The first drawing is a street, "Pisa 1791." Miss Berry was happier with buildings than with trees, which she drew with spectacular unsuccess. Village churches were her forte and there are two views of Goodwood that delighted Walpole because of his affection for the Richmonds— his large correspondence with whom has so unfortunately disappeared. Miss Berry's sketch book is markedly inferior to Agnes's, which is also at Farmington, but one feels it is closer to Walpole. "You are learning perspective to take views; I am glad," he wrote Mary, "can one have too many resources in one's self? Internal armour is more necessary to your sex than weapons to ours. You have neither professions nor politics nor ways of getting money like men, in any of which, whether successful or not, they are employed. Scandal and cards you will both always hate and despise as much as you do now; and though I shall not flatter Mary so much as to suppose she will ever equal the extraordinary talent of Agnes in painting, yet as Mary like the scriptural Martha is occupied in many things, she is quite in the right to add the pencil to her other amusements."

INTER FOLIA FRVCTVS

MARY BERRY

Bookplate of Mary Berry's Sketch Book.

"South Front of Goodwood" by Mary Berry.

Our chief interest in Miss Berry's later life is what she did for Walpole's reputation. It was not forgotten that she had been the closest friend of his declining years and, allegedly, might have been his wife. She was at the center of the talk that began when his will was read. It was said that he had left too much to the Duchess of Gloucester, too little to Kirgate, and nothing at all, Pinkerton objected, to Pinkerton; he was blamed for the death of Chatterton; he had been hateful to Mme du Deffand; J. W. Croker and Lord Liverpool agreed that he was "as bad a man as ever lived" because he had, they said, poisoned history at its source. Byron came to his rescue with equal extravagance in the Preface to *Marino Faliero*, 1821: "It is the fashion to underrate Horace Walpole; firstly, because he was a nobleman, and secondly, because he was a gentleman, but to say nothing of the composition of his incomparable letters, and of the *Castle of Otranto*, he is the 'Ultimus Romanorum,' the father . . . of the first romance and of the last tragedy in our language, and surely worthy of a higher place than any living writer, be he who he may."

Twelve years later in 1833 came Macaulay's attack on Walpole in the *Edinburgh Review*. Macaulay, rising thirty-three, boasted to his sister, "I have laid it on Walpole so unsparingly that I shall not be surprised if Miss Berry should cut me." Two or three weeks later, however, he is off to Miss Berry's soirée. "I do not know whether I told you that she resented my article on Horace Walpole so much that Sir Stratford Canning advised me not to go near her . . . You know that in *Vivian Grey* she is called Miss Otranto. I always expected that my article would put her into a passion, and I was not mistaken; but she has come round again, and sent me a most pressing and kind invitation the other day."

Macaulay's essay has had more influence on Walpole's reputation than all other comments on him combined. It is a caricature, but as in all good caricatures the victim is recognizable. Although every page contains untrue statements, there does emerge a distorted likeness. Miss Berry answered it seven years later in Bentley's edition of Walpole's *Letters*. Macaulay's picture of Walpole's character, she said, was "entirely and offensively unlike the original." She dismissed the untrue charges one by one, ending with the most serious, Walpole's alleged coldness of heart. She had decided to publish his letters to her and her sister to give proof "that the warmth of his feelings, and his capacity for sincere affection, continued unenfeebled by age."

There is no record of Macaulay and Miss Berry dining amicably after her defence, but there is at Farmington a statement not without interest written by George Bentley, the son of Miss Berry's publisher. It was given me by our hostess at Upton, Mrs Richard Bentley. "Miss Berry," George Bentley wrote, "had inoculated [the first Richard Bentley] with a feeling of affection for Walpole's character, and he could never bear to hear him ill spoken of . . . It was his great wish that his letters should be collected and chronologically arranged.

"Macaulay was consulted on the subject. His character of Walpole is well known, but Macaulay's opinion had modified in his later days as he confessed to Miss Berry, and as Miss Berry told my father."

Choice 19
Cole's Copy of *The Castle of Otranto*

When in March 1925 I went to London on my first Walpolian trip Chauncey Tinker, who had also just begun to collect, asked me to get him a first edition of *The Castle of Otranto*. "Any copy will do—a nice one of course." He paused, "and you may have the copy Walpole gave to William Cole." He picked on that one because Walpole's two letters about how he wrote the book were written to Cole, his chief antiquarian correspondent.

Maggs had a nice copy of the first *Castle of Otranto*, which I asked them to put with my books and to send Tink the next one they got. I justified this greediness by thinking, "Tink doesn't collect Walpole and I do." Fortunately, better behaviour saved me from what would have been an agonizing mistake, for on getting back to Farmington after giving the book to Tink I found a letter from Maggs that began, "We think you will be interested in a copy of *The Castle of Otranto* that has just come in. It is the copy Walpole gave William Cole." Cole wrote his name and "1765" on the title-page and below Walpole's pseudonym, "Onuphrio Muralto, Canon of the' Church of St Nicholas at Otranto," he added, "Wrote by the honble Horace Walpole, Esq." He also transcribed Walpole's two letters to him about writing the book. In the first one Walpole wrote, "If you will tell me how to send it, and are partial enough to me to read a profane work in the style of former centuries, I shall convey to you a little story-book, which I published some time ago, though not boldly with my own name, but it has succeeded so well, that I do not any longer entirely keep the secret: does the title, *The Castle of Otranto*, tempt you?" Two weeks later Walpole added,

I had time to write but a short note with *The Castle of Otranto*, as your messenger called on me at four o'clock as I was going to dine abroad. Your partiality to me and Strawberry have I hope inclined you to excuse the wildness of the story. You will even have found some traits to put you in mind of this place. When you read of the picture quitting its panel, did not you recollect the portrait of Lord Falkland all in white in my gallery? Shall I even confess to you

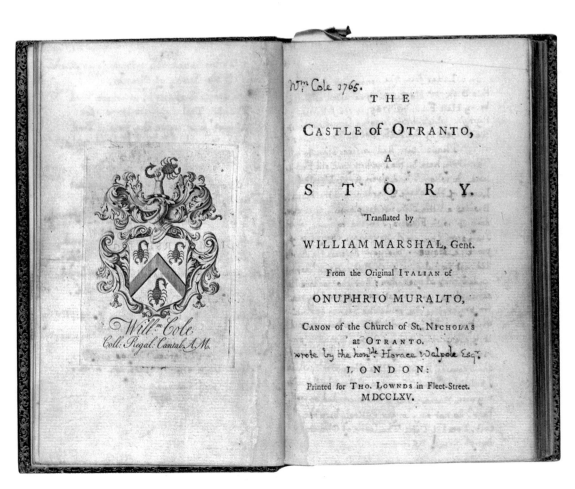

THE

CASTLE of OTRANTO,

A

S T O R Y.

Translated by

WILLIAM MARSHAL, Gent.

From the Original ITALIAN of

ONUPHRIO MURALTO,

CANON of the Church of St. NICHOLAS

at OTRANTO.

LONDON:

Printed for THO. LOWNDS in Fleet-Street.

MDCCLXV.

Title-page from William Cole's copy of *The Castle of Otranto*.

what was the origin of this romance? I waked one morning in the beginning of last June from a dream, of which all I could recover was, that I had thought myself in an ancient castle (a very natural dream for a head filled like mine with Gothic story) and that on the uppermost bannister of a great staircase I saw a gigantic hand in armour. In the evening I sat down and began to write, without knowing in the least what I intended to say or relate, work grew on my hands, and I grew fond of it—add that I was very glad to think of anything rather than politics—In short I was so engrossed with my tale, which I completed in less than two months, that one evening I wrote from the time I had drunk my tea, about six o'clock till half an hour after one in the morning, when my hand and fingers were so weary, that I could not hold the pen to finish the sentence, but left Matilda and Isabella talking, in the middle of a paragraph. You will laugh at my earnestness, but if I have amused you by retracing with any fidelity the manners of ancient days, I am content, and give you leave to think me as idle as you please.

This last was also addressed to us.

Cole transcribed verses "To the honourable and ingenious Author of the *Castle of Otranto*," that had appeared in the *St James's Chronicle*.

> Thou sweet Enchanter! at whose nod
>   The aery train of phantoms rise:
> Who dost but wave thy potent Rod,
>   And marble bleeds and canvas sighs.
>
> By thee decoy'd, with curious Fear
>   We tread thy Castle's dreary Round:
> Though horrid all we see, and hear,
>   Thy Horrors charm, while they confound.
>
> Full well hast thou persued the Road,
>   The magic Road thy master laid;
> And hast, with grateful skill, bestow'd
>   An off'ring worthy of his shade.
>
> Again his manners he may trace,
>   Again his characters may see,
> In soft Matild, Miranda's grace,
>   And his own Prospero in Thee.

This must have given Walpole great pleasure, for he said in the preface to the second edition of the book that Shakespeare was his model and he championed Shakespeare against Voltaire. How far Shakespeare's reputation in England ebbed in the eighteenth century is shown by Thomas

Davies's *Dramatic Miscellanies,* 1784. Davies quotes the passage in *Richard II* where the groom tells the deposed king how Bolingbroke, who deposed him, rode Richard's horse, Roan Barbary.

> Oh! how it yearn'd my heart when I beheld
> In London Streets . . .
> When Bolingbroke rode on Roan Barbary;
> That horse, which thou so often hast bestrid,
> That horse, that I so carefully have dress'd.

Davies observes: "This is one of those scenes which disgrace the tragedy of a great king." Walpole noted in the margin of his copy at Farmington, "Yet this is one of those exquisite and affecting touches of nature, in which Shakespeare excelled all mankind. To criticize it is being as tasteless as Voltaire."

Walpole borrowed freely from Shakespeare in the *Castle of Otranto.* "Angels of peace protect me!" cries Frederic upon seeing the figure from the other world, much as Hamlet cried before him, and Manfred shouts at the spectre, "Lead on! I will follow thee to the gulph of Perdition." Hippolita, "with a taper in her hand," enters the oratory alone in the manner of Lady Macbeth; Manfred bursts out about a phantom that might be Banquo's ghost at the feast and has to be reassured by his wife that "there are none here, but us, your friends." Isabella and Theodore creep about in caves like the one in *Cymbeline,* and are rescued in a scene that also ends with sword-play. When Frederic tells Theodore in the words of Friar Lawrence, "Young man, thou art too unadvised," when Matilda warns her lover in the balcony scene that "the morning dawns apace," readers are reminded of *Romeo and Juliet,* and they may see its nurse in Bianca. The only regrettable thing about the Walpole-Cole copy is that it was rebound in morocco by Rivière and one regrets the loss of Cole's binding, no matter how shabby it had become.

The easy runner-up in this Choice is John Carter's water-color drawing that Walpole described in "More Additions" to the '84 *Description,* "Procession in the Castle of Otranto, in water-color by John Carter." Carter added to this in the copy of the *Description* that Walpole bequeathed him and that is now at Farmington, "Was paid for it 20 guineas." On the back of the drawing Carter wrote, "Entry of Frederic into the Castle of Otranto, John Carter, inv. and del., 1790" and he showed it at the Royal Academy Exhibition of that year. Walpole's willingness to pay such a large sum for a water-color drawing proves his continuing affection for

John Carter's "Procession in the Castle of Otranto."

the book. He chose Carter to illustrate it because Carter was an antiquarian, the author of *Specimens of the Ancient Sculpture and Painting now
remaining in this Kingdom,* 1786, which he dedicated to Walpole. He
wrote, "[I] first found in you a Patron. Your kind encouragement gave
wings to my ambition to continue their [the *Specimens'*] publication, and
under your Auspices, and the Public's generous Assistance, I have been
able to bring to a Conclusion the first Volume: which with Gratitude and
Respect I dedicate to you, as some acknowledgment for the great obliga-
tions conferr'd on, Sir, Your very much obliged and faithful humble
Servant, John Carter. Nov. 1786." Its frontispiece, in which Edward the
Third and his family attended by warriors, courtiers, etc., makes a regal
entrance into a courtyard, foreshadows Frederic's entry into the courtyard of Otranto. Manfred ordered the gates

to be thrown open to [Frederic] and his train . . . In a few minutes the caval-
cade arrived. First came two harbingers with wands. Next a herald, followed
by two pages and two trumpets. Then an hundred foot-guards. These were
attended by as many horse. Two heralds on each side of a gentleman on horse-
back bearing a banner with the arms of Vicenza and Otranto quarterly—a
circumstance that much offended Manfred—but he stifled his resentment. Two
more pages. The knight's confessor telling his beads. Fifty more footmen, clad
as before. Two knights habited in complete armour, their beavers down, com-
rades to the principal knight. The 'squires of the two knights, carrying their
shields and devices. The knight's own 'squire. An hundred gentlemen bearing
an enormous sword, and seeming to faint under the weight of it. The knight
himself on a chestnut steed, in complete armour, his lance in the rest, his face
entirely concealed by his visor, which was surmounted by a large plume of
scarlet and black feathers. Fifty foot-guards with drums and trumpets closed
the procession, which wheeled off to the right and left to make room for the
principal knight.

How to get all this on a sheet of 23 by 19 inches would have daunted
a lesser Goth than Carter, but he managed it beautifully. Frederic's retinue
that has already arrived can be seen riding and marching into the distant
parts of the castle that had been inspired by King's College Chapel and
an Eleanor Cross (Carter ignored Walpole's hint in his second preface
that the Castle was Strawberry Hill). Walking beside Frederic is his
beadsman telling his beads; behind may be glimpsed the fifty footguards
with drums and trumpets. Immediately in front of him are men (hardly
a hundred) carrying the great sword, with Frederic in full armor, visor

down, lance at rest, entering on a superbly caparisoned horse. Gazing at him from a dais across the courtyard is Manfred, the villain, understandably perturbed, with Isabella, Frederic's daughter and the heroine of the tale, and Friar Jerome who is, I think, a portrait of Horace Walpole himself. Behind Manfred are the plumes of the giant helmet that crushed, no one knew how, Isabella's betrothed, the fifteen-year-old sickly Conrad, Manfred's only child. In the foreground, guarded by armed men with armor and weapons, is the castle's orchestra playing away. It includes a blind harpist, a bearded man thumping Turkish tabors, another man with a tuba, and two graceful girls, scantily clad, one of whom is playing a two-horned instrument, the other striking a triangle. Above and beyond the gate and drawbridge are towers inspired by German castles. I haven't begun to do justice to the drawing, but I hope I've suggested that it is the quintessence of the Gothic Revival and deserving of serious attention.

It was bought at the Strawberry Hill sale by the Rev. Horace Cholmondeley and descended to his great-grandson, the late General Sir Henry Jackson, a Dorset neighbor of Owen Morshead who brought us together. General Jackson very kindly let me have not only the drawing, but one of Walpole's copies of Watteau mentioned in Choice 3 and his annotated copy of McArdell's print after Walpole's portrait by Reynolds, which is Choice 26. The three pieces hang in our side hall and are a daily reminder of the General and Owen Morshead as well as of Horace Walpole, John Carter, and Watteau.

According to the first reviewers, the book's success was owing to its "highly finished" characters (*Monthly Review*) and the "spirit and propriety" of the narrative (*Critical Review*). Thomas Gray reported to Walpole from Cambridge that it made "some of us cry a little, and all in general afraid to go to bed o'nights." The first Lord Stanley of Alderley, a quarter of a century later, wrote to his sister how he read *The Castle of Otranto* to his party as they rowed from one of the Faroe Islands to another. "The scene," he reported, "was suitable to the subject. The fog just let us see the high rocks by which we rowed, and against which the sea broke into foam. We reached our ship . . . sorry to leave off the story before we knew to whom the great enchanted helmet belonged." The interest of the book's early readers was in the story itself.

The continuing success of *The Castle of Otranto* is one of the phenomena of English literature. There have been ninety editions of it, fifteen of them in this century including a recent one of 50,000 copies in Russia. The first of seven American editions was published in New York in 1801; later nineteenth-century editions appeared in Philadelphia and Hartford; three editions have been published in France, two in Germany, four in Italy where Bodoni of Parma printed the finest in 1791. Walpole's copies of it and of the handsome 1795 translation in London are at Farmington in morocco bindings worthy of them. Two of the five or six printed by Bodoni on vellum are also at Farmington.

In my Introduction to the edition published by the Oxford University Press in 1964 I quoted, as commentators on the *Castle of Otranto* always do, Walter Scott's praise of the book in his 1811 edition. He called it "remarkable not only for the wild interest of the story, but as the first modern attempt to found a tale of amusing fiction upon the basis of the ancient romance of chivalry," and he conceded to Walpole the applause "which cannot be denied to him who can excite the passions of fear and of pity." I am struck by his speaking of "the wild interest of the story," for I confess, quite quietly here, I have never felt any fear or pity in it; instead, I marvel how such a lucid and entertaining writer as Horace Walpole could have written so confused and clumsy a book. Gray's and his friends' delight in it came, I think, from the novelty of the book's setting, its pseudo-mediaeval speech, and its supernatural events. Richardson, Fielding, and Smollett had nothing like that. I am convinced by Henry James's transitions to the supernatural, but I find Walpole's ludicrous. Alfonso sighing and stepping out of his portrait is arresting, but when Manfred cries, "Lead on! I will follow thee to the gulph of Perdition," I do not yield to "the style of former centuries," but find Alfonso his own parody. Carter's drawing, on the other hand, leads us into a magical courtyard with Horace Walpole as Friar Jerome watching us from behind Manfred and Isabella as Frederic clanks across the drawbridge into the court and is welcomed by the Otranto heralds and orchestra. When Walpole was writing his letters he was talking easily to his correspondents, but when he wrote his novel he was being "literary." *The Castle of Otranto* must continue to be read by students as a landmark of English literature, yet it is not, I think, for others.

The eighteenth century's high regard for it is shown not only by the eighteen editions published then, but by contemporary illustrations of the story. There are thirty-four of them at Farmington bound in various copies of the book. Among them are two that suggest the artists failed to understand that Alfonso stepped off the canvas and down on to the floor, for they brought the whole picture down, frame and all. Much the best of these illustrations are four by Bertie Greatheed, aged fifteen, of Guy's Cliff, Warwick. Walpole wrote his father,

I have seen many drawings and prints made from my idle—I don't know what to call it, novel or romance—not one of them approached to any one of your son's four—a clear proof of which is, that not one of the rest satisfied the Author's ideas—It is as strictly, and upon my honour, true, that your son's conception of some of the passions has improved them, and added more expression than I myself had formed in my own mind; for example, in the figure of the Ghost in the Chapel, to whose hollow sockets your son has given an air of reproachful anger, and to the whole turn of his person, dignity. Manfred, in the last scene, has an uncertain horror, that shows he has not time to know what kind of agony he feels at what he has done. Such delineation of passions at so very youthful a period, or rather in boyhood, are indubitably indications of real genius, and cannot have issued from the instructions or corrections of a master.

Was there any way, Walpole asked, in which he might secure the originals or copies of them? The rest of the correspondence is missing, but the drawings—which make one think of Blake—were bound by Walpole in his copy of Bodoni's 1791 edition published in London by J. Edwards and are now at Farmington. These four drawings are far superior to the efforts of Greatheed's older amateur contemporaries and we join Walpole in lamenting the early death of the outstanding amateur of his time.

Choice 20

Walpole's Portfolio for His *Historic Doubts of the Life and Reign of Richard III*

"It occured to me," Walpole wrote in the Preface to his *Historic Doubts,* "that the picture of Richard the Third, as drawn by historians, was a character formed by prejudice and invention. I did not take Shakespeare's tragedy for a genuine representation, but I did take the story of that reign for a tragedy of imagination. Many of the crimes imputed to Richard seemed improbable; and, what was stronger, contrary to his interest."

"All I mean to show," Walpole began, "is that though [Richard] may have been as execrable as we are told he was, we have little or no reason to believe so. If the propensity of habit should still incline a single man to *suppose* that all he has read of Richard is true, I beg no more, than that person would be so impartial as to own that he has little or no foundation for supposing so.

"I will state the list of the crimes charged on Richard; I will specify the authorities on which he was accused; I will give a faithful account of the historians by whom he was accused; and will then examine the circumstances of each crime and each evidence; and lastly, show that some of the crimes were contrary to Richard's interest, and almost all inconsistent with probability or with dates, and some of them involved in material contradictions.

SUPPOSED CRIMES OF RICHARD THE THIRD.

1st. *His murder of Edward Prince of Wales, son of Henry the Sixth.*
2d. *His murder of Henry the Sixth.*
3d. *The murder of his brother George Duke of Clarence.*
4th. *The execution of Rivers, Gray, and Vaughan.*
5th. *The execution of Lord Hastings.*
6th. *The murder of Edward the Fifth and his brother.*
7th. *The murder of his own queen.*

To which may be added, as they are thrown into the list to blacken him, his intended match with his own niece Elizabeth, the penance of Jane Shore, and his own personal deformities.

Walpole became convinced as a young man that Richard had been maligned by the Lancastrian and Tudor historians who reported his reign; that is, Richard was an underdog and should be championed. When two eminent antiquarians called his attention to what they believed was the coronation roll, which showed that Edward V, far from having been murdered in the Tower by his uncle Richard, had walked at his coronation, Walpole determined to clear Richard of "the mob-stories" that put him "on a level with Jack the giant-killer." In his Preface he waved away possible criticism: his attempt, he said, was "mere matter of curiosity and speculation" of an idle man; he was ready to yield to better reasons, but not to " 'declamation.' " Unfortunately, the coronation roll turned out to be a wardrobe account of no relevance. This was disappointing, but it didn't weaken Walpole's desire to defend Richard.

Why did he get so excited about him? An explanation was given me years ago in London by the psychoanalyst Dr M. J. Mannheim that goes deeper than Walpole's stated wish to rescue Richard from the cupidity of Lancastrian and Tudor historians. This is that Walpole loved and hated his father; part of him regarded his father as a monster who had treated his adored mother badly; Richard was a monster; by defending Richard, Walpole was atoning for his suppressed hatred of Sir Robert. We are here at the point in biography beyond which, Plutarch tells us, there "is nothing but dark unpassable bogs, or Scythian cold, or frozen sea."

Walpole summed up his attitude towards Richard in a letter to a fellow-antiquary fifteen years after *Historic Doubts* appeared.

Give me leave in my own behalf to say, that if I am prejudiced, as probably I am, it is *against* those historians, not *for* Richard III. I did apprehend originally that I should be suspected of the latter, because when one contests popular prejudices, one is supposed to run into the contrary extreme. I do believe Richard was a very bad man—but I could not think him a weak one, which he must have been, had he acted in the absurd manner imputed to him. I am aware on the other side, that in so dark and ferocious an age, he and others may have acted very differently, and ventured on many steps, that would be preposterous in a more enlightened time—but then we ought to have a very good evidence of their having done so—and such evidence is very defective indeed.

Walpole's notes for the book are at Farmington. He kept them in the Glass Closet in a portfolio I am rescuing as this Choice. The 1842 Sale Catalogue called it "A portfolio containing original letters, deeds, extracts, etc. on the subject of the Historic Doubts on the Life of Richard III, written by Mr Walpole." It named some of his correspondents and added that the portfolio contained the proof sheets of the books' first edition, but it failed to mention Walpole's notes on the sources he used to write the book. Boone bought the lot for Lord Derby who put it into a linen case. The letters to Walpole about the book were those that Major Milner laid out around the billiard table for me at Knowsley in 1935. He didn't show me the other manuscripts in the portfolio, but their significance would have been lost on one unfamiliar with the immense complexities of Richard's story. Maggs bought the lot for me at Sotheby's in the 1954 Derby Sale. The reviewer of the sale in the *Times Literary Supplement* singled out the proof sheets, the only Walpolian ones I know of except those for the second edition of the *Royal and Noble Authors* already mentioned, but Walpole made few corrections in them and they are less interesting than other pieces in the lot.

The portfolio is now in a case worthier of its contents, but they have yet to be studied by a fifteenth-century specialist. His task will not be light, for Walpole jotted down his notes on slips of paper and left them in a general jumble. We'll see the same casual confusion when we come to his memoirs. Here in the portfolio is a scrap of six by four inches with 46 miscellaneous notes crowded to the margins on both sides. Next is a small card with five notes, including "H[enry] 7 did not reverse his Queen's Bastardy." A more extensive note quotes the late Lord Bolingbroke as saying "that the Ambassadors of France and Venice who were present at Richard's coronation wrote to their respective superiors that Richard was a handsome well made Prince." "By the favour of the Duchess of Choiseul," Walpole wrote, "I have had the Depot des affaires étrangères at Versailles carefully examined by the learned and ingenious Abbé Barthelemi, and with the same truth with which I have conducted this inquiry, I must declare that no such account is to be found among the state papers of the King of France. If I discover anything that makes against my own arguments, I shall declare it with the same impartiality. It is indifferent to me on which side the truth may come out, all my aim has been to lead to the discovery of it."

There are twelve and a half pages of manuscript references to the Harleian Manuscripts in the British Museum. Walpole listed them from

Memoranda, from Catalogue of Harleian MSS.

Vol. 1.

No. 16–22. | 18. Parliam. of Rich. 3?
No. 25. 31. | 28. a book in blue velvette — see it.
ib. | 29. old Annals.
No. 31.–35. | 33. a book that belonged to Humphrey D. of Gloster.
No. 35. — | 30. a letter of Sr Rob. Cecil. ✗
ib. — | 31. a letter of D. Essex. ✗
No. 36. —— | 27. a letter from Q. Eliz. to Czar, begging repres.
| 52. Instruct. to Willm Waad.
| 56–57. Letters of Sr R. Cecil ✗
| 59. Letter of Sr John Holles. ✗
| 60. letter of Sr R. Cecil. ✗
| 64. A Diary of Burleigh printed in ——— their papers ✗
No. 37. | 4. charge of Sr W. Mildes. & his answer ✗
39 — | 4. lett from Q. Eliz. to D. Treas. ✗
39–40 | 45. speech of Cath. Q. of Hertf. at her death. see it.
40.–42 | 3. print of Anne Boleyn's Coron. dinner. see it.
| 8. Kts of the Carpet.
| 12. persons present when Edw. 4ths son made Kt of Bath.
46.–49 | 3. 4. pieces relating to burial of Rich. D. of York.
| 5. a french letter abt Sr Ant. Widville. ✗
49–52 | a book that belonged to Rich. D. of Gloster.
50 | battle between E. of Salisb. son's & E. of North. sons.
69. | Challenges & Tilts.
| 17. Earl Tiptoft's Statutes. ✗ with pictures see them.
| 24 &c relating to Pr. Arthur & Q. Catherine.
| 37. Proclam. ag. Gentlemen, not to.
70. | 50. Writ by Rich. 1. to Archbp. for a tournament.
70–71. | 11. Catal. of Paul Dewes's books. 1610.
76.78 | 6. 7. 8. 9. relating to Sr T. Wyat. & his trial & epitaph.
| 12. letter of the Earl of Surrey. ✗
| 14. Verses by Sr T. Wyat.
| 27. note, Chaucer is called the laureat Poet. popishly laureat a corruption.
98. | 4. Dawson ——————
| 98. Manor of Ixworth.
98–99 | ———————————— W.

his printed copy of the *Catalogue,* which came to Farmington from the Library of Congress by exchange. So we have, most happily, not only Walpole's notes but his annotated source for them. The list of manuscripts has his characteristic crosses and dashes and an occasional "See it." That he went to the Museum to do so is proved by his quotations in *Historic Doubts* from the Harleian Manuscripts. For example, a footnote on page 39 of *Historic Doubts* exculpates Richard from charging his mother publicly with adultery. Walpole quoted an affectionate letter from Richard to her in Harleian Manuscript, no. 433.6. How, Walpole asked, could a son who wrote such a letter have said his mother was an adulteress? Opposite the reference to the letter in his copy of the printed *Catalogue* Walpole made a large asterisk in ink; and in his manuscript list he added "See this book" after "Letter of Richard 3d to his Mother." He confused matters by getting the Harleian Manuscript number wrong in his footnote and printing 2236.6 instead of 433.6, an error apparently unnoticed until now.

Dodsley published twelve hundred copies of *Historic Doubts* in 1768 and sold them so fast he began printing a second edition of one thousand copies the following day, a remarkable sale for the time. The book is a quarto with two illustrations by Vertue. The original of one of them, Richard and his Queen in its Walpolian frame, came to Farmington from Sotheby's in 1936. When I got the catalogue of the sale the drawing stood out as a "must" for me, but what was it worth? This was twenty years before Walpoliana shot into the stratosphere and the limit of £100 that I gave Maggs seemed extravagant, but it proved to be ample, for the drawing was knocked down to us at £2, less than half of what Miss Burdett-Coutts gave for it in 1842. The surviving collectors of the thirties look back to that time as to a lost paradise.

Historic Doubts caused a furor in the learned world when it appeared, for it is a pioneer work that challenged the traditional picture of Richard as a figure of unmitigated evil. Gray and Cole stood loyally by; Gibbon praised Walpole highly, but shared Hume's belief that Sir Thomas More's account of Richard was closer to the truth than Walpole's. Gibbon's copy, which Walpole gave him, is at Farmington, but has, alas, no notes. Among our other eighteen presentation copies are many to Walpole's antiquarian friends whose notes and comments in their copies will be of interest to future editors of the work, which continues to be, and doubtless always will be, controversial.

One of the strongest dissidents in 1768 was Dean Jeremiah Milles,

Richard III and His Queen by Vertue.

President of the Society of Antiquaries, of which Walpole was a member; another was the Rev. Robert Masters. He and Milles expressed their views in *Archaeologia,* the Society of Antiquaries' annual volume, whereupon Walpole rather foolishly resigned from the Society. He printed a *Reply to Dean Milles,* in six copies only, one of which is at Farmington.

His dismissal of Masters occurs in a letter to Cole, 7 April 1778, a letter that played an accidental part in launching the Yale Edition of Horace Walpole's Correspondence. In a talk to the Modern Language Association at New Haven in 1932 on the need for the new edition, a talk sponsored by Frederick A. Pottle, I pointed out that no one could open any edition of Walpole's letters at random and not need help a dozen times on the first page he read. I made this test and turned up the letter to Cole about Masters's attack on *Historic Doubts.* Walpole wrote, "I have now seen the second volume of the *Archaeologia.* . . . with Mr Masters's answer to me. If he had not taken such pains to declare it was written against my *Doubts,* I should have thought it a defence of them, for the few facts he quotes make for my arguments, and confute himself; particularly in the case of Lady Eleanor Butler; whom, by the way, he makes marry her own nephew, and not descend from her own family, because she was descended from her grandfather. This Mr. Masters is an excellent Sancho Panza to such a Don Quixote as Dean Milles! but enough of such goosecaps!" To explain all this a footnote of 500 words was ultimately written in the Yale Walpole.

Masters's attack in *Archaeologia* turned up again in 1944 after *Life Magazine* printed a six-page article, "Life Explores World's Finest Walpole Library." It was read by Mr Harold H. Nelson, Field Director of the Oriental Institute at Luxor, Egypt, which is part of the University of Chicago. He kindly wrote to say Walpole's own copies of the first twelve volumes of *Archaeologia* were in their Library. When I replied that I also had the twelve volumes in excellent condition and asked if there was any possibility of the Institute following other public institutions and exchanging their copies for mine, the librarian replied that he would be delighted to do so, but that the decision rested with Professor John A. Wilson at the University of Chicago. I began my letter to him, "Dear John, When we were exchanging little notes in the O.S.S. I had no idea that I would one day be writing you on a really important matter." He replied that so far as he was concerned I was more than welcome to Walpole's set, but that the person who had the final say about it was Professor Jesse H. Shera of the University Library. So I wrote, "Dear Jesse," for he had been my number one assistant in the O.S.S.'s Central Intelligence Division. The

Doutes historiques sur la vie et le règne de Richard III.

par Mr Horace Walpole

a Londres
chez J. Dodsley
dans le ~~Pall mall~~
1768

L'histoire n'est fondée que sur le témoignage des auteurs qui nous
l'ont transmise. Il importe donc extrêmement, pour la bien écrire,
de bien connoître que ce sont les auteurs. Rien n'en a négliger sur
ce point; le temps où ils ont vecu, leur naissance, leur patrie, la part
qu'ils ont eu aux Affaires, les moyens par les qu'ils ils ont été instruits, et
l'intérêt qu'ils y pouvoient prendre, sont des circonstances essentielles
qu'il n'est pas permis d'ignorer : de la dépend le plus ou moins d'autorité
qu'ils doivent avoir; et sans cette connoissance, on court risque très
souvent de prendre pour guide un historien de mauvaise foy, ou du
moins mal informé.

Hist. de l'Académie des Inscriptions Vol. X

Preface

La plusparst des historiens sont si incompetents pour le sujet qu'ils
encreprennent, qu'on pourroit mettre en doute, si les noms des temps
passés, qu'ils soient été capables de connoître les
évenements de leur propre temps, comme de la manière nous sont transmises par
l'ignorance et la mauvaise représentation. Toute l'histoire forte ancienne
sont de véritables fables, excepté celle des Juifs écrit par l'esprit saint.
Elles sont écrites
par des Prêtres, et ressemblées d'après leur rapport, et calculée seule-
ment pour donner une beauté idée de l'origine de chaque nation. les
Dieux et les demi Dieux sont les principaux acteurs, et on doit attendre
rarement de trouver la verité dans une histoire où les personnages sont les acteurs. les
historiens Grecs n'ont d'avantage, sur les Peuviens, que par la beauté
de leur langage, ou par ce qu'elle nous est plus familière.
Manço capac le fils du soleil est aussi sûrement l'âge sacré d'une
maison Royalle, que l'ancetre des Heraclides. Qui s'attend
à la vérité quand l'identité des personnes est incertaine? les actions d'une même
personne sont attribuées à plusieurs, et celles de plusieurs à une. On ne sait
pas s'il n'y a eu qu'un seul Hercule ou s'il y en a eu vingt.

First page of Louis XVI's translation of *Historic Doubts*.

Egyptian Government were much more loath to let the books come to
Farmington, but after a year they arrived. You can imagine with what
feelings I opened the second volume and hurried to Masters's article. I
was certain Walpole had annotated it profusely and I was quite right, but
he did so in pencil and some tidy custodian had carefully erased every one
of his notes.

Therefore, Walpole's set of *Archaeologia* is not the runner-up in this
Choice, nor is his copy (one of six only) of the *Historic Doubts* that he
printed at the Press in his 1770 *Works,* even though at the end of it he
bound in the manuscript of "Postscript to My Historic Doubts, written in
Febr. 1793" that was published in his 1798 *Works.* The Postscript begins,

It is afflictive to have lived to find in an Age called not only civilized but enlightened, in this eighteenth century, that such horrors, such unparalleled
crimes have been displayed on the most conspicuous Theatre in Europe, in
Paris, the rival of Athens and Rome. . . . by a Royal Duke, who has actually
surpassed all the guilt imputed to Richard the 3d: and who . . . will leave it
impossible to any future writer, how ever disposed to candour, to entertain
one historic doubt on the abominable actions of Philip Duke of Orleans.

After long plotting the death of his Sovereign, a victim as holy as, and infinitely superior in sense and many virtues to Henry 6th, Orleans has dragged
that sovereign to the block, and purchased his execution in public, as in public
he voted for it.

"That sovereign" provided the runner-up in this Choice. When Mme
du Deffand received her copy of the book from Walpole she was *extasiée,*
yet not as much as she wished to be because she had no English. She failed
to find a translator and died twenty years before the first French translation appeared in 1800. Walpole did not live to see it either, and so missed
what I think might have meant more to him than anything else in his
life. This was the knowledge that he had indirectly eased the last weeks of
the translator as he revised his manuscript while waiting for the mob to
come and drag him away to the guillotine. For the first French translator
of *Historic Doubts of the Life and Reign of Richard III* was Louis XVI,
and his much worked over manuscript is now at Farmington.

Choice 21

Manuscript of Walpole's Journal for 1769

The manuscript of Walpole's journal for 1769 came from Upton along with the manuscripts of Walpole's first and last memoirs, fragments of his printed memoirs, and many notes "written flying" for all of them. The title-page for the manuscript I am saving is, "Journal/of the most remarkable Events/ of/the reign of King George the third,/ from the beginning of the year/ 1769/ being a Supplement/to/The memoirs of/Mr Horace Walpole/carried on by Himself." It continues into 1771 with scattered jottings and newspaper cuttings. The whole runs to some 70,000 words, mostly on folio sheets. How Walpole used his journals is seen by the entry for 5 March 1770: "The House of Commons went on the affairs of America. Lord North proposed to repeal all the late duties but that on teas. Mr Conway was for the repeal of that also, as most men were persuaded a partial repeal would produce no content. Grenville so far agreed with the Rockingham part of the Opposition as to condemn a partial repeal, but too stiff to yield to any repeal, he went away without voting." This passage became in the *Memoirs of George III,* "On the 5th of March the House of Commons went upon the consideration of America. Lord North proposed to repeal all the late duties, but that on tea. *Mr Conway advised the repeal of that also,* most men believing that a partial repeal would produce no content. Grenville agreed in condemning, as the Rockingham party did too, a partial repeal; but, too obstinate to consent to any repeal, went away without voting, and the motion passed."

The manuscript of Walpole's first memoirs, which I believe he began in 1745, has the title, "Memoires. From the Declaration of the War with Spain," in 1739. The manuscript runs to about 7000 words with an epigraph that fits all the subsequent memoirs and journals, "Nothing extenuate nor set down aught in malice. Othello." Gray's letter of 15 December 1746 shows that he knew Walpole was engaged on this undertaking. "Among all the little folks, my godsons and daughters," he wrote, "I cannot choose but to inquire more particularly after the health of one; I mean

Page of Walpole's notes for his *Memoirs* 1769.

(without a figure) the Memoirs. Do they grow? Do they unite, and hold up their heads, and dress themselves? Do they begin to think of making their appearance in the world, that is to say, fifty years hence, to make posterity stare, and all good people cross themselves?"

"The War with Spain" has yet to be published, but when it appears readers will see that Walpole's intention in his later memoirs was already formed. "I write for Posterity, not for my contemporaries," he announced in this earliest of his memoirs, "and profess speaking my opinion for their information. . . . The intention of this work being to let my Readers rather into the character of the Actors, than into the minute Events of the Drama. The Laborious two hundred years hence may draw out a journal of what month the miscarriage happened before Toulon; or on what day the Battle of Dettingen was fought." Horace Walpole, who lived at the center of affairs and who knew all the chief persons in them, was revealing to us not only what happened, but how it happened. Let "the laborious," the drudges of history, look up the date of Dettingen, he would show us the characters of the men who brought it about.

He recorded in "Short Notes" that "about this time [1751] I began to write my memoirs. At first I intended only to write the history of one year." Gray wrote him in October 1751, "I rejoice to find you apply (pardon the use of so odious a word) to the history of your own times. Speak, and spare not. Be as impartial as you can; and after all, the world will not believe you are so, though you should make as many protestations as Bishop Burnet," who wrote in the Preface to the *History of His own Time*, "I writ with a design . . . to lay open the good and bad of all sides and parties as clearly and impartially as I myself understood it . . . without any regard to kindred or friends, to parties or interests. For I do solemnly say this to the world, and make my humble appeal upon it to the great God of truth, that I tell the truth on all occasions, as fully and freely as upon my best inquiry I have been able to find it out."

Far from ending his memoirs in 1751, Walpole carried them on forty years longer. Early in 1752 he recorded, "I sit down to resume a task, for which I fear posterity will condemn the author, at the same time that they feel their curiosity gratified. On reviewing the first part of these Memoirs, I find the truth rigidly told." They were, he said, his "favorite labor," yet only Gray, Bentley, Montagu, Mme du Deffand, and probably Conway knew he was writing them. He thought a great deal of their final disposition, ending up with a memorandum to his executors written less than a year before his death. A copy of it in Miss Berry's hand came to Farmington in the second Waller Sale. Walpole directed, "Not to be opened till after my will." The memorandum begins,

In my Library at Strawberry Hill are two wainscot chests or boxes, the larger marked with an A, the lesser with a B. I desire, that as soon as I am dead, my Executor and Executrix will cord up strongly and seal the larger box, marked A, and deliver it to the Honourable Hugh Conway Seymour, to be kept by him unopened and unsealed till the eldest son of Lady Waldegrave or whichever of her sons, being Earl of Waldegrave, shall attain the age of twenty-five years; when the said chest, with whatever it contains, shall be delivered to him for his own. And I beg that the Honourable Hugh Conway Seymour, when he shall receive the said chest, will give a promise in writing, signed by him, to Lady Waldegrave, that he or his Representatives will deliver the said chest unopened and sealed, by my Executor and Executrix, to the first son of Lady Waldegrave who shall attain the age of twenty-five years; the key of the said chest is in one of the cupboards of the Green Closet, within the Blue Breakfast Room, at Strawberry Hill, and that key, I desire, may be delivered to Laura, Lady Walde- grave, to be kept by her till her son shall receive the chest.
                                        (Signed) Hor. Walpole, Earl of Orford.
August 19, 1796.

These directions were carried out by his executors, Mrs Damer and her uncle Lord Frederick Campbell.

When Chest A was opened by the sixth Earl Waldegrave in 1810 it was found to contain twenty-three folio volumes of memoirs and journals from 1746 to 1791, a total of some three million words.

Memoirs of the Last Ten Years of the Reign of George the Second was published by John Murray in 1822. I have the drawings Bentley and Müntz made for them, thanks to Mrs Hallam Murray and the good offices of John Hodgson. Walpole describes the frontispiece, "The Author lean- ing on a globe of the world between Heraclitus and Democritus, presents his book to the latter. In the Landscape is a view of the Author's villa at Strawberry Hill near Twickenham, where the Memoirs were chiefly written." Richard Bentley brought out *Memoirs of the Reign of King George the Third* in 1845 and *Journal of the Reign of King George the Third from 1771 to 1783* in 1859. The manuscripts of them from 1784 to 1791 are at Farmington and will appear for the first time in the Yale Edi- tion of Horace Walpole's Memoirs.

The memoirs have suffered from their editors who cut out passages they thought indelicate, offensive to living persons, or just plain dull, and al- though they said they had indicated these omissions they often failed to do so. Doran, the editor of Walpole's Last Journals, printed newspaper cuttings Walpole pasted on the manuscript as if they were written by Walpole himself. One of Doran's footnotes is a classic of nineteenth-century editing. Walpole wrote of a naval engagement in which the English attacked the French with nineteen sail, the correct number. Doran printed the *nineteen* as *thirty-nine* and then accused Walpole of gross exaggeration. The reader flounders about in the *Memoirs* without the help of dates or references. The easy style of the letters is abandoned for historical austerity as may be seen by comparing Walpole's lively letter to Hertford of 15 February 1764 about the great debate on general warrants and the commitment of Wilkes to the Tower with Walpole's stark report of the session in the *Memoirs*. But help for the reader is on the way. Fortunately, Walpole preserved earlier drafts, or what he called "foul copies," which are with the final draft at Chewton. The Yale Edition of Horace Walpole's Memoirs is being edited by the man best qualified to do it, John Brooke, the co-editor with the late Sir Lewis Namier of the *History of Parliament, House of Commons, 1754–1790,* and the official biographer of George III. He is editing from Walpole's original manuscripts, the "foul copies," and notes that have been miraculously preserved. About eighty-five percent of the manuscripts still belong to Lord Waldegrave; the remainder were inexplicably kept by the first Richard Bentley at Upton instead of being returned with all the memoirs and journals after publication to the Lord Waldegrave of the time and they are now at Farmington.

When the new edition of the memoirs appears students of eighteenth-century politics will know at last what Walpole actually wrote. He made stylistic amendments, but did not bring his views and prejudices up to date. He did add "characters" of leading personages and reflection and comment. Some of these insertions are at variance with what he had written earlier, but instead of trying to conceal his altered views he states that the *Memoirs* are full of "contradictory opinions" that are accounted for by their having been written at different periods and by his changing his mind about the persons described. There is sometimes a lapse of three or four years between the events and his report of them. "If I had any personal causes for changing my opinion," he wrote, "I have told them fairly that the fault may be imputed to my passions, rather than to those I speak of." He might, he admitted, have made his book "more uniform by correction; but the natural coloring would have been lost; and I should rather have composed than written a history. As it stands an original sketch, it is at least a picture of my own mind and opinions. That sketch may be valuable to a few who study human nature even in a single character." The *Memoirs,* you see, are as much a "sketch" of Walpole as of his time, the great events of which tend to become merely the background of his life and its leading actors supporting members of his cast.

When *The Memoirs of the Reign of George the Second* came out in 1822 Walpole was criticized for the severity of his judgments on his contemporaries. They seem savage to us also, but we must remember that he was following the tradition of his time, when, as he wrote, "Similes and quotations, metaphors" in the House of Commons "were fallen into disrepute," but "it was not the same with invectives. . . . Debates, where no personalities broke out, engaged too little attention." There was also what Virginia Woolf calls, "the presence of obsolete conventions inherited from an earlier and still more ferocious time." One of these conventions was unbridled personal abuse and the memoirs are less remarkable for their savagery than for Walpole's uneasiness about the effect of his savagery on us. That concern is something new.

The interest of us non-specialists in the memoirs flags because Walpole assumed that his readers would be thoroughly familiar with the politics of the time and because, apart from his "characters," he was not writing at his best. We become confused and bored by the detailed accounts of the dismissal, resignation, and appointment of ministers, the reports of debates, and the passage or defeat of bills that mean nothing to us. We may read Walpole's letters with ease and pleasure even if we know little or nothing of the people and events in them because they were written with wit, grace, and, for the most part, good nature. This is not true of his *Memoirs.* He wrote them for us, posterity, yet only for those of us who would be the historians of the period, a small but formidable jury.

Today, the common reader's interest in the memoirs picks up when he comes to a cadenza on an individual such as the one on Walpole's uncle, "Old" Horace Walpole. "He was still," his nephew tells us,

one of the busiest men in Parliament; generally bustling for the Ministry to get a Peerage, and even zealous for them when he could not get so much as their thanks. With the King he had long been in disgrace, on disputing a point of German genealogy with him (in which his Majesty's chief strength lay) whose the succession of some Principality would be, if eleven or twelve persons then living should die without issue. He knew something of everything but how to hold his tongue, or how to apply his knowledge. As interest was in all his actions, treaties were in all his speeches. Whatever the subject was, he never

lost sight of the peace of Utrecht, Lord Bolingbroke, and the Norwich manu-
factures; but his language and oratory were only adapted to manufacturers. He
was a dead weight on his brother's Ministry; the first to take off that load on
his brother's fall; yet nobody so intemperately abusive on all who connected
with his brother's enemies; nobody so ready to connect with them for the least
flattery, which he loved next to money—indeed he never entirely forgave Lord
Bath for being richer. His mind was a strange mixture of sense alloyed by absurdity, wit by mimicry, knowledge by buffoonery, bravery by meanness,
honesty by selfishness, impertinence by nothing.

The 1822 edition of the *Memoirs* indicates a passage has been omitted at
this point by two lines of asterisks. Macaulay's copy of that edition is at
Farmington. In the margin at this point Macaulay wrote, "The words
omitted might as well have been published 'His body was more uniform;
for that was throughout burlesque and uncouth.' The asterisks led [John
Wilson] Croker to suspect, not altogether without reason, that something
very gross had been left out. See the Quarterly Review. Except in very
rare cases, a hiatus is more injurious to all parties than the whole text
would be."
    Here is another of Walpole's characters.

The Countess of Northumberland was a jovial heap of contradictions. The
blood of all the Percies and Seymours swelled in her veins and in her fancy,
while her person was more vulgar than anything but her conversation, which
was larded indiscriminately with stories of her ancestors and her footmen. Show
and crowds and junketing were her endless pursuits. She was familiar with the
mob, while stifled with diamonds; and yet was attentive to the most minute
privileges of her rank, while almost shaking hands with a cobbler. . . . She
had revived the drummers and pipers and obsolete minstrels of her family; and
her own buxom countenance at the tail of such a procession gave it all the air of
an antiquated pageant of mumming. She was mischievous under the appearance
of frankness; generous and friendly without delicacy or sentiment.

    How do you feel about that? If the blood of all the Percys and Seymours
swells in your veins it doubtless strikes you as being in bad taste, but if
you have never heard of the lady before, you may be entertained and
not care whether it is just or not. If you have read her *Journals* after she
became Duchess of Northumberland you will find confirmation of Walpole's "character" of her, and if you pursue your study of her further you
will not find him contradicted anywhere. You may feel that, even so, this
is not the way for a man to talk about a woman. If you are annoyed *and*
an historian you may re-examine other passages in the spirit that filled

Walpole himself when he set out to prove established historians prejudiced and untrustworthy. In his *Memoirs* he threw off the restraint that guarded his letters. When writing Lady Ossory or Cole he wanted to keep their respect. They and others were saving his letters and one day they would be printed. That was a sobering thought. He did frequently let himself go in his letters, particularly when writing to Mason who brought out his worst side, but he usually ended by apologizing or laughing at himself and so toned down his asperities.

Although he was under no such restraint in the *Memoirs,* he feared for their reception. He did not worry about his statements of fact because he knew "the laborious" would verify them; the Duke of Grafton when Prime Minister said that there was no one from whom he "received so just accounts of the schemes of the various factions" as from Walpole or "had so good means of getting the knowledge of what was passing." What Walpole worried about were his "characters." They had honorable precedents in Clarendon and Bishop Burnet who had also written in passion. Some of Walpole's readers would enjoy his severity, but "I am aware," he wrote, "that more will be offended at the liberty I have taken in painting men as they are: and that many, from private connections of party and family, will dislike meeting such unflattered portraits of their heroes or their relations." He warded off criticism on this score. "Few men," he pointed out, "can sit for patterns of perfect virtue." He had taken posterity into the secret councils of the time and exposed its principal actors, yet he feared his strictures might hurt him as much as the people he was exposing and he longed for our approval of his work and himself. He was like a man who has written many letters in anger that he prudently did not send, but who on re-reading them later is torn between shame of his intemperance and admiration of his force. The *Memoirs* gave him a sense of power. In the library at Strawberry working secretly at night, he was settling the reputations of his more powerful political contemporaries. He could not make history, but he could write it, and posterity would learn from him how the events of his time came about.

Choice 22

Lord George Gordon at Newgate by Richard Newton

After twenty years of editing the Yale Edition of Horace Walpole's Correspondence it was clear we needed a collection of eighteenth-century satirical prints and drawings. Their artists are the photographers of the time who show us its streets and rooms and the tacit assumptions of everyday life. I said to Annie Burr, "Study of satirical prints and drawings is a virtually unexplored continent and our print room could be its capital."

In 1953 Dick Kimball divided our squash court with a floor; the lower room, which is below grade, contains stacks for 10,000 books; the upper room has stacks for 4000 books, cases for 20,000 prints, and roller shelves for our Hogarth and Bunbury collections of prints and drawings. The old squash court gallery acquired a sink and a thymol cabinet made by the Yale Art Gallery in which prints and books are placed to kill the destructive mold on paper. The end wall of the upper room is almost covered by an oil conversation piece, Thomas Patch's "The Golden Asses," the name of a dining club in Florence that met in the 1760s with the British minister, Sir Horace Mann, Walpole's chief correspondent. Its name came from Machiavelli who 200 years earlier called the visiting English "The Golden Asses" because they were so rich, confident, and ignorant, an insult that delighted their elegant successors. In the picture, which is dated 1761, the members are seated at supper tables or are standing and talking with the self-assurance that fascinated Patch. Mann is standing at the left with the Duke of Roxburghe. Patch, who always included himself in his conversation pieces, is to the far right, astride a golden ass on a pedestal with Machiavelli's remarks engraved on it. Patch is holding his pallet and has raised his brush in triumph, but no one is taking any notice of him. Nearly all the sitters in his pictures are in profile except himself and are slightly caricatured if they didn't mind.

We have hung several prints whose figures were identified by Walpole:

"Eloquence or the King of Epithets" under which Walpole wrote, "Christie, the Auctioneer, 1782"; on Patch's "Sterne and Death" he wrote "Sterne, Author of Tristram Shandy, Done at Florence," and he identified the Prince of Wales upon whose prostrate body the Dukes of Grafton and Richmond are standing while the younger Pitt stands on their shoulders and reaches for the Crown. I regard the print of Christie with special affection. It was given me by Dr Rosenbach when I stayed with him in Philadelphia many years ago. The tour of the house ended in his bedroom which had magnificent iron gates and an enormous bed once the property of a Medici. "Why have you never told me about that?" I asked, pointing to the print of Christie. "Why should I?" Rosenbach answered. "Look at the note on it." Rosenbach did so and burst out, "Any fool can see that's Horace Walpole's handwriting. Here, take it," and he hauled the print off the wall and put it in my hands.

My brother-in-law, Hugh D. Auchincloss, gave to Yale his great collection of nearly 5000 English caricatures for our new print room, and another superb gift of 1700 caricatures was given Yale for us by Augustus P. Loring of Boston. It is the major portion of the collection formed by his grandfather, Alfred Bowditch, who was one of the first in this country to see the importance of eighteenth-century satirical prints. He added learned and beautifully written notes on the mats. Gus Loring, a loyal Harvard man and member of the Walpole Society, gave the collection to Yale for Farmington because he believed that it would be more useful here than elsewhere. No such gift was ever made more generously, for Gus emphasized that the new owners were free to sell or trade any of the prints to strengthen the collection. Walpole's blessing on this gift was revealed when four of the prints turned out to have his annotations. George Suckling, the London printseller, let me have the bulk of his eighteenth-century caricatures. Other consignments of over 1000 prints came from Maggs and The Old Print Shop in New York. These en bloc accessions put us ahead of the British Museum's collection of English satirical prints from 1740 to 1800.

Yale transferred to Farmington the print collection of many thousand portraits, country houses, and views of London that had been given to the University Library by Joseph Verner Reed who applauded the transfer. Identified prints solve many problems. One recognizes quickly the leading politicians of any era, but since eighteenth-century artists did not label their figures, help is needed with the lesser known.

By 1971 it became necessary to add a fourth room to the old squash

ELOQUENCE

OR THE KING of EPITHETS

*Let me entreat —Ladies—Gentlemen—permit me
to put this inestimable piece of elegance under your protec-
tion, — only observe, — — — The inexhaustable Munificence
of your superlitively candid Generosity must HARMONIZE
with the refulgent Brilliancy of this little Jewel.! — ? —.)*

Pub.d Jan.y 1.st 1782 by H.Humphrey N.o 18 New Bond Street

Christie, the auctioneer. 1782.

Christie, the auctioneer.

court to store the files for more than 100,000 cards and provide space for four desks. At the end of the room above the shelves, stretches a print over seven feet long that records a dinner party with the Prince of Wales and Mrs Fitzherbert sitting next each other and 69 other men and women of the first rank talking volubly.

On my first trip to London to collect Walpole in 1925 I bought a book that belonged to Lord George Gordon, the instigator of the 'Gordon Riots' in 1780. The book is *Scotland's Opposition to Popery,* 1780. It is bound in green morocco with gold tooling, front and back. The front cover shows Our Lord, right hand upraised, above a cluster of thistles that surround an inscription "For the Right Honbl Lord Geo. Gordon," which is framed by standards of flags and stacked arms and angels blowing trumpets above them. I bought this book because I remembered how Walpole watched from afar the fires set by the Gordon rioters in East London and how his account of them brought back to me San Francisco burning from the Mission to North Beach on the night of 19 April 1906, as I, aged ten, watched from across the bay. I also liked owning such a beautiful book that had belonged to so celebrated a madman. I met him again in the twenties when Vernon Watney, who lived in Walpole's Berkeley Square house, showed me the iron bars Walpole added to its front door during the Gordon Riots. Subsequently, I rescued the door itself, bars and all, when the house was pulled down in 1937 and it is now in our long hall at Farmington.

In our print room is one of the twenty-six choices the Almighty is allowing me to save, a water-color drawing by Richard Newton of Lord George Gordon entertaining fifteen fellow-political prisoners in his dining-room on "the Master's side" at Newgate Prison where the privileged prisoners had their private quarters. He is wearing the beard he grew after he became a Jew and is seated on a dais above his socially inferior guests at one end of the table. He and all but three of them are smoking clay pipes, a defiance of contemporary manners as striking as going to a formal dinner-party today in blue jeans. You could not be more *avant garde* than Lord George Gordon and his friends.

Most librarians in 1929 believed that the place for prints and drawings was in a museum, not a library; nor did many scholars, other than art historians, pay serious attention to them. In 1929 R. W. Chapman of Oxford stared with disgust at our drawing of Lord George. *"Why,"* he asked, "did you buy that *horrible* thing?" It is different today. When Andrew Wilton, then of the British Museum and now at Yale, saw the drawing he

Lord George Gordon at Newgate by Richard Newton.

burst out, "Why, that's a *Newton!*" And when Charles Montgomery, Curator of the Garvan and Related Collections of American Art at Yale, saw it he was astonished that it had so many Windsor chairs with such curious stretchers and induced the Registrar of Winterthur Museum, who was writing on Windsor chairs, to make a trip to Farmington to see them. Prints and drawings are documents that have messages for those who can read them.

A portrait by Nathaniel Hone in the English National Portrait Gallery introduced me to the study of pictures. The Hone was labelled, "Horace Walpole, Earl of Orford, Historian of English Painting and Author of a considerable correspondence." At lunch one day in the thirties I asked Henry Hake, the Director of the Gallery, "Why do you think the sitter in your Hone is Horace Walpole?" He was staggered. "Good God! don't you think he is?" and then he asked me who I thought he was? "Just a nasty little man with a bad cold." Hake looked grave. "We must have an inquest," he announced.

The inquest was held in the cellar of the Gallery. The jury were Hake, Kingsley Adams, the Assistant Director, and myself. I was installed in a great chair before a screen round which curious visitors to the Gallery peered. The questioned picture was flanked on the screen by Eccardt's and George Dance's portraits of Walpole, both unquestionably "right." Hake, magisterial in a wing collar and black tie, presided at the left of the screen. We began. When and how had the picture come to the Gallery? By purchase, Adams reported, at the sale of Lord James Stuart's pictures in 1865. This was a point in my favor since a portrait of Horace Walpole was the last thing a Stuart would have owned. How old was the sitter? Not over thirty, we thought. When was he painted? Hake and Adams agreed that it must have been after 1760 when rolled collars came in. Thirty from 1760 is 1730 and our Horace Walpole was born in 1717. Hake asked when I thought the Eccardt of Walpole was painted. I guessed 1754 or 1755 because Strawberry Hill appears in the background with its Refectory and Library, which were finished in 1754. I asked if they had looked at the back of the picture: "No, why should we?" "Because I think you'll find Walpole dated it." The picture was brought down and Walpole had written on the back,

Horace Walpole
youngest son of Sir R. Walpole
by Eckardt
1754.

We returned to the questioned portrait. I guessed it was Walpole's first cousin, Horace Walpole, the eldest son of "Old" Horace for whom our Horace was named and for whom the extinct Earldom of Orford was revived after our Horace's death; that is, the two men had the same name and title. Adams produced a mezzotint of Cousin Horace in old age from a portrait by the excellent Norfolk painter Henry Walton that he and Hake agreed was the man Hone had painted years earlier. The Hone was carried away in disgrace and the postcards of it were removed from public sale. "Where," I asked, "is the original of Walton's portrait?" "That," Hake replied, "is for you to discover." I did so ten years later in the dining-room of the American Embassy at Canberra. Like the Gallery's Hone it was labelled, "Horace Walpole, Earl of Orford," which was correct so far as it went. When our Ambassador in Canberra learned that the sitter was not the letter-writer, but his undistinguished cousin, he let the picture recross the Pacific to Farmington where it hangs in our New Library next to cousin Horace's father, "Old" Horace Walpole by Jean Baptiste Vanloo.

Shortly after the inquest Hake asked me to join him and Adams in making an iconography of Walpole. When I protested my ignorance he waved it away, "Adams and I'll take care of all the technical business," he said, "but we can't do Horace Walpole without you." So I accepted happily. At Farmington we had identified most of Walpole's portraits and their artists and knew when they were painted, but we didn't know when and where they had been sold and resold and to whom and for how much and where and when and by whom they had been exhibited. Nor did we have all the engravings of them.

I asked to see some of the iconographies that the Gallery had done. Hake was embarrassed. "This will be the first."

"But there must be a standard work I can look at?"

Hake brightened up. "There is. It's of your great General George Washington," I nodded knowingly, "by an American, John Hill Morgan."

"Who," I said, "lives a quarter of a mile from us at Farmington, Connecticut, and is with his wife next door to us at Brown's Hotel this minute. Won't you lunch with us tomorrow?" Iconography is a small world, after all. It also takes time, I was to learn. Our iconography of Horace Walpole was delayed by the War, Hake's death, and Adams's succession to him as Director of the Portrait Gallery. It was not until Adams retired that our work appeared in the Walpole Society volume for 1968–1970, thirty years after we began it.

The question of my assistant in our new Print Room was settled quickly because Annie Burr had proved her flare for iconography as Vice Regent for Connecticut in the Mount Vernon Ladies' Association of the Union. She also changed a label in the English National Portrait Gallery itself. The label on their portrait of Bishop Berkeley stated that its background was Bermuda. "But," Annie Burr pointed out, "Bishop Berkeley never got to Bermuda. He stayed at Newport, and that," she added, pointing to a ridge in the background of the picture, "is Paradise Rock there." Later in the summer she photographed Paradise Rock as it appears in the picture and sent it to Hake who gratefully corrected the Gallery's howler. When I talked to Annie Burr about iconography I was talking to one who knew more about it than I did.

Her appointment as Curator of Prints in the Lewis Walpole Library was made by a standing vote of the Yale Corporation, perhaps the only appointment ever so voted in Yale's history. She learned how to catalogue and index our material from Lawrence Wroth of the John Carter Brown Library at Providence who had devised a system for his Library's eighteenth-century prints. Our subject file grew as Annie Burr became more and more informed and she anticipated what the users of the index would be seeking. Three recent queries have been for prints showing corkscrews, candle-snuffers, and country dances, and all three enquirers said they were "overwhelmed" by the number of prints, all new to them, that we produced. The subject file answered a question I was asked at a meeting of the Winterthur Museum Board: Did curtains in colonial America come down to the floor in heaps and piles and mounds of silk as they then did at Winterthur and most American Wings? I doubted that they touched the floor in eighteenth-century England and if that was so they didn't come down to the floor in this country, which followed English fashion. Annie Burr's index answered the question in two minutes when thirty-eight prints between 1712 and 1800 proved that they never touched the floor.

The fears of the time appear in its prints. One was dismemberment of the Empire. An article by Edwin Wolf 2d in the *Proceedings of the American Philosophical Society* that marks the 250th anniversary of Benjamin Franklin's birth shows that the well-known print, "Magna Britannia her Colonies Reduc'd," was instigated by Franklin to encourage the repeal of the Stamp Act. In the print Britannia is leaning against a world globe; her spear and shield lie beside her, quite useless because her arms and legs, labelled "Virginia," "Pennsylvania," "New York," and "New England," have been chopped off. Her expression is understandably wan. The British navy is beached in the distance; the British oak in the foreground has lost its leaves. Over the globe and Britannia is a ribbon inscribed "DATE OBOLUM BELISARIO." A lengthy EXPLANATION points out that the valiant Belisarius who saved Rome under Justinian was mutilated by that ungrateful Emperor and forced to beg, "Give Belisarius a penny." The Explanation is followed by a MORAL that leaves nothing to the imagination. When I took this to our print room, an earlier dismembered Britannia just happened to be lying on a table. In it her arms, labelled "Cape Breton" and "Gibraltar," are lying on the floor and she is being disemboweled for good measure. Annie Burr found still another print in which the British lion has lost a paw, "Minorca," and is about to lose two others, "Nova Scotia" and "Oswego." Franklin's print attacking the Stamp Act by showing Britannia dismembered preyed on the fear Englishmen had of losing their Empire.

In the four years left Annie Burr to work on her index she made upwards of 12,000 cards, adding to them whenever she could right up to the end. She used to wonder if anyone would ever use them, but we have had many visitors, some as far from Farmington as Peru, Ceylon, and South Korea. The subjects of the prints range from "Abolition of slave trade" to "Zoo." Annie Burr laid out a six-lane highway straight across the vast and relatively unexplored continent that will be travelled as long as the Lewis Walpole Library exists. Her work has been carried on by devoted people who have developed it to a point that is not, so far as I know, duplicated elsewhere. We have over 60,000 cards for the collection of satires and 50,000 for our "straight" portraits. Each satire has at least six cards for its date, title, persons shown in it, artist and engraver, printer and publisher, and subject. The largest number of cards for a single print is 43.

To help scholars explore the virtually unknown continent of English eighteenth-century satires, we shall reproduce photographically the 1200 in our library from 1740–1800 that are not described in the British Museum's *Catalogue of Political and Personal Satires*. We shall then avoid the costly drudgery of writing descriptions that inevitably overlook details of interest to specialists—such as the Windsor chairs at Lord George Gordon's dinner-party. I believe the twenty-first century will find our print room the busiest part of the Library, that more rooms will have been added to it, and that its contents will continue to be studied by visitors from all over the world.

Choice 23
Hogarth's First Oil Sketch for *The Beggar's Opera*

This is the first of six oils by Hogarth of Gay's *Beggar's Opera,* Act III, Scene IX with Lucy Lockit, her father the Warden of Newgate, Macheath the highwayman, Polly Peachum, and her father. The scene shows the two girls begging their fathers to save their lover from hanging. Walpole wrote a note on the back of the picture that he copied in the *Description of Strawberry Hill:* "Sketch of The Beggar's Opera as first performed: Macheath, in red, by Walker. Polly kneeling, in white, by Miss Fenton, afterwards Duchess of Bolton; Lucy in green, her face turned away, by Mrs. Eggleton; Peachum, in black, by Hippisley; Lockit, by Hall. Amongst the audience, on the left hand, Sir Thomas Robinson of Rokeby, a tall gentleman with a long lean face; on the right Sir Robert Fagge, profile, a fat man with short grey hair, much known at Newmarket. Painted by Hogarth. H.W." Walpole added in his copy of the '84 *Description,* "Bought at the sale of John Rich, the well-known harlequin, and master of the theatres in Lincoln's-inn-fields and Covent-garden, for whom the picture was painted." He also added in his copy of the '74 *Description* "with prices of such pieces as I can recollect" that he paid five guineas for the picture. When it was sold in the Lowther Castle Sale in 1947 Annie Burr bought it for me through Messrs Spink and it hangs now in the long hall at Farmington beside a black and white chalk drawing of Sir John Perrott, an Elizabethan Deputy of Ireland, that Walpole hung next to it in the Great North Bedchamber at Strawberry Hill. Our *Beggar's Opera* was reproduced by the Harvard and Yale University Presses in a portfolio that Philip Hofer and I made of Hogarth's six versions of the scene in 1965. We also reproduced Walpole's copy of Blake's print of it that is at Farmington.

Walpole gave Hogarth a chapter to himself among "Painters in the Reign of King George II" in the fourth volume of the *Anecdotes of Painting.* "Having dispatched the herd of our painters in oil," the chapter begins, "I reserved to a class by himself that great and original genius, Hogarth; considering him rather as a writer of comedy with a pencil, than

Hogarth's "Beggar's Opera," Act III, Scene IX.

as a painter. If catching the manners and follies of an age *living as they rise,* if general satire on vices and ridicules, familiarized by strokes of nature, and heightened by wit, and the whole animated by proper and just expressions of the passions, be comedy, Hogarth composed comedies as much as Molière. . . . He is more true to character than Congreve; each personage is distinct from the rest, acts in his sphere, and cannot be confounded with any other of the dramatis personae." In the Hogarth chapter we see Walpole the patriot who wrote in the *Anecdotes,* "This country which does not always err in vaunting its own productions," a sentiment quoted by the British Walpole Society in its notebooks. It also inspired the leading collectors of early American antiques in 1910 to adopt his name when starting the private American Walpole Society. Patriotism is one of Walpole's attractive qualities that has been missed by his detractors.

The panegyric of Hogarth in the *Anecdotes* has a mildly disparaging notice of Hogarth's *Analysis of Beauty,* 1753. "So little had he eyes to his own deficiencies," Walpole wrote, "that he believed he had discovered the principle of grace." Walpole's copy of the *Analysis,* which was given me by R. W. Chapman, has no notes by Walpole, but he did paste in the subscription ticket to it, "Columbus Breaking the Egg," as a frontispiece. The chapter on Hogarth in the *Anecdotes* ends with a very severe criticism of his "Sigismonda," which, Walpole wrote, "was no more like Sigismonda than I to Hercules. Not to mention the wretchedness of the coloring, it was the representation of a maudlin strumpet just turned out of keeping, and with eyes red with rage and usquebaugh, tearing off the ornaments her keeper had given her. . . . I make no more apology for this account than for the encomiums I have bestowed on him. Both are dictated by truth, and are the history of a great man's excellences and errors." Not to offend Hogarth's widow, Walpole held up the publication of the volume for nine years until pressure from the subscribers to the *Anecdotes* forced him to publish it. The letter he sent Mrs Hogarth with the book is missing, but at Farmington is a copy of it in Kirgate's hand on which Walpole wrote, "Copy of my letter with the 4th volume of my Anecdotes of Painting to Mrs Hogarth. She returned no answer. H.W." He pasted it into his copy of John Nichols's *Biographical Anecdotes of William Hogarth,* 1781, opposite Nichols's passage on the "Sigismonda."

Walpole and Hogarth were not on the best of terms. Walpole wrote Montagu 5 May 1761,

. . . the true frantic œstrus resides at present with Mr Hogarth; I went t'other morning to see a portrait he is painting of Mr Fox—Hogarth told me he had promised, if Mr Fox would sit as he liked, to make as good a picture as Vandyke or Rubens could. I was silent—"Why now," said he, "You think this very vain, but why should not one speak truth?" This *truth* was uttered in the face of his own Sigismonda, which is exactly a maudlin whore tearing off the trinkets that her keeper had given her, to fling at his head. . . . As I was going, Hogarth put on a very grave face, and said, "Mr Walpole, I want to speak to you"; I sat down, and said, I was ready to receive his commands. For shortness, I will mark this wonderful dialogue by initial letters.

"H. I am told you are going to entertain the town with something in our way [the *Anecdotes of Painting.*] W. Not very soon, Mr Hogarth. H. I wish you would let me have it, to correct; I should be sorry to have you expose yourself to censure. We painters must know more of those things than other people. W. Do you think nobody understands painting but painters? H. Oh! So far from it, there's Reynolds, who certainly has genius; why, but t'other day he offered £100 for a picture that I would not hang in my cellar; and indeed, to say truth, I have generally found that persons who had studied painting least, were the best judges of it. . . . I wish you would let me correct it—besides, I am writing something of the same kind myself, I should be sorry we should clash. W. I believe it is not much known what my work is; very few persons have seen it. H. Why, it is a critical history of painting, is it not? W. No, it is an antiquarian history of it in England; I bought Vertue's MSS, and I believe the work will not give much offence. Besides, if it does, I cannot help it; when I publish anything, I give it to the world to think of it as they please. H. Oh! if it is an antiquarian work, we shall not clash. Mine is a critical work; I don't know whether I shall ever publish it—it is rather an apology for painters—I think it owing to the good sense of the English, that they have not painted better. W. My dear Mr Hogarth, I must take my leave of you, you now grow too wild"—I left him—if I had stayed, there remained nothing but for him to bite me.

Walpole believed he had the largest collection of Hogarth's prints in existence, 365 in number. It may have been the largest when he made the claim, but after the painter's death Walpole wrote Cole that George Steevens "ransacked" Mrs Hogarth's collection of the prints. Steevens's collection is now at Farmington. It has 469 prints with 236 additional satires of Hogarth's prints by Bickham, Ireland, and Paul Sandby. Steevens pasted the prints into three elephant folios. He discriminated the states of the early tradesman's cards and exhibition announcements and included lists of the prints priced by Hogarth and his widow. Steevens be-

queathed his collection to William Windham of Felbrigg Hall in Norfolk, where it remained until Wyndham Ketton-Cremer's uncle sold it at
Sotheby's in 1919 to Dyson Perrins whose estate resold it at Sotheby's in
1959. I bought it in memory of Annie Burr and so it has joined the collections of Hogarth at Farmington formed by Queen Charlotte and Lord
Kinnaird. According to Ronald Paulson, we are now second only to the
British Museum's collection, which includes a large proportion of the
prints from Strawberry Hill. Thirteen of them are at Farmington. They
include drawings of Dr Misaubin and Dr Richard Mead, prints of "the
Black Girl in Bed," and "Humours of Oxford," which turned up in Lady
Ossory's copy of Walpole's *Fugitive Pieces in Verse and Prose*. We also
have the copperplates for "The Sleeping Congregation," and Hogarth's
portrait of himself painting the Comic Muse. His plates are rare because
so many of them were melted down for bullets in the dawn of the New
Dark Ages.

The runner-up in this Choice is Walpole's collection of prints and
drawings by Henry Bunbury. I owe it to John Carter, who bought it for
me from an undergraduate at King's. It is bound in two elephant folios,
each with a special title-page printed at the Strawberry Hill Press: "Etch-
ings/by/Henry William Bunbury, Esq; and/ After His Designs." We
hear of it first in Walpole's letter to Lady Ossory of 13 July 1776: "I am
obeying the Gospel, and putting my house in order, am ranging my prints
and papers, am *composing* books, in the literal sense, and in the only sense
I will compose books any more, I am pasting Henry Bunbury's prints into
a volume." After he filled the first volume he started the second and went
on adding to it as long as he lived. He referred in the *Anecdotes of Painting,* to "the living etchings of Mr H. Bunbury, the second Hogarth, and
first imitator who ever fully equalled his original." This astonishing
encomium did not prevent Bunbury from falling into long neglect, but
owing in large part to my colleague in the Yale Walpole, John Riely,
whose paper on him, "Horace Walpole and the Second Hogarth," appeared in *Eighteenth Century Studies,* Fall 1975, he has been brought
back to respectful notice.

Bunbury was the son of a clerical baronet and the younger brother of
Sir Charles Bunbury, the husband of Walpole's friend, Lady Sarah Lennox.
After Westminster and St Catharine's Hall, Cambridge, Bunbury went on
the Grand Tour and was painted by Patch at Florence as the central
figure in a comical conversation piece that no doubt delighted its first
viewers, but whose humorous references are lost on us today as we pass

ETCHINGS

BY

Henry William Bunbury, Eſq;

AND

AFTER HIS DESIGNS.

Bunbury's prints and drawings, with a special title-page printed at Strawberry Hill.

it in our long hall. Bunbury went to Rome for a few months to study drawing before returning to Cambridge. In 1771 he left the University to marry one of the beautiful Hornecks who had been painted by Reynolds and whose family were intimate with Goldsmith and the Johnson circle. Bunbury's etching of Goldsmith annotated by Walpole is at Farmington.

I was introduced to Bunbury in 1915 when, a Sophomore at Yale, I joined Mory's, a pleasant eating-club that cultivated an olde English coffee-house atmosphere with the aid of one eighteenth-century caricature, "The Coffee-House Patriots." Its chief figure is a fat gormandizing man said to be Dr Johnson, who is staring at us with an open mouth; with him are a dog and half a dozen men arguing. I glanced at it daily, not because I liked it particularly, but because it was that strange and alluring world, the eighteenth century. Thirteen years later when Annie Burr and I married, an old and dear friend, Leonard Bacon, gave us the original drawing for the print, which is signed, "H. W. Bunbury, 1780."

There are forty-seven of Bunbury's drawings at Farmington. They range from five that were drawn for Boydell's *Shakespeare Gallery,* to servants playing billiards, wood-gatherers, and the younger Horace Mann, having lost his way being escorted home by a farmer's wife. Of special interest is *La Cuisine de la Poste,* which was exhibited at the Royal Academy Exhibition in 1770. Walpole noted on it in his copy of the catalogue, "All the characters are most highly natural, and this drawing perhaps excels the Gate of Calais by Hogarth in whose manner it is composed." Bunbury's drawing has come to Farmington since I began this Chapter. Eleven years after it was drawn Bunbury exhibited his "Richmond Hill" at the Royal Academy and presented it to Walpole in a note after the Exhibition was over. Walpole wrote him,

I am just come, Sir, from the Royal Academy, where I had been immediately struck, as I always am by your works, by a most capital drawing of Richmond Hill; but what was my surprise and pleasure—for I fear the latter preceded my modesty—when I found your note, and read that so very fine a performance was destined for me! This is a true picture of my emotions, Sir, but I hope you will believe that I am not less sincere when I assure you that the first moment's reflection told me how infinitely, Sir, you think of overpaying me for the poor though just tribute of my praise in a trifling work, whose chief merit is its having avoided flattery. Your genius, Sir, cannot want *that,* and, still less, my attestation; but when you condescend to reward *this,* I doubt I shall be a little vain, for when I shall have such a certificate to produce, how will it be possible to remain quite humble? I must beg you, Sir, to accept my warmest and most grateful thanks, which are doubled by your ingenious delicacy in delivering me, in this very agreeable manner, from the pain I felt in fearing that I had taken too much liberty with you. I am, etc., Hor. Walpole.

Bunbury's high place in Walpole's collection of talented ladies and gentlemen is seen in our Print Room. I believe his reputation will grow as more and more discover his good-natured drawings and prints that give us characters in all walks of eighteenth-century life going about their daily business with the "touches of nature" that won the encomiums of the first historian of his country's artists.

Choices 24 and 25
Ramsay's Portrait of Walpole and
Berwick's of Conway

One day in the summer of 1931 Annie Burr and I had tea at Nuneham Park with the dowager Lady Harcourt. Nuneham was a place of pilgrimage for me because it was the house that I think Walpole most enjoyed visiting. He delighted in everything about it, its "own beauties," its gardens, which he called "the quintessence of nosegays," and its talented owner, George Simon 2d Earl Harcourt and his wife who wrote verses.

Harcourt was an amateur artist who Walpole said etched landscapes "in a very great style" and whose views of his other house in Oxfordshire, Stanton Harcourt, were "the richest etchings I ever saw, and masterly executed." Walpole begged Lady Harcourt in vain to let him print her verses, which he said were written "in a very natural style." I was eager to see "the paradise on earth" and Walpole's letters to Harcourt, fifty-seven in number, which were there. On our first visit Lady Harcourt asked the housekeeper to produce them, a request carried out with marked distaste. The housekeeper told us darkly that an American who said he was a professor came to see the letters years before and she was sure he had made off with some of them. The most common explanation for the disappearance of family papers in England is a fire; the second most common explanation is the visit of an American professor.

I didn't touch the letters, but admired the portraits in oval frames above the library shelves, Locke, Pope, Gray, and so on, including an unrecorded portrait of Horace Walpole, "By Gogain, after Allan Ramsay." Since it was the custom in the eighteenth century to give copies of one's portraits to friends it was not surprising to find Walpole at Nuneham, but in 1931 I was still uninitiated in the science of iconography and assumed that the copy couldn't be of Walpole because it doesn't appear in the Toynbees' edition of his letters. When a few years later I found in the house of a Walpole relation a second Gogain of Ramsay's portrait in-

224

Allan Ramsay's portrait of Horace Walpole.

scribed on its frame "The Hon. Horace Walpole copied from an original picture of him at Nuneham," I was still too uninstructed to do more than wonder mildly about the original Ramsay.

I found it ultimately through the Agony Column of the *Times* when in 1936 my advertisement brought this letter:

Dear Sir

Accidently I heard you were interested in Strawberry Hill. My family and I have a larg [*sic*] number of painting and watercolors from the great sale and by inheritance. Angelica Kaufmans and Paul Sandbys. Aylesbury tapestries etc If you are sufficiently interested I shall be glad to show you some of them at least My grandfather and Anne Seymour Damer were close connections
Nothing for sale

Yrs faithfully
H. Campbell Johnston.

Campbell Johnston was a promising name, allied to the Argyll family in which were Lord Frederick Campbell, Walpole's executor, and his sister Lady Ailesbury, Conway's wife. They were uncle- and aunt-in-law of Sir Alexander Johnston of Carnsalloch, Dumfriesshire, the enlightened re-organizer of Ceylon early in the nineteenth century.

H. Campbell Johnston was one of his descendants, as I discovered when I called on him in Kensington. His flat (third floor back), his clothes, his chastened manner, indicated one who had seen better days. He admitted that the Walpoliana did not belong to him, but to a younger brother, D. Campbell Johnston. However, he went on earnestly, his brother would show them to me at tea, and he did so a few days later in his big house in Hans Road. Also present in the drawing-room besides the elder brother was a younger sister. My entrance was irregular because on walking into the room I saw several objects from Strawberry Hill and acknowledged them by a cry of recognition before greeting my host. There are dead-pan collectors who suppress such cries hoping to pay less for the coveted objects, but I think I have gained by my undisguised delight on seeing them. In the drawing-room were Müntz's sketch of Walpole in the library at Strawberry Hill, two drawings of Conway at Park Place by Paul Sandby, Eccardt's conversation piece of Conway, Lady Ailesbury, and Mrs Damer, when a child, and two of Lady Ailesbury's needlework tapestries in silk. The flame of hope rose in the elder brother as my enthusiasm invested the family treasures with transcendent value. I was aware of this and also that in the bosom of the younger brother no friendly response stirred, a disappointment, since it was clear that his was the deciding voice in the family councils. The sister was amused by my and her elder brother's eagerness to have something come of the call besides tea and by her younger brother's evident decision that nothing should. I made notes of the Walpoliana, but not, unfortunately, of the conversation. My inquiries in 1937 and 1938 to the younger brother about Walpole's letters to Lord Frederick Campbell received terse replies that he did not have them.

When I was in London in 1942 the Campbell Johnstons had disappeared from all works of reference and I did not pursue their Walpoliana until 1951 when, fortunately, I mentioned them to Owen Morshead who discovered immediately that the objects I saw in Hans Road had descended to Commander Colin Campbell Johnston, who was living at Brighton, and there they were in his drawing-room when I arrived for lunch in a few days. In answer to the question about other members of the family who might own Walpoliana, my host suggested I write to the head of it, the Laird of Carnsalloch, Mr David Campbell Johnston. He replied that he had no Walpole letters, but kindly wrote out the list of contents of the five volumes of *Lord Orford's Works*, 1798, a not uncommon work. As an afterthought he mentioned that he owned Ramsay's portrait of Walpole. I urged him to get an appraisal from the most reputable dealers and auctioneers if he ever decided to part with it, but this gratuitous advice went unacknowledged. After a year I wrote again, sending a copy of my earlier letter, which I feared had gone astray. This time the Laird replied at once, saying there was no use in discussing the matter further unless I was prepared to give him £120 for the picture. When it reached Kingsley Adams's office at the National Portrait Gallery in London en route to Farmington it was discovered that much of it had been cut away—how much appears from Ramsay's preliminary sketch in the National Gallery, Edinburgh, that shows Walpole at his desk holding a quill pen, only the tip of which survives. Despite its mutilation, the portrait ranks among the best known of Walpole because Professor George B. Cooper used it on the dust jacket of the selection of Walpole's letters he encouraged me to make for his large class at Trinity College, Hartford, and that is used in other classrooms as well.

The Laird of Carnsalloch informed a cousin in London, Miss Scholefield, that there was a mad American at Brown's Hotel who would pay anything for Walpoliana and that here was a chance to sell her Gainsborough of Henry Conway and repaint her dining-room. Miss Scholefield

wrote me she would be happy to show me the Gainsborough. I turned to
Kingsley Adams for guidance and support. He had succeeded Hake as
Director of the Portrait Gallery and the Gallery's records of Conway's
portraits were in his brief case when we rang Miss Scholefield's door-bell
a few days later. Among the Conway portraits was one that had been
exhibited at the New Gallery in 1890–91. It was signed "A. Berwick,"
who was a copyist, according to Whitley's *Artists and Their Friends in
England, 1700–1799.* Miss Scholefield opened her door promptly. She was
most cordial, but as we stood wedged in the tiny hall she announced we
were not to see the picture until Dr Lewis had passed a test. Adams
giggled rather wildly; I bowed acquiescence and Miss Scholefield opened
the door behind her and waved towards a scruffy old parrot at the end of
the room. The parrot was apparently the test Dr Lewis must pass. I
marched right up to its cage not to reason why, but to do or die. "Good
morning, Polly," I said distinctly and bowed. Polly turned on me the
unwinking gaze of a mature bird. After an appraisal that seemed quite
long, it said, "Oik?"

"Oh," Miss Scholefield interpreted, "Polly likes you!"

Encouraged, Dr Lewis told Polly that he trusted she was well and admired her feathers, a few of which she had discarded on the floor of her
cage. After another thoughtful pause she stepped delicately off her perch,
grasped the wires of the cage with her horrible claws, and turned upside
down, in which position she gazed up at Dr Lewis with an expression that
was unmistakably flattering.

"Why," Miss Scholefield exclaimed, "Polly likes you *very* much! *He*
has never done *that* for anybody." In spite of mistaking Polly's sex Dr
Lewis had passed the test.

Miss Scholefield led Adams and me to the small dining-room and the
commanding three-quarters-length portrait of Conway that dominated it.
As its head and shoulders had been engraved for Lord Orford's *Works,*
1798, they were familiar, but the engraving gives us only Conway the
soldier wearing a cuirass; in the portrait he is also the statesman, the
Secretary of State for the Southern Department that included the American Colonies. He is standing at a table on which is a red dispatch box, a
globe turned to North America, a manuscript copy of his "Free Port Bill"
that opened Spain's Caribbean colonies to the Boston merchants, and a
copy of the bill, which he also fathered, for the repeal of the Stamp Act.
A dark red curtain is at his back; a classical colonnade stretches away on
his right. Could the picture be taken down to see what was on the

Field Marshal Henry Seymour Conway by Berwick.

stretcher? Polly screamed assent from the drawing-room and the picture was taken down, a precarious business with Adams standing on a light chair, his arms spread across the picture embracing the frame as he teased it off its hook while Miss Scholefield and I, squatting below, heaved it up with little cries of caution and apprehension. The picture and Adams safely down, we found on the stretcher "A. Berwick pinxit," and the label of the Hanover Exhibition at the New Gallery in 1890–91. There was also a note that the picture belonged to "Mrs Campbell Johnston." Everybody was relieved and delighted. The moment had come to cross the valley of reticence and talk money.

The two principals were what auctioneers call, "A Willing Seller and A Willing Buyer." The latter advised Miss Scholefield to get the best professional advice for a valuation. She looked blank. I rolled off five possibilities: "Agnew, Colnaghi, Leggatt, Christie's, Sotheby's."

"Oh, *Sotheby's!*"

"You know them?"

"No, but I've always liked the name."

I telephoned Vere Pilkington, at that time the senior partner of Sotheby's. "Is he in a red coat?" he asked.

"Yes."

"Bad luck, I'm afraid that will add £20."

After the portrait reached Farmington I told Robert Vail, who was then Director of the New York Historical Society, that the Campbell Johnston family believed the original was painted for "the Town Hall of New York." He kindly explored the matter and found that it was the people of Boston, not New York, who on 18 September 1765, voted their thanks to Conway and requested his portrait for Faneuil Hall. The picture reached it after a delay of nearly two years—while the copy was being made for Conway's family?—but the original was lost during the Revolution. The copy descended to Miss Scholefield, who wrote its new owner to say how happy she was it had found such a good home. Her letter concluded, "Polly sends you the enclosed," which was a snapshot of Polly himself.

Who painted the portrait? Family tradition is not necessarily wrong and a very important critic has said the head at least may be by Gainsborough. The pose is similar to Gainsborough's portrait of Conway owned by the Duke of Argyll, the head of the Campbell clan. The trees seen through the colonnade have a Gainsboroughesque look. My guess is that before Conway sent his portrait to Boston he had the copy made in Gainsborough's studio where I understand A. Berwick was employed and of course I like to think that the head was painted by the master.

The Campbell Johnston connection with Farmington was not ended. In February 1955 a letter arrived from Colombo, Ceylon, signed "James T. Rutnam" who reported to Professor Wilmarth Sheldon Lewis that he owned "about 200 original letters written to Walpole by his cousin Field Marshal Henry Seymour Conway and his wife," Lady Ailesbury. Rutnam said he was a great admirer of Sir Alexander Johnston, the creator of the new Ceylon, and collected him and his family, how extensively was shown by his having bought the Conway letters because Lady Ailesbury was a Campbell into whose family Johnston had married. Rutnam hoped to have the letters published "along with a comprehensive memoir of Conway" and solicited Professor Lewis's "comments in this connection."

Professor Lewis's comments were encouraging. He had tried to find those letters, some seventy of which had been printed in *Fraser's Magazine* in 1850, but the originals had not been seen by Walpole's editors since. "I shall be more than willing to publish your letters in this edition," I assured him on the official letter-head. "Fortunately, it is not too late. Am I right in assuming you do not wish to sell them? If that is so, I hope very much that you will permit me to have them photostated at my expense for use in the Yale Walpole." I concluded by offering to give Mr Rutnam a duplicate set of the photostats and to send him a copy of *Collector's Progress*.

Mr Rutnam's reply was dictated to his wife from the hospital where he had gone with hepatitis. The letters were not for sale, but their owner was willing for them to be photostated and accepted the offer of a set for himself. "With regard to the final disposal of these letters, it is my intention to send them to a worthy library. As presently advised I may perhaps send them to the Yale University. I thank you for the offer of your book and I look forward to receiving an author's copy as early as possible," and also copies of *Life's* article on the Walpole library, Hazen's bibliographies of the Strawberry Hill Press and of Walpole's works.

Things moved swiftly. I had written the present Lord Harcourt who had just been staying with us at Farmington, that Conway's letters to Walpole had turned up in Colombo and he expedited the photostating of them by the Mercantile Bank of India. Letters flew back and forth between Colombo and Farmington. Mr Rutnam used business stationery that gave the telephone numbers of his Office, Stores, and Residence, and his telegraphic address, but did not say what his business was. He disclosed it in mid-May in a letter full of biographical details. He was fifty years of age with nine children, of whom the eldest, aged twenty-one, had become an American citizen and was a Corporal in the U.S. Marines stationed in the California desert, where Rutnam trusted I would call on him. Rutnam had many personal friends in the United States, the Ceylonese Ambassador and other ranking members of the Embassy; among his business friends were The Export Managers of Four Roses Whiskey and the Galban Lobo Trading Co. in New York. He described himself as "a business man, a merchant who very often strays into letters." His wife and second son had been in Boston the year before to meet members of the Congregational Mission there. Although Mr Rutnam was a pure Ceylonese three of his great-grandparents had taken the impeccable Connecticut names of *Dwight, Tappan,* and *Gardiner* on being converted to Christianity by Connecticut Congregational missionaries. He was doing some research in the history of the American Christian Mission to Ceylon during the early part of the last century and he was particularly interested in Sir Alexander Johnston and his family.

In a few days there arrived a column of "Cabbages and Kings," by "Walrus." "Cabbages and Kings" appeared in the Ceylon *Daily News.* "Walrus" was G. J. Padmanabha, who, Mr Rutnam explained, was his son-in-law. Walrus pointed out that "One of the most monumental publishing enterprises of the century" is the Yale Walpole and that "a local collector . . . businessman James T. Rutnam" had made a remarkable contribution to it. "In the course of a recent trip to England Mr Rutnam, a keen student of Ceylon history, did some research in the family history of Sir Alexander Johnson, in the course of which he discovered and acquired 178 letters written by Conway to Walpole, fifteen addressed to Walpole by Conway's wife, the Countess of Ailesbury, and a few miscellaneous items relating to this portion of the Walpole Correspondence. . . . The Conway letters are, we understand, ultimately earmarked for the great Walpole Library at Farmington, Connecticut, where Professor Lewis' own unrivalled collection of Walpoliana is housed."

This was most welcome news. Where, I wondered in my next letter to Rutnam, had he found Conway's letters? I presumed that they were in the younger Campbell Johnston's house in Hans Road when I called there in 1938 and had gone to a nephew or niece I had failed to identify. The answer to my question was silence for four years. It was broken by Mrs Rutnam who was in Boston again in the spring of 1959 and who telephoned me to ask if she might stop off at Farmington to see me and my wife. We couldn't have her because it was towards the end of Annie Burr's last illness. Mrs Rutnam answered most feelingly, made a vow for Annie Burr's recovery, and prayed for her every night thereafter.

Two years later Rutnam wrote that one of his daughters was ill in San Francisco of a serious heart ailment. Mrs Rutnam was with her. Could I be of assistance to them through my friends there? I got in touch with a medical fellow-trustee of the Thacher School, the dreaded operation was avoided, and Mrs Rutnam was able to move her daughter to Los Angeles where she had a married son living with his American wife. Mr Rutnam sent the Conway letters to Farmington as a gift and asked me to let Mrs Rutnam have whatever I thought they were worth; he would reimburse me when he could. I couldn't let him do that, so a check went to Mrs Rutnam, the daughter recovered, and Mrs Rutnam returned to Ceylon. But after a short illness she died, "leaving a message to inform Dr Lewis specially." Her heart-broken husband sent me a copy of the letter of condolence from the Prime Minister, Mrs Sirimavo Bandaranaike, and the press notices about Mrs Rutnam. Among them was, "Evelyn Rutnam, who moved unobtrusively in every circle, never losing the common touch, presided at a home at Cinnamon Gardens, Colombo, which was known to her friends as Freedom Hall where the white and the black, the brown and the yellow, the high and the low, the pious and impious, the gay and the reserved, the loyalist and the rebel, all met on a footing of equality and broke bread together."

Conway lived to 1795; his rescued letters to Walpole come down only to 1759. Where are the remainder? Perhaps they are in an undiscovered branch of the Campbell Johnston family; perhaps they have wandered off into quite a different family and are lying forgotten in a box or cupboard awaiting the arrival of the next searcher of Walpoliana from, it is to be hoped, the Lewis Walpole Library at Farmington. Meanwhile, Conway hangs in our long hall opposite his relations, Sir Robert Walpole and his first wife (Conway's aunt), Lady Mary Churchill with her husband and eldest son, Dorothy Clement, Princess Sophia of Gloucester, and the Allan Ramsay of Horace Walpole.

Choice 26

Walpole's Annotated Print of His Portrait by Reynolds, 1757

We come now to the final Choice, the copy of McArdell's print of Walpole engraved after Reynolds in 1757, which Walpole hung in his bedroom at Strawberry Hill. The Strawberry Hill sale catalogue records that "A Latin inscription, in the handwriting of Horace Walpole, is at the back of this engraving, rendering it particularly interesting." It was bought in 1842 by the Rev. Hon. Horace Cholmondeley, Walpole's cousin, and thanks to the friendly offices of Owen Morshead came to me in 1962 from General Sir Henry Jackson of Dorset, Horace Cholmondeley's grandson. The Latin inscription on the back in Walpole's most elegant hand is from *Historia sui temporis* by Jacques Auguste de Thou (1553–1617), historian and statesman. The Warden of All Souls, Mr John Sparrow, kindly translated it for me:

In far distant times, one will look with wonder on the green turf that covers the grave where my ashes are buried, and will say: "It was his lot to be born in a bed of down, blessed with ample means, with favor and resources surpassing those which nowadays all wonder at from their earliest years: the glories of his time, his natural ambition, and the fresh fame of his illustrious father, all gave grounds to hope that he would excel the example of his ancestors which he strove to imitate; yet, despite all this, he preferred to seek the obscure, easeful retreats of the Muses, to shun the rocks and storms of Court and to despise the insubstantial vanities that men contend for: he chose the ivy and the laurel that grow wild rather than the spoils of battle or triumphs that batten on a hungry peace."

One feels Walpole's pleasure as he copied out that passage with its remarkable parallels to himself. Like de Thou he would be talked about "in far distant times," not for the insubstantial vanities that men strive for, but for the enduring awards of the Muses; he would be remembered for his letters and memoirs as well as for his contributions to the arts,

I. Reynolds pinx.t   *Ia M.cArdell fecit 1757*

Horace Walpole

Youngest Son of S.r Rob.t Walpole Earl of Oxford.

Horace Walpole by McArdell after Reynolds with a Latin inscription on the back.

literature, and antiquarianism. The future owners of the objects mentioned in the *Description of Strawberry Hill* would enjoy them the more because he had owned them.

John Pinkerton in his *Walpoliana,* 1799, says that McArdell's print of Walpole "must have been very like, as strong traces of resemblance remained, particularly about the eyes." Earlier Pinkerton wrote, "The person of Horace Walpole was short and slender, but compact and neatly formed. When viewed from behind, he had somewhat of a boyish appearance, owing to the form of his person, and the simplicity of his dress. His features may be seen in many portraits; but none can express the placid goodness of his eyes, which would often sparkle with sudden rays of wit, or dart forth flashes of the most keen and intuitive intelligence." One is reminded of General Fitzwilliam's witness to Walpole's "natural talents, his cheerfulness, the sallies of his imagination, the liveliness of his manner."

The accessories that Reynolds chose to suggest Walpole's interests give us the virtuoso and writer as well as the man of the world. The tall table on which he is leaning and displaying the ruffles at his wrist has a print of his antique marble eagle that was dug up in Rome in 1742. The *Description of Strawberry Hill* calls it "one of the finest pieces of Greek sculpture in the world," and assures us that "the boldness and yet great finishing of the statue are incomparable. The eyes inimitable. Mr Gray has drawn the flagging wing. It stands on a handsome antique sepulchral altar, adorned with eagles too." Reynolds's portrait also gives us the writer with a quill and inkpot and two or three of his books tumbled together on the tall table.

Hanging next it in our side hall is a lightly colored copy by John Thomas Smith (1766–1833) of the drawing by George Dance in 1793. The first entry in Joseph Farington's diary tells how we went "in company with Mr George Dance and Mr Samuel Lysons to Lord Orford's at Strawberry Hill, where we breakfasted with his Lordship," and how in the forenoon Dance "made a drawing of his Lordship's profile, an excellent resemblance." Dance's original drawing of Walpole is now in the National Portrait Gallery and played a part in Choice 22 when we discarded the Gallery's Hone of Walpole. In our side hall Smith's Walpole is regarding the McArdell print with charitable amusement; one feels that the sober man of seventy-five is studying the elegant forty-year-old virtuoso of Reynolds's painting with approval.

At Farmington is an example of an *objet de virtù* that appears in the

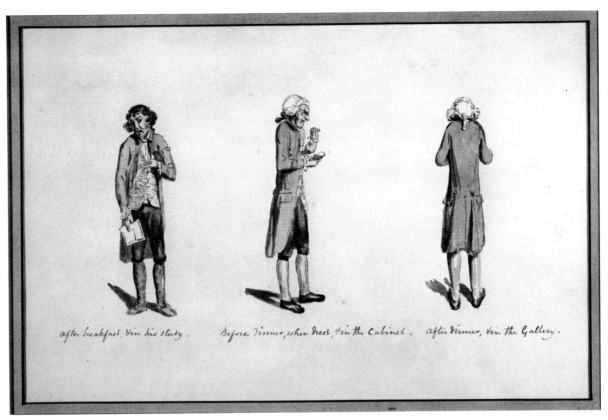

after breakfast, & in his study.   Before Dinner, when drest, & in the Cabinet.   After dinner, & in the Gallery.

Horace Walpole by Carter, "after breakfast," "before dinner," and "after dinner."

sale catalogue, 23rd day, lot 25: "A REMARKABLY FINE OLD BOULE COFFER, a splendid specimen of this work at an early period, the front elaborately finished with tortoise-shell ground work, massive or-molu mountings, masque handles, chased rosette corners, and lined with blue silk, on a pedestal *en-suite*, with richly worked boule back and stand for porcelaine." It stood in the Round Drawing Room where the *Description of Strawberry Hill* merely notes, "A trunk of tortoise-shell and bronze; by Boul, on a frame of the same" and says nothing about what Walpole kept in it. Above the coffer today hang four drawings of Walpole. The topmost one is a second drawing by Dance that belonged to his great-granddaughter. Below it are three sketches of the elderly Walpole that John Carter hurried off as he followed his host about the house. Carter labelled them, "after breakfast and in his study," "before dinner when dressed in the Cabinet" (in the act of taking snuff), and "after dinner, and in the Gallery." Walpole is standing in all three sketches, erect, spare, and wrinkled, an old man still full of purpose. The Carter trio is the runner-up in this Choice to Walpole's print of Reynolds's stylish portrait engraved by McArdell.

Well, there they are, my twenty-six choices. It has taken me two years to pick them out and write them up. I have gone rather far in describing other objects related to them, but the Almighty's punishment has been limited to two consignments for repairs in the Hartford Hospital.

If Walpole came to Farmington I don't doubt he would be pleased, not only to see that so many of his favorite objects have been reunited, but to find himself accepted as a major source of his time by twentieth century historians. You may recall that in his earliest memoirs, "The War with Spain," he said, "I write for posterity," and now posterity is reading him with ever-increasing respect and pleasure, just as he planned. He would share my satisfaction with Raymond Mortimer's pronouncement that the Yale Edition of Horace Walpole's Correspondence "is the most impressive monument ever erected to any English author," and see that its index of a million entries will serve as an encyclopedia to the eighteenth century and be supplemented by the twenty-odd volume edition of his memoirs. He would receive with pleasure the pilgrims who come to Farmington to pay their respects to him from places as far away as Lima, Osaka, Colombo, and Cape Town. Ambitious as he was, he couldn't ask for more recognition of his lifelong labor to leave posterity a full account and picture of his time.

The contents of Strawberry continue to reach us at Farmington although much more slowly. Many objects that were at Strawberry, its glass and china, for example, have lost their identity; many other objects that never saw Strawberry have been placed there by owners and vendors —the amount of bogus Walpoliana I have been offered would fill the Metropolitan Museum.

Nevertheless, I close with the hope—and belief—that some reader of this page will rescue a true piece in the vast mosaic for us and set all the bells of Walpoleshire ringing with joy and gratitude as the Almighty Himself nods approval.

Index